FUNDAMENTAL
English Grammar Review

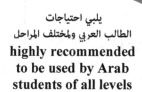

يلبي احتياجات
الطالب العربي ولمختلف المراحل
**highly recommended
to be used by Arab
students of all levels**

نظرة ومعالجة شاملة لتراكيب
اللغة الإنجليزية
**comprehensive
treatment of the
structures and usages**

مرجع للطالب والمعلم (ولمن
يستعد لاختبار
(ECL, TOEFL)
serves both students and
teachers

Indispensable for home, office and class

عوني شاتي العطيــــوي

First Edition
2011

The Hashemite Kingdom of
Jordan
The Deposit Number at The
National Library
(2011/3/1115)

425
Etaywe, Awni S.
   Fundamental English Grammer Review / Awni S.
Etaywe.- Amman. Dar Zahranco,2011
P. (   )
Deposit No. : 2011/3/1115
Descriptors : English Language // Grammar//Education

المتخصصون في الكتاب الجامعي الأكاديمي العربي والأجنبي
دار زهران للنشر والتوزيع

تلفاكس : 5331289 – 6 – 962+، ص.ب 1170 عمان 11941 الأردن
E-mail : Zahran.publishers@gmail.com
www.darzahran.net

ACKNOLEDGMENTS

I would like to express my great appreciation to Dr. Owayed Rata'an (a person of myriad skills with Ph.D in TEFL) for his encouragement, continuing support, constructive suggestions, and keen perceptions.

I am also indebted to Mr. Adnann AlEtaiwy (Instructor, Advisor and Translator at Dhofar University- Sultanate of Oman) for his constructive suggestions and comments.

I am really thankful to my students from Jordan. They taught me as much as I taught them. They have been proactive participants in their classrooms. Their questions and suggestions have been acting as a trigger that generates brilliant ideas and even a guidance to the required final structure of the material of this book. To them I send all my respect.

A special thank you is due to Sue Maggee (English Trainer at the British Council-Jordan) for her assistance. And to my friends who championed this work I say 'thank you'

Finally, I would like to mention how grateful I am to my wife, for her encouragement and infinite patience during the long gestation of this book.

FOREWORD

It is said that teaching a language without grammar is like having a chicken walking without bones. Unlike teachers of the mother tongue, the teachers of foreign languages do not question the necessity for teaching grammar.

It is no exaggeration to say that the author of *'Fundamental English Grammar Review'* spared no pains to come up with this work. It is a comprehensive treatment of the structures and usages of English grammar needed by Arab learners of English.

In fact, the book covers with fullness a plethora of grammar points and areas where students have particular difficulties. It also provides enough explanation in Arabic and is written in a way that allows students to study on their own.

This book is highly recommended to be used by beginning, intermediate and advanced students of English as a foreign language. Teachers may also find it useful for reference.

This work will surely serve the end for which it has been intended, and that both students and teachers will gain many benefits from it.

Enjoy reading it.

Dr. Owayed Awad Rat'an
(A Textbook Writer &
A Supervisor of English)
14th July, 2009

إهـــــداء...

أهدي هذا الكتاب إلى أمي التي حوتني منذ كنت نطفة حتى تخلَّقتُ عظاماً اكتسى لحماً ثم ربتني حتى بلغت الرابعة- تلك السنة من عمري التي اختار اللـه فيها أمي لجواره. فهيهات أمي عني تغيب بصحو بنومٍ ما بين السطور، بقلبي تعيشُ بخفق الصدور.. أدعوه عز وجل أن يجعل هذا العمل المتواضع في ميزانِ حسناتها، وأن يتغمدها برحمته إنه نعم المولى ونعم الوكيل

ابنك عوني

Contents

- "Allah will exalt in degree those of you who believe, and those who have been granted knowledge"

V (11); Surat Al-Mujadilah; The Holy Quran

"يرفع الـله الذين آمنوا منكم والذين أوتوا العلم درجات"

1. The English Alphabet

الحروف بالإنجليزية (ولفظها)

English language has twenty six letters which have small and capital forms. Those letters are:

اللغة الانجليزية تشتمل على (26) حرفا لكل منها رسم كبير وآخر صغير، وهذه الحروف هي:

Aa Bb Cc Dd Ee Ff Gg Hh Ii Jj Kk Ll Mm Nn Oo Pp
Qq Rr Ss Tt Uu Vv Ww Xx Yy Zz

1.1 Groups of English Letters   مجموعات الحروف في اللغة الانجليزية
The English letters are divided into two groups:
1.   Vowels (a, e, i, o, u).
2.   Consonants (the rest of the letters).

تقسم الحروف الانجليزية إلى مجموعتين: الأولى وتشمل حروف العلة المتحركة الواردة في المجموعة الأولى أعلاه، والثانية وتضم الحروف الساكنة الصحيحة وتشمل بقية الحروف.

1.2 Phonetic Symbols   الرموز الصوتية

1.2.1   The following are the symbols which are used to show how the English consonant letters sound in words:

الجدول التالي يبين الرموز المستخدمة كمفاتيح لفظ للحروف الساكنة الصحيحة، و كل حرف وضع في كلمة هي مثال يرد فيه ذلك الحرف.

ملاحظة: يوضع الرمز الصوتي بين خطين مائلين / / .

/p/	put	/b/	best
/v/	van	/t/	tell
/⊠/	three	/d/	day
/ð/	this	/k/	cat/kilo
/s/	sell	/g/	good
/z/	zoo	/tʃ/	cheese
/ʃ/	ship	/dʒ/	just
/ʒ/	measure	/n/	next
/h/	house	/⊠/	song
/m/	must	/l/	love
/r/	rest	/j/	you
/w/	will	/f/	fan

1.2.2   The following are some of the symbols which are used to show how vowels are pronounced.

الجدول التالي يعرض بعض الرموز المستخدمة كمفاتيح لفظ للحروف المتحركة/حروف العلة، و كل حرف وضع في كلمة هي مثال يرد فيه ذلك الحرف (قد تجد الرموز التالية تختلف من مرجع الى آخر).

ملاحظة: يوضع الرمز الصوتي بين خطين مائلين / /.

/æ/	c**a**t	/e /	b**e**t
/ə/	**a**nother	/I/	s**i**t
/ɒ/	t**o**p	/ʌ/	c**u**t
/ʊ/	b**oo**k	/i/; /i:/	s**ee**m
/U/; /U:/	m**oo**n	/eI/	s**ay**
/aI/	d**ie**	/ɔI/	b**oy**
/ɔ/	l**aw**	/əʊ/	**o**pen
/aʊ/	n**ow**		

1.3   **Basic rules for reading and pronunciation (c, g, qu, kn, wr, tion, sion, final s/ es/ d/ ed)**   قواعد أساسية للقراءة واللفظ

The following are some rules that help you read letters and words correctly: (*Remember that every rule has an exception*)

تالياً بعض القواعد التي تساعدك على قراءة الحروف والكلمات بالشكل الصحيح.

(تذكر أن لكل قاعدة شواذ)

● 'C' is pronounced /s/ when it is followed by (e, i, or y), as in; city, circle, ceiling, and Bicycle. When followed by any other letters, it is pronounced /k/, as in: can, car, company, close, and case.

'c'يلفظ (س) إذا جاء بعدها احد الحروف التالية (e, i, y) كما في كلمة (city, ceiling, bicycle)

'c'يلفظ (ك) إذا جاء بعدها أي حرف غير (e, i, y) كما في كلمة (can, car, company, close)

● 'G' is pronounced /dʒ/ when it is followed by (e, i, or y), as in general, giant, gym, and geography. When followed by any other letters, it is pronounced /g/, as in: gate, good and glance.

'g' يلفظ (ج) إذا جاء بعدها احد الحروف التالية (e, i, y) كما في كلمة (general, giant, gym).

إذا جاء بعدها غير هذه الحروف فإنه يلفظ كما في اللهجة المصرية كما في كلمتي (gate, good).

● 'Qu' is pronounced /k / when it comes at the middle or at the end of the word, as in; anti**qu**e, and eti**qu**ette. And it is pronounced as /kwa/ when it comes at the beginning of the word, as in; **qu**estion, **qu**iz, and **qu**iet.

'qu'يلفظ (ك) إذا جاء في منتصف أو آخر الكلمة كما في كلمة (antique, etiquette)

'qu'يلفظ (كوَ) إذا جاء في بداية الكلمة   كما في كلمة (question, quiz)

● 'Kn' in word like '**kn**ock' is pronounced /n /.

'kn'يلفظ (ن) كما في كلمة (knock)

● 'Wr' is pronounced / r/, as in '**wr**ite'.   'wr'يلفظ (ر)كما في كلمة (write)

- 'Ck' is pronounced /k /, as in (kno**ck**, lo**ck** and che**ck**).

'ck'يلفظ (ك) كما في (kno**ck**)

- 'tian' and 'tion' sound /ʃin/, as in (Egyp**tian** and na**tion**).

'tian/ tion' يلفظ (شن) كما في (Egyp**tian**/ na**tion**)

- 'sion' is pronounced /ʒin/, as in (televi**sion** and vi**sion**) .

'sion' يلفظ (چن) كما في (televi**sion**/ vi**sion**)

- The final 'e' of a word is not pronounced, as in (have, late, love, make, give, same).

'e' لا يلفظ إذا جاء آخر الكلمة.

- **The final s/ es:**
  - Final 's' is pronounced /s/ after a voiceless letter, as in (seat**s**, hat**s**, book**s**, ask**s**)

's' يلفظ (س) إذا جاءت في آخر الكلمة وبعد حرف غير صوتي/ حرف **مهموس**
(لا تهتز عند ذكره الأوتار الصوتية) وهذه الحروف تضم:

  (t, s, k, p, h, f, c, t,ch= /ᵗʃ/,th=/⊠/, sh= /ʃ/)

  - Final 's' is pronounced /z/ after a voiced letter, as in (bag**s**,   home**s** , mile**s**, day**s**, agree**s**)

's' يلفظ (ز) إذا جاءت في آخر الكلمة وبعد حرف صوتي/ حرف **مجهور**
(تهتز عند ذكره الأوتار الصوتية) وهذه الحروف تضم:

  (b, g, d, j, l, m, n, v, z, th=/ð/)

  - Final 'es' or 's' is pronounced /ez/ after (sh, ch, s, z, ge), as in (wish**es**, dish**es**, catch**es**, match**es**, ris**es**, cours**es**, siz**es**, priz**es**, edg**es**, judg**es**)

's/es' يلفظ (إز) إذا جاءت في آخر الكلمة وبعد sh, ch, s, z, ge

- **The final d/ed :**

  - Final 'ed' is pronounced /t / after voiceless letters, as in (loo**ked**, hel**ped**, pu**shed**, lau**ghed**)

'ed'يلفظ (ت) إذا جاءت آخر الكلمة و بعد حرف مهموس كما في كلمة (loo**ked**, hel**ped**)

  - Final 'ed' is pronounced /d / after voiced letters, such as: filled, dried, and enjoyed .

'ed' يلفظ (د) إذا جاءت آخر الكلمة و بعد حرف مجهور كما في كلمة (fi**lled**)

  - Final 'ed' is pronounced /ed / after d and t, for instance, nee**ded**, wai**ted**, loa**ded**, and coun**ted**.

'ed' يلفظ (إد) إذا جاءت بعد (d, t) كما في (**needed, counted**)

Fundamental English Grammar Review

Exercise (1)

Select the appropriate answer:

1. The underlined letter in the word *'books'* is pronounced:

    a. /s /   b. /z/   c. /ez/

2. The underlined letter in the word *'days'* is pronounced:

    a. /s /   b. /z/   c. /ez/

3. The underlined 'Kn' in the word *'know'* is pronounced:

    a. /n /   b. /k/   c. /kn/

4. The underlined letter in the word *'city'* is pronounced:

    a. /s/   b. /k/   c. /z/

5. The underlined letter in the word *'company'* is pronounced:

    a. /s/   b. /k/   c. /z/

6. The underlined letter in the word *'bag'* is pronounced:

    a. /k/   b. /g/   c. /j/

7. The underlined letters in the word *'helped'* is pronounced:

    a. /t/   b. /d/   c. /et/

Exercise (2)

According to the sound of the underlined letter(s), write the words in the correct column:

played	cheap	consumption	painted	sacked
entangled	van	laughed	affected	sharp
repeat	these	receive	deduction	thin

/t/	/d/	/ð/	/i/	/θ/	/ʌ/	/v/	/ʃ/	/ed/

2. Word Classes, and English Sentence

أقسام الكلمة، والجملة في اللغة الانجليزية

2.1 Word Classes/ parts of speech   أقسام الكلام

There are eight word classes in English language. This includes the following: هناك ثمانية

أقسام للكلمة في اللغة الانجليزية وهذا يشمل

Word Classes	Examples
Noun أسم	Robert, prevention, college, house, table, Jordan
Pronoun ضمير	she, they, it, me, which, who
Adjective صفة	rich, terrible, fantastic, handsome, boring
Adverb ظرف	politely, yesterday, always, very, where, very, well
Verb فعل	see, helped, taught, married, is, could, seem
Preposition حرف جر	on, at, in
Conjunction أداة ربط	before, then, after, then, so, if, but
Determiner محدد	a, the, few, all

1.   Noun is a word that can act as a subject or an object of a verb, or as an object of a preposition; examples include:

    a. **Prevention** is better than cure.

        subject

    b. Don't *show* **laziness** to your boss.

               object

    c. She has something *of* **courage**.

                  object

الاسم: وهو كلمة تعمل عمل الفاعل كما في مثال (1) أوعمل المفعول به للفعل مثال (2)، أو عمل المفعول به

لحرف جر مثال (3).

2.   Pronoun is a word used instead of a noun, as in:

الضمير يستخدم ليحل محل الاسم، كما في المثال التالي:

Melissa sold the cassette to **her** brother.

3.   A verb is a word which describes an action or a state, as in:

الفعل يعبر عن حدث أو حالة معينة، كما في الأمثلة التالية:

- He **plays** well.   - They **are** quick.

4.   An adjective is a word that qualifies a noun or pronoun, as in:

الصفة هي كلمة تصف وتعرف الاسم أو الضمير، كما في المثال التالي:

Rami is a **quiet** man.

She is **beautiful**.

5.   An adverb is used to modify a verb, an adjective and another adverb. Examples

include: الظرف يصف الفعل أو الصفة أو ظرفا آخر، كما في الأمثلة

    a. I spoke **politely**.

    b. I'm **very** *well*.

    c. The programme was **very** *boring*.

6. A preposition is a word which shows a relationship between objects or actions, as in: حرف الجر يبين العلاقة بين الأجسام أو الأحداث

The book is **on** the table.

He looked **at** me.

He arrived **in** time.

7. A conjunction is a word that connects words, clauses or sentences, as in:

أداة الربط تستخدم لربط كلمة بأخرى أو جملة بأخرى كما في الأمثلة

Aidah is clever **but** she always fails.

Aidah **and** Maya are close friends.

8. A determiner is used to modify a noun (the quantity, the definition, possession, etc...), as in:

المحددات تعرف بالاسم (كميته، معرفة أم نكرة...) كما في الأمثلة التالية:

The lady I saw was kind.

Some sons are unkind to their parents.

2.2   English Sentence   الجملة في اللغة الانجليزية

The sentence is at the top of the hierarchy of grammar. All the other elements, such as words, phrases and clauses go to make up sentences. It is a unit of grammar that can stand alone and make sense and obeys grammatical rules. For example:

'The old man is exhausted'

   Subject   Predicate

'The old man is exhausted' is a sentence that is made up of a subject *'The old man'* and a predicate *'is exhausted'*.

تقع الجملة الانجليزية في رأس الهرم لموضوع القواعد، وإن كل العناصر والأجزاء الأخرى كالكلمات وأشباه الجمل ما هي إلا أجزاء تعمل على تكوين الجملة. فالجملة هي وحدة قواعدية مستقلة ذات معنى تام. كما في المثال أعلاه حيث أن الجملة مكونة من:

- 'The old man' وهي شبه جملة عملت كفاعل للجملة ومن

- 'is exhausted' وعملت كتتمة ووصف للفاعل.

Note: Predicate means all the parts of a clause or a sentence that aren't contained in the subject.

يطلق المصطلح 'predicate' على أجزاء الجملة التي ليست جزءا من الفاعل.

Note: In English statements, the subject precedes the verb.

في الجمل الخبرية في الانجليزية (ليست الجمل الأمرية ولا الاستفهامية) فان الفاعل يسبق الفعل.

2.3   The Main Parts of English Sentence   الأجزاء الرئيسة للجملة

Any English sentence consists of different parts. The following are the main parts from which we usually form sentences:

تتألف أية جملة في اللغة الانجليزية من أجزاء مختلفة، والواردة في الجدول التالي هي الأجزاء الأبرز التي عادة ما نصيغ منها الجملة الانجليزية.

The main parts	Examples
- verb phrase شبه الجملة الفعلية	- can run, is playing, has got
- noun phraseشبه الجملة الاسمية	- this tooth, the bed, a man, this book, a glass of milk
	- absolutely horrible
- adjective phrase شبه جملة الصفة	- upstairs, outside
- adverb phrase شبه جملة ظرفية	- in the city, on Saturday
- prepositional phrase شبه جملة الجار والمجرور	

- A verb phrase is a group of verb forms that has the same function as a single verb, as in *'We **have been running**'*, *'have been running'* is a verb phrase.

شبه الجملة الفعلية هي مجموعة أفعال بأشكال وصيغ مختلفة تعمل عمل الفعل المكون من كلمة واحدة.

- A noun phrase is a group of words containing a noun as its main word and functioning like a noun in a sentence. It may contain determiners (the, a, this, etc.), adjectives, adverbs, and/or nouns. It doesn't begin with a preposition.

شبه الجملة الاسمية هي مجموعة كلمات تحتوي أسما كجزء أساسي فيها، و تعمل عمل الاسم في الجملة. فهي تحتوي على محدد أو صفة أو ظرف أو اسم.

In the sentence *'She is **a complete fool**'*, *'a complete fool'* is a noun phrase. Similarily in 'I lost an ***invaluable ring***'.

ففي المثال أعلاه 'a complete fool' هي شبه جملة اسمية وتحتوي أسما كجزء أساسي فيها وهو 'fool'.

- An adjectival phrase describes a noun/ pronoun, as in 'He is absolutely ***idle***'.

- An adverb(ial) phrase usually describes a verb, as in: 'We meet the boss *regularly*.' ('*regularly*' describes '*meet*')

شبه الجملة الظرفية تصف الفعل ويمكن لها أن تصف الاسم أو ظرفا اخر- كما مر سابقا.

- A prepositional phrase consists of a preposition+object, as in "I was **in the library**", "in the library" is a prepositional phrase.

شبه جملة الجار والمجرور تتكون من حرف جر+ اسم (مفعول به) كما في In the library

2.3.1   The normal sentence pattern in English is as the following:

الصيغة الاعتيادية للجملة في اللغة الانجليزية كالآتي:

Subject (فاعل)	Verb (فعل)	Object (مفعول به)	Modifier (محدد)
George	ate	a sandwich	last night

The subject is the person or thing that performs the action of the sentence. Every sentence in English language must have a subject. The subject may be a single noun (as in sentence 1), a noun phrase (as in sentence 2) or a pronoun (as in sentence 3).

1. **Tea** is my favourite drink.
2. **The Housing Bank** was closed yesterday.
3. **She** works very hard.

الفاعل هو الشخص أو الشيء الذي يقوم بالحدث الذي تعبر عنه الجملة. وكل جملة في اللغة الانجليزية يجب أن تحتوي على فاعل. حتى الجملة الأمرية يكون الفاعل فيها مضمنا يفيد الضمير المخاطب "أنت - you".

والفاعل يكون إما اسم مكون من كلمة واحدة كما في المثال (1) أو يكون شبه جملة كما في المثال (2) أو يكون ضميرا كما في مثال(3).

The verb shows the action of the sentence. Every sentence must have a verb. That verb may be a single word (as in sentence 1) or a verb phrase (as in sentence 2 and 3).

1. John **loves** Haya.
2. John **is eating** Kabab.
3. John **has been watching** a football match.

الفعل يبين الحدث في الجملة. وكل جملة في اللغة الانجليزية يجب أن تحتوي على فعل. والفعل يكون إما كلمة واحدة كما في المثال (1) أو شبه جملة كما في المثال (2، 3).

The object completes the verb as a complement. It is usually a noun, a noun phrase or a pronoun. Not every sentence requires an object. It depends on whether the verb is transitive or intransitive. This complement doesn't begin with a preposition, and it answers the question what? or whom?

1. Mr. Dove ate **a cake** last night.
2. Jim was driving **a brand new car**.
3. Mary called **him**.

المفعول به يكمل الفعل. وهو يكون في حاله كالفاعل إما كلمة واحدة كما في المثال (1) أو شبه جملة كما في المثال (2) أو يكون ضميرا كما في مثال (3). وليس كل جملة تتطلب مفعولا به وهذا يعتمد على نوع الفعل إذا ما كان لازماً أو متعديا. وهذه التكملة (المفعول به) تجيب عن السؤال بـ: what/ whom (ما، من، ماذا).

A modifier tells the time (as in sentence1), place (as in sentence 2 and 3), or manner of the action (sentence 4 and 5). It answers the question when? where? or how? It is usually a prepositional phrase (a group of words that begins with a preposition and ends with a noun) or adverbial phrase as in :

1. I saw my fiancée **at eight o'clock**.
2. Mary met Sally **at the roundabout**.
3. Samar was swimming **in the pool**.
4. She drove her car **very fast**.
5. Ali works **carefully**.

المحدد يخبرنا عن زمن الحدث كما في المثال (1) أو عن مكان الحدث (مثال 2،3) أو لأسلوب وكيفية وقوع الحدث (مثال 4،5). وهو يجيب عن السؤال بـ (متى؟ أين؟ وكيف؟)

وهو عادة ما يكون بصيغة شبه جملة جار ومجرور (وهي مجموعة كلمات تبدأ بحرف جر وتنتهي باسم كما في الأمثلة 1، 2، 3) أو بصيغة شبه جملة ظرفية أو ظرف كما في الأمثلة 4 ، 5.

Note: **Intransitive verbs** are verbs that do not take direct objects, as in:

الأفعال اللازمة هي التي لا تأخذ مفعولا به على الإطلاق أو لا تأخذ مفعول به مباشر كما في الأفعال:

(go, agree, and walk):

- I go to school every Monday. Things *changed*.
- I agree with you.
- He walked.

Transitive verbs are verbs that take direct objects. In the sentence:

"Sam *bought a book*".

verb   object

'a book' is a direct object and so, 'bought' is a transitive verb.

الأفعال المتعدية هي التي تأخذ مفعولا به مباشر، كما في المثال أعلاه،حيث أن bought فعل أخذ مفعولا به مباشر.

Note: Many verbs can be either transitive or intransitive, according to the context. Thus 'change' is intransitive in 'Things changed' but transitive in 'Sam changed his plan'.

العديد من الأفعال قد تكون لازمة وقد تكون نفسها متعدية وحسب السياق الواردة فيه، مثل 'changed' حيث أنه جاء لازما في الجملة الأولى و متعديا في الثانية:

1. Things changed.
2. Sam changed his clothes.

2.3.1.1 A noun clause is a subordinate that performs a function in a sentence similar to a noun or noun phrase. It can act as a subject, an object or a complement of a main verb. It can be preceded by any of these connectives (that, what, why, when, where, which, who, how many, how old, how often, how long, and how much).

العبارة الاسمية هي عبارة تابعة (ليس لها معنى كامل أو مستقل) و تعمل عمل الاسم أو الضمير. وهي يمكن أن تعمل كفاعل، أو مفعول به، أو تكملة لبعض الأفعال على أن لا يسبقها اسم أو ضمير موصوف وإلا أصبحت جملة موصولة/ جملة وصفية (تم تخصيص وحدة منفصلة للبحث في الجمل الموصولة). والعبارة الاسمية تأتي ضمن الجملة المعقدة وبعد أحد أدوات الربط التالية:

(that, what, why, when, where, which, who, how many, how old, how often, how long, and how much).

Examples include:

1. We asked **why he objected**. (*why he objected*) is a noun clause used as an object.

2. **When he leaves** is his own business. (*when he leaves*) is a noun clause used as a subject.

3. That is **what I want**. (what I want) is a complement.

الجمل الاسمية المكتوبة بالخط العريض في الأمثلة الثلاثة أعلاه هي جمل اسمية عملت في الأولى عمل المفعول به وفي الثانية عمل الفاعل وفي الثالثة عملت كتكملة وتتمة لفعل رئيس.

2.4   Types of English Sentence   أنواع الجملة في اللغة الانجليزية

a. Simple Sentence

The simple sentence cannot be broken down into other clauses. It generally contains a finite verb, as in:

الجملة البسيطة: وهي لا يمكن تجزئتها لجمل أخرى وهي تحتوي على فعل واحد و محدد ولها معنى كامل، كما في الأمثلة التالية:

The man stole the red car.

I saw a wonderful island.

She studies so hard.

Note: A clause is a group of words containing a finite verb, which can form a part of a compound or complex sentence.

العبارة: هي مجموعة كلمات تتضمن فعل محدد، ويمكن أن تكون جزءا من جملة مركبة أو معقدة.

Note: **A finite verb** is a verb that has a tense and agrees with a subject in number and persons for example 'look' is finite in *The man looks ill'*. The non-finite verb includes: the present participle, the gerund, the past participle and the infinitive verb.

الفعل المحدد هو الفعل الذي له زمن محدد وفاعله يتفق معه في العدد (يطابقه في الإفراد والجمع)، أما الفعل غير المحدد فهو إما يكون التصريف الثالث للفعل، أو مصدر الفعل أو فعل بصيغة - صيغة الاستمرارية (ing + فعل).

The following are the main sentence patterns of simple sentences:

تاليا القوالب الرئيسية المتبعة في صياغة الجمل في الإنجليزية

*The Patterns	Examples
S+ V	- The sun rose. - He has been sleeping. - He is swimming.
S+ TV+ DO	- Hassan writes novels. - He bought a house. - You can rely on Martin. - Asma is reading a fairy tale.
S+ TV+ DO+ IO	- The chief granted me a medal.
S+ IV+ Adverbial/ Prepositional phrase	- Ali arrived at 10 o'clock. - My pen is on the table. - The cat is in the kitchen. - Veronica is arguing again. - Helena is coming to lunch.

S+ LV+ Adj	- The lesson was interesting. - To go further became more exciting. - He is a teacher. - She was kind.
S+ V+ to infinitive (+ Complement)	- Jane hesitated to phone the office. - Tom likes to arrive early. - Tom loves to do the household chores.
S+ V+ V-ing/ gerund	- Noah quit smoking. - I admitted stealing from the store.
S+ TV+ DO+ to infinitive	Tony hates his wife to lose her temper.
S+ TV+ DO+ V-ing/ gerund	John regrets Sali's leaving.
S+ TV+ DO+ Prepositional phrase	- I cleared the pavement of rubbish. - The waiter confused his name with my friend.
S+ TV+ DO (clause)	Bill had decided what to do next.

* S= Subject; Verb= V; DO= Direct Object; IO= Indirect Object;   Adj= Adjective; TV= Transitive Verb; IV= Intransitive Verb; LV= Linking Verb

b.   Compound Sentence

A compound sentence is a type of sentence with more than one independent clause and linked by a coordinating conjunction such as, *and, but, or, or else, otherwise, either...or, neither...nor*, as in:

الجملة المركبة: وتتكون من جملتين بسيطتين لكل منها معنى كامل مستقل ويربط بينهما بإحدى أدوات الربط كالتالية:

(*and, but, or, or else, otherwise, either...or, neither...nor*)
- *I went to the cinema **but** I didn't enjoy the film.*
- *Yaseen quit school **and** joined the navy.*
- *Take this ball **or** drop that one.*
- *I should arrive in time; **otherwise** I will be in trouble.*
- *You must drive carefully **or else** you will have an accident.*
- *He will **either** play football **or** watch TV.*
- *He **neither** got his car fixed **nor** bought a new one.*

c.   Complex Sentence

A complex sentence is a type of sentence in which there is a main/ independent clause, which can stand alone and make some sense, and one or more subordinate/ dependent clauses which can't stand alone. The two clauses are joined by co-ordinating conjunctions of adverbial clauses and relative clauses; such as (*although*, *because*, *despite*, *so*, *before*, and *who*). The subordinate clause can be a relative clause, or an adverbial clause.

الجملة المعقدة: تحتوي على جملة رئيسة مستقلة، ذات معنى تام إذا ما ذكرت وحدها وتسمى Main / independent clause وأخرى تابعة ثانوية ليس لها معنى تام ما لم تذكر مع جملة رئيسة وتسمى (subordinate/ dependent clause) ويتم ربط الجملتين بأداة ربط قد تدل على: علاقة السببية، النتيجة، التناقض، الشرطية (وهي كلها جمل ظرفية) أو أداة تسبق جملة وصفية. ومن الأمثلة على هذه الأدوات:

(*although*, *because*, *despite*, *if*, *while*, *so*, *before*, *who*)

فالجملة التابعة تكون عادة إما ظرفية أو وصفية.

الجملة التالية مثلا تتألف من جملتين إحداهما رئيسة مستقلة وأخرى تابعة (ظرفية تفيد التناقض):

'*We went to visit my cousin although he had been unfriendly to us*' is a complex sentence since it is composed of:

- **a main clause**- جملة رئيسية: (*we went to visit my cousin*).
- **a subordinate clause**-جملة ثانوية: (*although he had been unfriendly to us*).

تاليا المزيد من الأمثلة التي توضح ذلك ، لاحظ أن الجملة التابعة تقع بعد أداة الربط.

More examples include:

- <u>If I can help you</u>, <u>I will try</u>.

  Subordinate clause   main clause

- <u>He drove his car</u> <u>while he was using his cell phone</u>.

  Main clause   subordinate clause

- <u>Although the car is old</u>, <u>it is still serviceable</u>.

  Subordinate clause   main clause

d. Compound Complex- Sentence

The compound complex sentence consists of two or more independent clauses, one of which is complex. As in: "*The hurricane stopped, and we went to Shumari Wild Reserve where we had lost our team leader.*"

الجملة المعقدة المركبة: هي جملة تتألف من جملتين مستقلتين رئيسيتين أو أكثر إحداها تكون جملة معقدة كما في المثال التالي:

The hurricane stopped, and we went to Shumari Wild Reserve where we had lost our team leader.

الذي يمكن توضيحه بتجزئته كالتالي:

<u>The hurricane stopped</u>, <u>and we went to Shumari Wild Reserve</u>

Independent clause1   Independent clause2

<u>and we went to Shumari Wild Reserve where we had lost our team leader.</u>

Complex sentence

Fundamental English Grammar Review

Exercise (3)

A. Define the underlined words: (noun, verb, adjective, adverb, preposition, determiner, pronoun, or conjunction).

1. I <u>helped</u> an old man.
2. <u>She</u> usually drinks milk.
3. That lady is really <u>rich</u>.
4. I'm lucky to have <u>a few</u> friends in Pakistan.
5. <u>If</u> I were you, I wouldn't join that nasty group.
6. <u>Robert</u> should see the doctor.
7. Alison is <u>very</u> upset.
8. Mr. Brown will be sitting <u>at</u> the bus stop.

B. Identify the subject, verb, complement, and the modifier in each of the following sentences.

1. <u>Fadi is buying a new house in Amman.</u>
2. <u>Eddi has been shopping downtown.</u>

Exercise (4)

Write the name of the underlined phrases next to every sentence:

1. I <u>was playing</u> volleyball.   (   )
2. <u>Macbeth</u> usually drinks milk. (   )
3. He is <u>absolutely idle</u>.   (   )
4. She is <u>in the pool</u>. (   )
5. I will move <u>before you arrive</u>. (   )

Exercise (5)

Read the following sentences and write the sentence type next to each one. (simple, compound or complex)

1. I like to feed the homeless. (   )
2. Why Mohammad is kind with her is not my problem. (   )
3. Erick does the painting and designs the models. (   )
4. Before Sara turned the radio off, her husband got annoyed. (   )
5. The maintenance of the arrivals terminals will take more time.(   )
6. Adam sleeps early every night. (   )
7. It is an ancient piece of metal, but it is a precious one. (   )
8. I can remember what you told me. (   )

3. Verbs
الأفعـــــال

English verbs are classified as main verbs and auxiliaries, including: *state* verbs (I *have* a car), *be* (is, are, was, were, am) *have* (have, has, had), *do* (do, does, did), *dynamic* verbs (I *play* football regularly),*and modals* (I *must* go right now). Consider the following examples:

الأفعال بالانجليزية تصنف إلى أفعال رئيسة وأخرى مساعدة. والأفعال الرئيسية تشمل أفعال الكينونة والتملك والعمل والحال وأفعال أخرى تعبر عن نشاط. تأمل الأمثلة التالية:

'She/He *is* angry.'; 'I *am* an English teacher.'; 'I/He/She *was* awesome.'

'We/They/You *are* humble.'; 'We/They/You *were* outstanding.'

'She *did* her best.'; '*Do* me a favor.'; 'He *does* painting.'

'She *has* a nice car.'; 'I/ We/ They *have* fashionable glasses.'

'She is *laughing*.'

3.1 Auxiliary Verbs

An auxiliary verb is used in forming tenses, moods and voices of the verbs. These include 'be: is, are, am, was, were', 'do: do, does, did', 'have: have, has, and had'.

الأفعال المساعدة: تستخدم لصياغة الأزمنة والمبني للمجهول والمعلوم وللتعبير عن حالة معينة. وتشمل الأفعال المساعدة أيضا (أفعال الكينونة والتملك والعمل).

The verb 'to be'   عائلة أفعال الكينونة

في الزمن المضارع Present	في الزمن الماضي Past	في المستقبل Future
I am (I'm)	I was	I will be (I'll be)
You are (singular) (You're)	You were	You will be (You'll be)
He is (He's)	He was	He will be (He'll be)
She is (She's)	She was	She will be (She'll be)
It is (It's)	It was	It will be (It'll be)
We are (We're)	We were	We will be (We'll be)
You are (plural) (You're)	You were	You will be (You'll be)
They are (They're)	They were	They will be (They'll be)

The verb 'to have'   عائلة أفعال التملك

Present	Past	Future
I have (I've)	I had	I will have (I'll have)
You have (singular) (You've)	You had	You will have (You'll have)
He has (He's)	He had	He will have (He'll have)
She has (She's)	She had	She will have (She'll have)
It has (It's)	It had	It will have (It'll have)

We have (We've)	We had	We will have (We'll have)
You have (plural) (You've)	You had	You will have (You'll have)
They have (They've)	They had	They will have (They'll have)

The verb 'to do'   عائلة أفعال العمل

Present	Past	Future
I do	I did	I will do (I'll do)
You do (singular)	You did	You will do (You'll do)
He does	He did	He will do (He'll do)
She does	She did	She will do (She'll do)
It does	It did	It will do (It'll do)
We do	We did	We will do (We'll do)
You do (plural)	You did	You will do (You'll do)
They do	They did	They will do (They'll do)

a. The *verb 'to be'* is used as an auxiliary verb with the 'ing' form of the main verb to the progressive tense, as in 'We *are living* in NY nowadays'.

أ. تستخدم أفعال الكينونة كفعل مساعد مع صيغة:

الفعل +Ing ، لصياغة الزمن المستمر (المضارع المستمر و الماضي المستمر)، مثال

'We *are living* in NY nowadays'/ 'We were living in NY.'

b. The *verb 'to be'* is used as an auxiliary verb with the past participle of the main verb to form the passive voice, as in:

'My chairs *are made* in Jordan'.

ب. تستخدم أفعال الكينونة كفعل مساعد مع التصريف الثالث للفعل لصياغة المبني للمجهول كما في المثال أعلاه.

c. The *verb 'to be'* is used as an auxiliary verb with the main verb to form negative sentences, for example:

'I *am not taking* the chance'.

ج. تستخدم أفعال الكينونة كفعل مساعد مع الفعل الرئيسي لتكوين النفي (لنفي الجمل)، كما في المثال أعلاه.

d. The *verb 'to have'* is used as an auxiliary verb with the past participle of the main verb to form the perfect tenses, as in:

'They *have completed* the task.'

'He *had realised* the fault.'

د. تستخدم أفعال التملك كفعل مساعد مع التصريف الثالث للفعل لصياغة الزمن التام (مضارع تام أو ماضي تام)، كما في المثالين أعلاه.

e. The *verb' to do'* is used as an auxiliary verb with the main verb to form negative sentences. Example:

'She *doesn't believe* in her eldest brother'.

هـ. تستخدم أفعال العمل كأفعال مساعدة في صياغة نفي الجمل كما في المثال أعلاه.

f. The *verb 'to do'* is also used with the main verb to form questions, as in:

> ***Does*** she ***play*** well?

و.   تستخدم أفعال العمل مع الفعل الرئيسي لصياغة سؤال، كما في المثال أعلاه.

g. The *verb 'to do'* is used to form sentences in which the verb is emphasized, as in:

> He ***does like*** shopping.

ز.   تستخدم أفعال العمل للتأكيد على الفعل الرئيسي كما سيأتي في الوحدة (25)، كما في المثال أعلاه.

3.2   Modal Verbs

A modal verb is a type of auxiliary verb that helps the main verb to express a range of meanings including possibility, probability, wants, wishes, necessity, permission, suggestions, etc. The main modal verbs include: *can, could, may, might, will, would, shall, ought to, should, must.* Modal verbs have only one form, and they are followed by the base form of verbs.

الأفعال الشكلية: هي أحد أنواع الأفعال المساعدة التي تساعد الفعل الرئيسي لينقل التعبير عن الإمكانية، الرغبة، الاحتمالية، التمني، الضرورة، الطلب، الاستئذان، العرض، وكلها لها شكل واحد وثابت لا يتغير سواء كان الفاعل مفرد أو جمع، مذكر أم مؤنث، ويتبعها فعل مجرد/ تصريف أول. وأهم هذه الأفعال:

can, could, may, might, will, would, shall, ought to, should, must

Examples of modal verbs include:

- We ***should*** leave right now.
- I ***must*** arrive by dawn.
- ***Could*** you give him a message?
- You ***can*** have another bike.

3.3   Linking Verbs

A linking verb links a subject with its complement. Unlike other verbs, linking verbs don't denote an action but indicate a state. Linking verbs are also called *'copula'*. The following are examples of linking verbs:

أفعال الربط: وتربط الفاعل بتتمة الجملة التي تصف الفاعل، وهي تعبر عن حالة وليس حدث، ويأتي بعدها تكملة أو صفة. وهي تضم:

'look', 'become', 'be', 'appear', 'seem', 'feel', 'keep', 'remain', 'smell', 'sound', 'taste', 'stay', 'turn', and *'grow'.*

As in:

> He **looks** well.
>
> He **became** a Muslim.
>
> You **are** a fool.
>
> Sue **seems** an intelligent person.

3.4 Contracted forms of pronouns with auxiliary verbs

The following table shows how to write the short/ contracted form of pronouns with verb 'to be', 'to have', 'will' and 'would':

Note: contracted forms are used in informal language.

الجدول التالي يعرض كيف تكتب الشكل المختصر للضمائر مع أفعال الكينونة و الملكية والفعل
will/ would .

Pronouns	Contractions	Examples
he, she, it	's (is/ has)	he's, she's, it's
you, they, we	're	you're, they're, we're
I	'm	I'm
I, you, they, we	've	I've, you've, they've, we've
I, you, we, they, he, she	'd (had/ would)	I'd, you'd, we'd, they'd, he'd, she'd, it'd
I, you, we, they, he, she	'll (will/ shall)	I'll, you'll, we'll, they'll, he'll, she'll, it'll
let	's (us)	let's

ملاحظة: تستخدم الصيغ المختصرة هذه في اللغة غير الرسمية، أما في أسلوب اللغة الرسمية فتكتب الأفعال كاملة دون اختصارات.

- **Can you lend me your book?**

  No, I'm sorry. (informal style)

  No, I can't. (informal style)

  No, I am sorry. (formal style)

  No, I cannot. (formal style)

4. Tenses

الأزمنــــة

4.1 Tense is the form of verb that is used to show the time at which the action takes place. (See the following two tables which show the tenses, their forms, use, and adverbs of frequency briefly and straightforwardly).

الزمن يقصد به شكل الفعل المستخدم الذي يعبر عن زمن وقوع الحدث. و يعرض الجدولان أدناه الأزمنة في اللغة الانجليزية: شكلها واستخدامها وظروف التكرار المستخدمة معها والدالة عليها باختصار وبأسلوب مباشر:

<u>Table (1). This table shows the verb form that each pronoun takes in different tenses using the same base verb (**drink**)</u>

الجدول التالي يبين كيفية تغير صيغة الفعل مع تغير الفاعل (الضمير) ليعبر عن الأزمنة المختلفة

Simple present	I, we, you, they	drink	coffee every morning
المضارع البسيط	He, she, it	drinks	coffee every morning
Present progressive	I	am drinking	coffee now
المضارع المستمر	We, you, they	are drinking	coffee now
	He, she, it	is drinking	coffee now
Simple past	I, we, you, they, he, she, it	drank	coffee yesterday
الماضي البسيط			
Past progressive	We, you, they	were drinking	coffee when Ann came back
الماضي المستمر	He, she, it, I	was drinking	coffee when Ann came back
Present perfect	We, you, they, I	have drunk	coffee for ten years
المضارع التام	He, she, it	has drunk	coffee for ten years
Past perfect	I, we, you, they, he, she, it	had drunk	coffee before Jeff left
الماضي التام			
Present perfect progressive	We, you, they, I	have been drinking	coffee for three hours
المضارع التام المستمر	He, she, it	has been drinking	coffee for three hours
Past perfect progressive	I, we, you, they, he, she, it	had been drinking	coffee for three hours
الماضي التام المستمر			
Simple future tense	I, we, you, they, he, she, it	will drink	coffee tomorrow morning
المستقبل البسيط			

<u>Table (2). The tenses</u>

الأزمنة

Note: Base form and **bare infinitive** are used interchangeably in the book.

استخدمت المصطلحات base form, bare infinitive في الكتاب كمترادفات لتعني شيئا واحدا وهو (الفعل المجرد/ مصدر الفعل).

Table (2) Tenses: adverbs of frequency and examples

Note: Base form and **bare infinitive** are used interchangeably in the book.

Tense: Present Simple

Form: "_he, she, it+ base form of verb+ (s)/ or (-es)_", if the verb ends in, s, ss, sh, ch ,x."

"_I, they, we, you+ base form of verb_"

Adverbs of frequency/ time expressions: _always, usually, sometimes, never, habitually, hardly ever, every+ time, occasionally, rarely, seldom, daily, weekly, yearly, annually, scarcely, regularly, frequently, once/ twice + time (once a week)_

يستخدم المضارع البسيط للحديث عن الحقائق، العادات، الروتين اليومي، أحداث تحدث طوال الوقت (للحديث عن شي دائم)، وللحديث عن خطط مستقبلية، وأحداث ضمن جدول زمني

Use	Examples	Yes/ No question
1. To express facts/ general statements	1. The sun _rises_ from the east.	* Does+ he, she, it+ base form+ object/ complement? -_Does_ he _speak_ English?
2. To talk about Routine/ actions happen all the time/ habits	2. She _washes_ her face regularly. - We always _visit_ our cousins.	* Do+ I, they, we, you+ base form of verb+ object/ complement?
3. Permanent actions	3. I _live_ in Jordan.	-_Do_ you _like_ swimming?
4. Arrangements as per a time table	4. The train _leaves_ at 10 am.	

Tense: Present Progressive

Form: _(I) am , (he, she, it) is, (they, we, you) are + verb+ ing_

Adverbs of frequency/ time expressions: _now, at the moment, right now, this+time(this month, listen!, look!, see!, be careful!_

المضارع المستمر يصف حدثاً بحالة الاستمرارية وقت الحديث عنه، للحديث عن خطط وقرارات مستقبلية، لوصف شيء مؤقت

Use	Examples	Yes/ No question
1. To describe an action in progress at the time of speaking	1. I _am writing_ a letter at the moment. - Look! He's studying.	* am+ I/ is+ he, she, it/ are+ they, we, you + verb+ ing? - _Is_ he _playing_ football?
2. Future actions for which arrangements	2. She is leaving tomorrow morning.	- Am I _going_ tonight?

have already been made 3. *To describe temporary actions*	3.They are living in Irbid.	- Are you *watching* T.V now?

Tense: Past Simple

Form: he , she, it, you, they , we, I+ past simple form of verb

(e.g. walked, ran, drank)

Adverbs of frequency/ time expressions: Yesterday, ago, last+ time (last month), past dates (1989), before

الماضي البسيط: يستخدم للتعبير عن حدث بدأ وانتهى بالماضي، لذكر سلسلة أحداث تمت بالماضي، ولوصف عادة معينة كانت بالماضي وتوقفت

Use	Examples	Yes/ No question
1. To express the idea that an action started and finished in the past (completed action)	1. He slept for eight hours last night. - They *bought* a new house yesterday. - I *studied* French when I was a child.	* Did+ subject+ base form of verb+ O/ complement? - *Did* she *sleep* for eight hours? - *Did* they *buy* a new house?
2. To list a series of completed actions in the past	2. She *called* Dove before she hit the car. - I *finished* work at 8:00, *went* to the beach and *met* a friend at 10:30.	

Tense: Past Progressive

Form: - I, she, it, he+ was+ v+ ing

- we, they, you+ were+ v+ing

Adverbs of frequency/ time expressions: while, as, when

الماضي المستمر يصف حدث تخلله حدثاً آخر بالماضي، لوصف حدث كان بحالة الاستمرارية عند نقطة معينة بالزمن الماضي، وللتعبير عن عدة أحداث كانت متزامنة في وقت الوقوع في الماضي، للتعبير عن شيء مزعج كان يتكرر حدوثه في الماضي always, constantly ومع كلمات مثل:

Use	Examples	Yes/ No question
1. To describe an interrupted action in the past (an action happened in the past and was going on when another action happened)	1. He *was brushing* his teeth when she called.	*Was+ he, she, it, I / were+ we, you, they+ v+ ing? - *Was he brushing* his teeth?
2. To describe an action that was in progress around a particular time in the past	2. They *were playing tennis* at 6:30 last night.	

3. To express the idea that the actions are parallel- were happening at the same time	3. While Allen was telling her father's a story, Janet was watching TV.	- *Were they waiting* for Sammy when the earthquake started?
4. With words such as 'always' or 'constantly' to express the idea that something irritating often happened in the past	4. She was always coming to class late. - Sue was constantly talking. She annoyed me.	

Tense: Present Perfect

Form: (he , she, it)+ has (we, they, you, I)+ have+ p.p

Adverbs of frequency/ time expressions: since , for , already, yet, just, so far, all my life, how long, recently, before, this (year)

ارع التام يصف حدثا وقع في الماضي لكن له نتائج حاضرة، ويستخدم للحديث عن انجازات و تجارب، ولوصف حدث ما وقع في الماضي وانتهى للتو، ووصف أحداث اكتملت بالماضي القريب

Use	Examples	Yes/ No question
1. To describe an activity that began in the past and just ended	1. Sam to his father: I've just reviewed me lessons.	*Has/ have+ subject+ p. p?
2. To talk about experiences and achievements	2. I *have written* three novels since 1999.	- *Has he reviewd* his lessons? - *Have* you *been* to Jerash before?
3. To describe an activity that happened in the past but it has present results/ consequences	3. I have cut my finger.	

Tense: Present Perfect Progressive

Form: - he, she, it+ Has+ been+ verb+ ing

you, they, we, I+ have+ been+ verb+ ing

Adverbs of frequency/ time expressions: since, for, yet, just, recently, this (year), how long, this+ time, all+ time

المضارع التام المستمر يصف أحداثا طويلة ومتكررة في الماضي القريب، يصف حدثا وقع بالماضي وما زال ممتدا حتى الوقت الحاضر (لم تكتمل بعد)، ويستخدم ليشير الى كم طال حدوث شيء ما، ولاستنتاج حدوث شيء ما في الماضي القريب من خلال عواقب ونتائج أو اثار ذلك الفعل.

Use	Examples	Yes/ No question
1. To describe prolonged/ repeated actions; to describe incomplete/ not finished	1. He *has been listening* to music for a long time. - They *have been sleeping* all day.	* Has/ have+ subject+ been+ verb+ ing? - *Has he been listening*

action 2. To deduce the occurrence of actions in the recent past from their present consequences and results	2. I am really tired. I have been running. - There is an ashtray on the desk. Someone has been smoking. - I see a lot of spots on Sam's shirt. He has been painting all day.	to music for a long time? - You look wet. *Have you been running* in the rain? - She has a stomachache. *Has she been eating* too many sweets?

Tense: Past Perfect

Form: He, she, it, I, they, you+ had+ p.p

Adverbs of frequency/ time expressions: when , as soon as, the moment, before, after, by the time, already

الماضي التام يصف حدثا تم قبل حدث آخر بالماضي

Use	Examples	Yes/ No question
To describe something which happened before another action in the past	- He *had* already *cooked* lunch by the time his father came home. - We *had learnt* two languages before we went to school.	* Had+ subject+ p.p? - *Had you learnt* Arabic before you went to school?

Tense: Past Perfect Progressive

Form: He, she, it, I, they, we, you+had+ been+ verb+ ing

Adverbs of frequency/ time expressions: by/ at that time, by then, for, since

الماضي التام المستمر يصف حدثا طويلا أو متكررا في الماضي، أو حدث توقف قبل لحظة الحديث عنه

Use	Examples	Yes/ No question
To describe repeated or prolonged action in the past; to describe an action that happened for long in the past and stopped before a specific time in the past	- I was tired because *I had been driving* since 7 o'clock.	* Had+ subject+ been+ v+ ing? - *Had you been washing* your clothes since she left home?

Tense: Simple Future

Form: I, we+ shall+ infinitive/ he, she, it, they, you+ will+ infinitive

Adverbs of frequency/ time expressions: tomorrow, next (year), dates in future (2080), today

المستقبل البسيط يستخدم للتعبير عن حدث سيقع بالمستقبل، أو للتنبؤ بحدوث شيء، أو لقطع وعد

Use	Examples	Yes/ No question
1. To talk about an	1. Rashid *will meet* his	* Will+ subject+ bare

action that will happen in the future	friends tomorrow. - They will meet their families next month.	infinitive? - *Will he meet* his friends tomorrow?
2. To predict something 3. To make a promise	2. It *will rain* tomorrow. 3. I *will buy* you a new house.	

Tense: Future Perfect

Form: He, she, it, I, we, they, you+ will have+ p.p

Adverbs of frequency/ time expressions: by, by the time, by then

المستقبل التام يصف حدثا سيقع ويكتمل قبل حلول موعد أو وقت معين في المستقبل

Use	Examples	Yes/ No question
To describe an event that will be completed before a specific future time	- I *will have retired* by August 2015. - They will have finished the task by next April.	* Will+ subject+ have+ p.p? - *Will you have retired* by August?

Tense: Future Progressive

Form: He, she, it, I, we, they, you+ Will be+ verb+ ing

Adverbs of frequency/ time expressions: tomorrow, next (month), this (month), until (6 o'clock)

المستقبل المستمر يصف حدثا سيقع قبل نقطة معينة في المستقبل وسيستمر بعدها، أو لوصف حدث سيكون بحالة استمرارية عند نقطة ما في المستقبل، وكذلك لوصف حدث سيقع كتحصيل حاصل

Use	Examples	Yes/ No question
1. To describe an event that will be in progress at a future point	1. At 6:30 tomorrow evening I will be sleeping.	* Will+ subject+ be+ verb+ ing?
2. To describe something that will happen as a matter of course	2. Do you need anything from the post office? I'll be passing on my way home.	- *Will you be reading* a novel by 10 a.m?
3. To describe an event that will happen before a future point of time and continues after that point	3. I *will be reading* a novel tomorrow morning.	

Tense: Future Perfect Progressive

Form: He, she, it, I, we, they, you+ will+ have+ been+ verb-ing

Adverbs of frequency/ time expressions: by+ future time, by the time, by then.

المستقبل التام المستمر يركز على حقيقة استمرارية الحدث الذي سيكون جارٍ قبل وقوع حدث آخر أو قبل حلول وقت آخر في المستقبل

Use	Examples	Yes/ No question
It emphasizes the duration of an activity that will be in progress before another time or event in the future	- Her husband will have been sleeping for five hours by the time she gets home.	* will+ subject+ have+ been+ verb-ing? - Will you have been studying by the time I arrive?

Future Tense with (Be going to)

Form: (I am/ he, she, it+ is/ they, you, we+ are)+ going to+ infinitive

Adverbs of frequency: tomorrow, next, today, now

هذه الصيغة تستخدم لوصف حدث سوف يقع بالمستقبل (ويكون مخطط له أو منوي القيام به بقرار سابق)

Use	Examples	Yes/ No question
To describe an action that will happen in the future (planned event/ intended to be done).	- I *am going to see* the dentist tomorrow	* Am/ is / are+ subject +going to+ base verb? - Are you going to see the dentist tomorrow?

Note: Never, ever, and yet in present perfect tense:

- We use '**never**, to say we have not done something at any time, as in:

. **I've never played basketball.**

تستخدم Never في المضارع التام لتفيد معنى: لم أقوم بشيء ما البتة/ على الإطلاق كما في المثال أعلاه والذي يعني: لم يسبق لي أن لعبت كرة السلة على الإطلاق/ لم ألعب كرة السلة من قبل.

- '**Ever**' means at any time in your past life, and it is used to ask other people about things they've done, as in:

Have you ever been to Paris?

تستخدم Ever في المضارع التام لتفيد معنى: في أي وقت **خلال حياتك**. كما في المثال أعلاه والذي يفيد معنى: **هل سبق لك أن زرت باريس؟** أي خلال حياتك.

- '**Yet**' is used in negative statements and in questions, as in:

I haven't visited Ali yet.   لم أقم بزيارة علي بعد.

Have you not visited Ali yet?   هل قمت بزيارة علي؟

Yet تستخدم في الجمل المنفية والسؤال بمعنى "بعد" أو "لغاية اللحظة". كما في الأمثلة أعلاه.

More examples of different tenses include:

- It snows in Syria.   (Simple present/ fact)
- I *watch* T.V *every day*.   (Simple present/ routine)
- It *snowed yesterday*.   (Simple past)
- I *watched* T.V *yesterday*. (Simple past)
- It *will snow tomorrow*.   (Simple future)
- He *will be playing* computer games when we get home. (Future progressive)
- He *is watching* a film *right now*. (Present progressive)
- I *have already eaten* apples. (Present perfect)
- I *had already drunk* tea when I arrived. (Past perfect)
- I *will have finished* when she arrives. (Future perfect)
- I *have been studying* for two hours. (Present perfect progressive)
- I *had been studying* for two hours before Fred came. (Past perfect progressive)
- I'll have been studying by the time you arrive. (Future perfect progressive)

The following examples are statements of facts, so that they are written in present simple tense:

الجمل التالية كلها تعبر عن حقائق لذا تم كتابتها بالمضارع البسيط:

1. Wood floats on water. 2. Man is mortal.
3. Man has reason.   4. Salt dissolves in water.
5. People inhale oxygen. 6. Water freezes at zero degree centigrade.
7. Chickens lay eggs.   8. A plant has roots.
9. Birds have wings.   10. Oil is flammable.

The following examples express habitual activities, so that they are written in present simple tense:

الجمل التالية كلها تعبر عن عادات لذا تم كتابتها بالمضارع البسيط:

Fundamental English Grammar Review
1. Rula visits Europe every ten years.
2. My classes begin at 7:30.
3. Huda never goes to bed before midnight.
4. I rarely go shopping in winter.

Fundamental English Grammar Review

Exercise (6)

Use the simple past tense or the past progressive in the following sentences as appropriate.

1. Amal ....(eat) dinner when her friend called.
2. While Asma was cleaning the room, her father.....(sleep)
3. At three o'clock this morning, Dan .....(study)
4. Josef ......(go) to Denmark last week.
5. While Harry was writing the daily report, Robert .....(look) for more information.

Exercise (7)

Use the simple past tense or the present perfect in the following sentences.

1. Bob ......(see) this movie before.
2. John ....(swim) in the pool last night.
3. Conrad ....(read) the newspaper already.
4. I.....(not, begin) to study for the final test yet.
5. Joan..... (travel) around the world by boat.

Exercise (8)

Use the simple past tense or the past perfect tense in the following sentences.

1. Bob ......(read) my letter after he .....(meet)me.
2. After John ....(wash) his clothes, he began to study.
3. Maria ....(join) the army after she had graduated from the School of Armor..

Exercise (9)

Use the simple present tense or the present progressive tense in the following sentences.

1. The train......(leave) at 7:30 every morning.
2. We always .....(go) skiing.
3. She rarely ....(get) home in time.
4. The sun .....(rise) from the east.
5. I......(work) in Kuwait nowadays.
6. She.....(buy) a new pair of shoes right now.

5. Regular Verbs, Irregular Verbs, and Gerund

الأفعال المنتظمة وغير المنتظمة وصيغة اسم الفاعل (Verb+ing)

5.1 Regular and Irregular Verbs

The past form of a verb could have either regular or irregular form.

⟹ The regular form ends in 'd'/ 'ed' in past and past participle form, as in:

الأفعال المنتظمة وغير المنتظمة و صيغة اسم الفاعل: إن صيغة الفعل الماضي قد يكون له شكل منتظم يتفق مع التصريف الثالث للفعل (الاسم المفعول)، وقد يكون له شكل شاذ عن التصريف الثالث للفعل. أما الشكل المنتظم للتصريف الثاني والثالث للفعل فينتهي اما بـ ed أو d كما في الأمثلة التالية:

Infinitive	Past	Past participle
act	acted	acted
walk	walked	walked
hope	hoped	hoped

⟹ Whereas the irregular verbs are written differently, as in:

بينما تكتب الأفعال الشاذة بأشكال مختلفة، كما في الجدول التالي- ولمزيد من الأمثلة راجع الملحق(1):

Infinitive	Past	Past participle
arise	arose	arisen
cut	cut	cut
catch	caught	caught

(see appendix 1 for irregular verbs)

- Some irregular verbs have two past tenses and two past participles which are the same (one ends in (e)d whereas the other does not), as in:

بعض الأفعال غير المنتظمة لها صيغتين للفعل الماضي وكذلك للاسم المفعول/ التصريف الثالث، وكما في الأمثلة التالية:

Infinitive	Past	Past participle
burn	burned/ burnt	burned/ burnt
hang	hanged/ hung	hanged/ hung
kneel	kneeled/ knelt	kneeled/ knelt
leap	leaped/ leapt	leaped/ leapt
learn	learned/ learnt	learned/ learnt

- Some irregular verbs have past tenses that don't end in (e)d and have the same form of the past participles, as in:

بعض الأفعال غير المنتظمة لها صيغة للفعل الماضي التي لا تنتهي بـ ed/ d وهو نفس شكل التصريف الثالث، وكما في الأمثلة التالية:

Infinitive	Past	Past participle
bend	bent	bent
sit	sat	sat
stick	stuck	stuck
flee	fled	fled
lose	lost	lost

- Some irregular verbs have regular past tense forms but two possible past participles, one of which is regular, as in:

بعض الأفعال غير المنتظمة لها صيغة منتظمة للفعل الماضي أما للتصريف الثالث فلها صيغتان إحداهما منتظم، وكما في الأمثلة التالية:

Infinitive	Past	Past participle
mow	mowed	mowed/ mown
prove	proved	proved/ proven
sew	sewed	sewed/ sewn
show	showed	show/ showed
swell	swelled	swelled/ swollen

- Some irregular verbs have past tense and past participle that are different from each other, as in:

بعض الأفعال غير المنتظمة لها فعل ماضي واسم مفعول مختلفان عن بعضهما في الصيغة، وكما في الأمثلة التالية:

Infinitive	Past	Past participle
arise	arose	arisen
begin	began	begun
freeze	froze	frozen
go	went	gone
give	gave	given

5.2   For forming present participle/ gerund out of a verb we add 'ing' to the infinitive, as in:

لصياغة اسم الفاعل من الفعل فإننا نضيف (ing) لمصدر الفعل، كما في الأمثلة التالية:

Infinitive	Gerund
act	acting
walk	walking
cut	cutting
cultivate	cultivating
study	studying
speak	speaking
tell	telling

5.3   Dealing with forming gerunds and the past (participle) forms of verbs is inevitable. Here are some **rules of how to spell '- ing' and 'ed' at the end of verbs:**

إن التعامل مع صياغة اسم الفاعل والتصريف الثاني والثالث للفعل أمر لا مفر منه. التالية هي بعض القواعد المفيدة في تهجئة الأفعال عند إضافة:ed أو ing لنهاية الفعل المجرد/ المصدر.

❖ Verbs that end in 'e':   الأفعال المنتهية بحرف e

   ● If the word ends in 'e', drop the 'e' to add- ing, as in:

      have= having

      date= dating

      hope= hoping

          اذا كان الفعل المصدر ينتهي بحرف e احذفه وأضف ing لصياغة اسم فاعل.

      If the verb ends in 'ee', the final 'e' is not dropped, as in:

      agree =   agreeing.

          اذا كان الفعل المصدر ينتهي بـ ee فلا تحذف أيا منها وأضف ing لصياغة اسم فاعل. وأضف d فقط لصياغة التصريف الثاني والثالث.

   ● If the word ends in 'e', add 'd' without dropping the 'e', as in:

      date= dated

      hope= hoped

          اذا كان الفعل المصدر ينتهي بحرف e فقط أضف ed لصياغة الفعل الماضي.

❖ In one syllable verbs that end in a vowel+ a consonant, double the last consonant to add 'ing' 'or' 'ed', as in:

   stop= stopping, stopped

   beg= begging, begged

   But in 'fix' you don't double the last consonant:

   fix = fixing, fixed

          في الأفعال التي تتكون من مقطع واحد والتي تنتهي بحرف علة يليه حرف صحيح كرر/ ضعف الحرف الصحيح الأخير. مع استثناء كلمات مثل fix.

❖ In 2nd syllable stressed two- syllable verbs that end in a vowel+ a consonant you double the last consonant, as in:

   control= controlling, controlled

   prefer= preferring, preferred

          في الأفعال التي تتكون من مقطعين والتي تنتهي بحرف علة يليه حرف صحيح ويكون فيها التشديد على المقطع الثاني من الفعل فانك تكرر/ تضعف الحرف الصحيح الأخير ثم تضيف ing/ ed .

❖ If the verb ends in two consonants, just add the 'ing'/ 'ed' , as in :

   start= starting, started

          اذا كان الفعل المصدر ينتهي بحرفين صحيحين أضف ed /ing للفعل.

❖ If the verb ends in 'y' that is preceded by a vowel, keep the 'y' and just add the 'ing' or 'ed', as in:

enjoy= enjoying, enjoyed

اذا كان الفعل المصدر ينتهي بحرف 'y' مسبوق بحرف علة، فقط أضف ing/ed.

But if the 'y' is preceded by a consonant, change 'y' to 'i' to add 'ed', and keep the 'y' if you want to add 'ing', as in:

study= studying, studied

أما اذا كان الفعل ينتهي بحرف y ومسبوق بحرف صحيح، فقط أضف ing، لصياغة اسم فاعل واقلب ال y الى i عند إضافة ed اذا أردت صياغة التصريف الثاني/أو الثالث للفعل.

❖ If the verb ends in 'ie', just add 'd' to form the past tense or the past participle; and change 'ie' to 'y' to add 'ing', as in:

die= dying, died

اذا كان الفعل المصدر ينتهي بـ ie ، فقط أضف d لصياغة التصريف الثاني/ الثالث، واذا أردت أضافة ing اقلب ie لتصبح y .

6. Non-Progressive Verbs

الأفعال غير المستمرة

6.1 While progressive verbs express activities in progress, non- progressive verbs express existing state. Non-progressive verbs can't be written in the '-ing form'. The following are non-progressive verbs, which include the following groups:

بينما تعبر الأفعال المستمرة عن نشاطات بحالة استمرارية فإن الأفعال غير المستمرة تخبر عن حالة و ing. وضع قائم حاليا. والأفعال غير المستمرة (لا تأتي بصيغة استمرارية): أي لا يضاف لمصدرها وهي تضم:

a. Mental State- Verbs. These include:

أفعال تصف حالة ذهنية/ عقلية، وتشتمل الأفعال أدناه:

know يعرف *realize* يدرك *understand* يفهم *believe* يعتقد *think* يعتقد

imagine يتخيل/يتصور *want* يرغب/ يريد *lack* يفتقر لـ/يعوزه *need* يحتاج

prefer يفضل *remember* يتذكر and *recognize* يدرك

For example:

- I *believe* in almighty God.
- She *needs* you.
- I *understand* your point.
- He *thinks* you are mistaken.
- He *imagines* weird things.
- I *remember* my father's advice.
- I *know* the truth.
- Ali *lacks* confidence.

b. Emotional State- Verbs. These include:

أفعال تعبر عن عاطفة أو شعور، وتشمل الأفعال التالية:

love يحب *hate* يكره *like* يحب *dislike* لا يحب *appreciate* يقدر *fear* يخاف and *care* يهتم/يرعى

As in:

- Ann *hates* articles about computer games.

('*hates*' is non progressive as it describes Ann's emotional state).

- I *like* swimming in the hotel pool.
- I *appreciate* your help.

c. Sense Perceptions- Verbs. These include: *smell* رائحة يبعث/ رائحته

taste مذاقا *feel* يشعر/ يعطي(له) مذاقه *see* يرى *hear* يسمع look يبدو seem يبدو notice يلاحظ

For example:

- This omelet smells nice.
- The sea food tastes delicious.
- He *seems* friendly.
- Janet *looks* so attractive.
- The cat *feels* soft.

d. **Possession- verbs** (أفعال التملك) as in: *possess* يمتلك *own* يملك *belong* ـ ينتمي and *have* يمتلك.

Examples include:

- I don't *belong* to this nation.
- Alia *owns* three apartment-buildings.
- She *possesses* a Mercedes company.
- They *have* plenty of food.

e. In addition to the following verbs بالإضافة للأفعال التالية: *cost, be, exist, owe, appear, contain, consist of, include, be worth,* and *weigh.*

For example:

- This car *is worth* $ 2000.
- That wallet *costs* 20 dollars.
- She *is* a great actor.
- My father *weighs* 200 pounds.
- Water *consists* of oxygen and hydrogen.
- This classroom *contains* 20 seats.
- Yousef *owes* me 20,000 Euro.
- Mount Nebo *exists/ is* in Jordan.

6.2 However, the following verbs can also be progressive to give a special meaning: *think, have, small, taste, see, feel, look, appear, weigh* and *be.*

على أية حال فان الأفعال التالية يمكن أن تأتي بصيغة الاستمرارية لتعطي معانٍ خاصة.
(*think, have, small, taste, see, feel, look, appear, weigh* and *b*)

For example:

(Think) in the following sentences:

- I am *thinking* of building a wooden house. (it refers to a mental activity)
- I *think* that my dictionary is lost. (*'think'* expresses a mental state)

فمثلا الفعل Think في المثال الأول جاء ليشير إلى نشاط عقلي، بينما في الجملة الثانية
استخدم بمعنى " يعتقد" ليعبر عن حالة ذهنية.

(Have) in the following sentences:

- We are *having* lunch. (it means the activity of *eating*)
- I have a farm. (it means *possess*)

فمثلا الفعل have في المثال الأول جاء بمعنى يأكل، بينما في الجملة الثانية بمعنى يملك.

7.   Causative Verbs (make, have, get, let...)

أفعال السببية

7.1 *'Make, have, get and let'* can be used to express the idea that someone causes another to do something.

تستخدم هذه الأفعال للتعبير عن فكرة مغزاها (أن شخصا ما يتسبب بجعل شخص آخر يؤدي فعل معين)، لاحظ الأمثلة التالية:

For example:

    a.   I *made* Ali *open* the door. (It means that Ali had no choice. I insisted that he open the door. I **forced** him to do it).

هذه الجملة تعني أن عليا لم يكن لديه خيار وإنما:**أجبرت عليا ليفتح الباب.**

    b.   I *had* Ali *open* the door. (It means that Ali opened the door because I **requested**/ asked him to do so).

هذه الجملة تعني أن عليا فتح الباب لأنني طلبت منه ذلك:جعلت عليا يفتح الباب.

Note: Causative ' have' and 'make' are followed by the bare infinitive.

لاحظ أن الفعل Have/make يأتي متبوعا بفعل مجرد/ مصدر.

    c.   I *got* Ali *to open* the door. (It means that I **managed to persuade** Ali to open the door)

هذه الجملة تعني: أنني تمكنت من إقناع علي ليفتح الباب.

Note: Causative 'get' is followed by 'to infinitive' (to+ simple form of a verb).

لاحظ أن الفعل get يأتي متبوع بمصدر مسبوق بـ to .

    d.   'Let' means 'permit/ allow'. 'Let' takes the base form of a verb (bare infinitive), whereas 'permit/ or allow' takes 'to-infinitive', as in:

let تستخدم بمعنى يسمح، الا أنها تأخذ فعلا مجردا (مصدر)، كما في المثال(1)، بينما allow أو Permit تأخذ فعل مصدر مسبوق بـto كما في المثال (2).

    1.   John let me swim in the pool.

(Subject+ let+ object+ base form of verb)

    2.   John allowed me to swim in the pool.

(Subject+ allow/ permit+ object+ to-infinitive)

7.2 Have/ get something done

We can use *'have'/get'* in a passive pattern to mean that *an arrangement made for someone to do something for you.*

نستخدم have/get في صيغة المبني للمجهول لنشير الى أن هناك ترتيبات يتم القيام بها

لتمكين شخص ما للقيام بأمر ما أو أن شخصا اخر يقوم بالفعل نيابة عنك باعتباره مختص أو يؤده لك كمساعدة.

Examples:

- I *had the furniture delivered.*

(someone else delivered the furniture)

لقد تم إيصال الأثاث. هذه الجملة تفيد أن شخصا ما قام بإيصال الأثاث نيابة عني.

- You should *have that video fixed.*

(by the technician)

تفيد أنه عليك أن ترسل جهاز الفيديو للتصليح. ترسله للتقني المختص.

- Mary *had a new house built.*

(not by herself)

تفيد هنا أيضا أن المنزل الذي تم بناءه لها لم تبنه هي بنفسها، وإنما المختص بأعمال البناء هو من بناه لها.

وكذلك الأمر في الأمثلة التالية:

- I must *get the furniture delivered.*

- I *got that video repaired.*

- I'm going to *get my eyes tested.*

- She is *getting her house decorated.*

Exercise (10)

A: Correct the verbs in brackets.

1. The student made Fredrick......(leave) the classroom.
2. Helena had Salim......(repair) the car.
3. Allen got Hamdan.......(type) her essay.
4. I had the students......(write) a formal letter.
5. Maria let Adnan.....(sign) the forms.
6. Mariam allows her sons....(play) for late hours.
7. Salamah permitted his daughter.....(swim) with her friends.

B: Study the following pair of sentences and answer the question below.

a. I've taken my shirt to be shortened.

b. I've shortened my shirt.

Which sentence indicates that the tailor/ not the speaker has shortened the shirt.
....

8. Gerund and to-infinitive (playing/ to play)

الفعل: بصيغة إسم الفاعل، ومصدره مسبوق بـto

A gerund is the -ing form of a verb, as in *'playing'*. An infinitive is 'to+ the simple base form of a verb, as in *'to play'*.

8.1 The uses of –ing form of verbs

The uses of the 'ing' form of verb include: صيغة اسم الفاعل تستخدم كما يلي

    a. A gerund as a **"noun"** which could be used as a subject/ or an object in a sentence, e.g.

- *Sleeping* early is good for the health. (*sleeping* is the subject)

- I'm talking about *visiting* Petra. (*visiting* is the object)

تستخدم كأسم والذي يمكن أن يستخدم كفاعل كما في الجملة الأولى، وكمفعول به كما في الجملة الثانية أعلاه.

    b. A participle to express an idea in present/ or past **progressive** tense, as in;

- Ann is *swimming*.

- Ralph was *painting*.

تستخدم لصياغة حالة الاستمرارية/ أو للتعبير عن فكرة ما في الزمن المضارع المستمر والماضي المستمر.

    c. A present participle used as an **adjective** تستخدم كصفة, as in;

- *surprising* events أحداث مفاجئة - developing countries دول نامية

- daring commander قائد شجاع - sleeping women نساء نائمات

    d. After some verbs, including: **smell, feel, taste, hear, see, listen, watch, notice, find, catch.** The following pattern is followed: (**verb+ noun/ object pronoun+ verb+ ing**)

بعد الأفعال أعلاه على أن يلي هذه الأفعال مفعولا به وتتبع النسق التالي (فعل+ مفعول به+ فعل بصيغة اسم فاعل) وكما في الأمثلة التالية:

Examples include:

- I *saw Hani **climbimg*** the mountain.

       v   o gerund (v+ ing)

- I heard you *crying* last night.

- I felt him *lying*.

- I found Shaza *punishing* a little child.

    e. After 'waste' and 'spend' when they are followed by time expressions, following this pattern (**waste/ spend+ expression of time+ verb+ ing**).

بعد الأفعال أعلاه على أن يلي هذه الأفعال تعبير عن الوقت وتتبع النسق التالي (الفعل+ تعبير عن الزمن+ فعل بصيغة اسم فاعل) وكما في الأمثلة التالية:

- Mr. Ibrahim *spent* *five weeks* ***looking*** for a new job.

          v time expression v+ ing

- Mrs. Ibrahim *wastes three hours a day watching* TV.

f.   After 'sit', 'stand' , and 'lie' when they are followed by place expressions, following this pattern **(sit/ stand/ lie + expression of place+ Verb+ ing)**.

بعد الأفعال أعلاه على أن يلي هذه الأفعال تعبير عن المكان وتتبع النسق التالي (**الفعل+ تعبير عن المكان+ فعل بصيغة اسم فاعل**) وكما في الأمثلة التالية:

- I *sat in the corridor revising* my new book
      V   place expression   V+ ing
- I stood there *thinking* about you.
- She lay in her bed *waiting* for her husband.

g.   After '**go**' to express an activity done for recreation, as in:

go shopping, go fishing, go hiking, go hunting, go canoeing, go dancing, go sightseeing, go skiing, go swimming, go sledding, go tobogganing, etc.

As in: "I usually go shopping at weekends".

بعد الفعل go للتعبير عن نشاطات ورياضات نقوم بها للترفيه كما في الأمثلة أعلاه.

h.   After certain verbs that are mentioned in paragraph (**8.3**).

بعد أفعال محددة كالواردة في الفقرة (8.3) لاحقا.

8.2   Verbs followed by to- infinitives

أفعال شائعة يتبعها أفعالا مجرده ومسبوقة بـ to .

a. Some verbs are followed immediately by to- infinitive, this includes: *plan, intend, decide, hope, promise, seem, agree, offer desire, attempt, prepare, tend, claim, forget, demand, hesitate, learn, refuse, appear, pretend, ask, afford, expect, want, need, advice* and *would like.*

Examples include:

- Ala *expects to begin* studying applied linguistics next month.
- I *learnt to swim* when I was ten.
- The chief *decided to postpone* the conference.
- Katrin *agreed to act* as a logistic officer.

To form a negative out of those verbs you put 'not' before the infinitive.

ويصاغ النفي من هذه الأفعال بإضافة Not بعدها وقبل الفعل المصدر/ المجرد والمسبوق بـ to ، وكما في المثال التالي:

As in: I *promised to arrive* early.

I *promised not to arrive* early. (Negative)

b. Some verbs are followed by a noun or pronoun (as an object) and then to- infinitive, including:

بعض هذه الأفعال يتبعها اسم أو ضمير ثم الفعل المجرد/ المصدر مسبوقا بـ to مثل:

"*tell, invite, require, beg, convince, expect, instruct, persuade, prepare, promise, urge, ask, permit, order, allow, warn, force, want, would like, encourage,* and *remind*", as in:

The boss *forced me to shout* at her.

I _told Benedict to leave_ at 7 am.

The teacher _encouraged the students to practice_ English in the classroom.

I _urged Leon to appear_ in class.

I _asked Bell to call_ me at noon time.

(Subject+ verb+ object form of pronoun/ noun+ to- infinitive)

8.3 **Verbs followed by the gerund**

الأفعال التي يتبعها فعل+ ing .

a. The following are common verbs followed by the gerund:

الأفعال التالية يتبعها فعل+ ing .

enjoy, appreciate, admit, report, postpone, resent, practice, resist, can't help, resume, recall, risk, mind, quit, finish, avoid, delay, keep, miss, recommend, consider, discuss, mention and _suggest_, as in;

- You should _keep running_.
- Noah _quit smoking_.
- I _admitted stealing_ from the store.
- You _enjoyed seeing_ your school friends.

b. Some verbs can be followed **by either the gerund or the to- infinitive with no change in meaning,** such as: _suggest, hate, regret, like, start, love, continue, try, dread, prefer, enjoy, hope, dislike,_ and _can't stand._

بعض الأفعال يمكن أن يتبعها فعل مجرد يسبقه to ويمكن كذلك أن يتبعها فعل بصيغة أسم فاعل دون أن يتغير المعنى تبعا لذلك.

- I _started to study_ after lunch.

    I _started studying_ after lunch.

- He _hates to ride_ bikes.

    He _hates riding_ bikes.

c. Some verbs can be **followed by either the gerund or the to- infinitive, but the meaning changes,** as in: stop, forget, and remember.

بعض الأفعال يمكن أن يتبعها فعل مجرد يسبقه to ويمكن كذلك أن يتبعها فعل بصيغة أسم فاعل إلا أن المعنى يتغير تبعا لذلك.

For example:

- Ali _stopped teaching_ English. (He is not going to teach anymore)

توقف علي عن تدريس الانجليزية (أي انه لن يدرس الانجليزية من الآن فصاعدا)

- Ali _stopped to teach_ English. (He stopped in order to teach English)

توقف علي لتدريس الانجليزية (أي من أجل أن يدرس الانجليزية)

d. **Some verbs are followed by a noun or pronoun and then the gerund.** However the noun or pronoun must appear in the possessive form (their calling, teacher's calling).

بعض هذه الأفعال يتبعها اسم أو ضمير ثم فعل يتبعه وهذا الاسم أو الضمير يكون بصيغة الملكية ويتبع هذا الإسم أو الضمير فعل بصيغة اسم الفاعل (Their calling, teacher's calling)

Examples include:

- He *regrets her leaving*.
- He *regrets Ali's leaving*.
- We are ***looking forward to** their visiting* next month.
- We are *looking forward to Hisham's visiting* next month.

(Subject+ verb+ possessive form of noun/ possessive adjective+ verb+ ing)

8.4 Adjectives followed by to- infinitives

Some adjectives are usually followed by infinitives, as in

'Surprised to' in: 'I was *surprised to see* Samia at the party'.

The following is a list of adjectives which are followed by infinitives as per this pattern (**Adjective+ to- infinitive**):

بعض الصفات يتبعها فعل مجرد ومسبوق بـ to وكما في النسق التالي

(**Adjective+ to- infinitive**) ومن هذه الصفات:

glad	fortunate	careful
happy	sorry	hesitant
pleased	ready	lucky

Examples include the following:

- I'm *glad to be* with you.
- Are you *ready to go*?
- She's *pleased to take part* in the championship.
- Fredrick was *lucky to meet* the king at the independence celebration.
- Ali speaks so fast that it's *difficult to understand* what he's saying.
- I found that box *heavy to lift*.
- I found the homework *easy to do*.

8.5 Verb+ prepositions followed by the gerund

If a verb+ preposition, adjective+ preposition, noun+ preposition, or preposition is followed directly by a verb, the verb will be in the gerund form.

إذا سبق الفعل حرف جر فإنه يصاغ بصيغة اسم الفاعل (verb+ing).

approve of	give up	insist on	succeed in	think about	think of
depend on	rely on	worry about	intend on	count on	object to
object to	confess to	afraid of	accustomed to	successful in	
choice of	excuse for	method for	possibility of	reason for	

- She has no excuse **for dropping** the boxes.
- Mike is afraid **of getting** married now.

8.6 Used to

a. 'Used to infinitive':

This pattern is used to refer to something that happened regularly in the past, but it doesn't any more, as in:

1. When I was a child, I *used to smoke* heavily.

2. I *used to drink* alcohol. (it means I gave it up)

'Used to+ infinitive'

تستخدم هذه الصيغة لتشير إلى شيء حدث بانتظام في الماضي إلا انه لم يعد موجودا. ففي المثال الأول تفيد الجملة (أنني كنت معتادا على التدخين عندما كنت في طفولتي، إلا أنني لا أدخن في الوقت الحاضر). وكذلك الجملة الثانية فتعني (كنت معتادا على شرب الكحول ولكن توقفت عن ذلك).

b. 'Be+ used to+ verb+ ing' pattern is used to mean 'accustomed to or familiar with'.

هذه الصيغة تفيد معنى (معتاد على).

As in:

Rasha *is used to driving* fast.

رشا معتادة على القيادة بسرعة.

Are you *used to walking* long distance?

هل أنت معتاد على مشي المسافات الطويلة؟

I *am* not *used to swimming* in the pool.

أنا لست معتادا على السباحة في البركة.

8.7 Hear+ object+ sing; hear+ object+ singing

We can use (see, hear, watch, feel, smell+ object) followed either by gerund or by infinitive without (to) to give specific meanings. For example:

(1) I **saw** Mary **killing** the thief. (I saw part of the action)

(2) I **saw** Mary **kill** the thief. (I saw the whole action)

يمكن أن يأتي بعد الأفعال:(see, hear, watch, feel, smell+ مفعول به) فعل+ Ing أو مصدر (فعل مجرد) ولكن لكل حالة منها معنى مختلف، مثلا في المثال أعلاه الجملة الأولى تعني أنني شاهدت جزءا من الحدث وهو قتل ماري للص، أما الجملة الثانية فتعني أنني شاهدت كل الحدث. وكذلك الأمر في الأمثلة التالية:

- I **heard** Hala **sing** in her bedroom.

  I **heard** Hala **singing** in her bedroom.

- I **watched** Obama **addressing** his people.

  I **watched** Obama **address** his people.

Exercise (11)

Using the verbs in brackets, choose the appropriate one to fill in the space in the following sentences

1. I am pleased ……from you. (to hearing/ to hear/ hearing)
2. I hope …….you soon. (to seeing/ see/ to see/ seeing)
3. I quit ……… (to smoke/ smoking)
4. The class bores the students. It is a …… class. (bored/ boring)
5. My dad made me…….. the house. (leave/ to leave)
6. I got Shirazi …… the items. (to fetch/ fetch/ fetching)
7. I had Kerry …..the ceiling. (to repair/ repair/ repairing)
8. When I was in the countryside, I used ….....10 miles a day.
    (to walk/ to walking)
9. Tim avoided…………….. (looking/ to look) at Rehab.
10. Do you enjoy………… (playing/ to play) soccer ?
11. Keep………….. (talking/ to talk). I'm listening to you.
12. I hope………….. (visiting / to visit) London next week.
13. Richard is expecting us….(to come/ coming) to class tomorrow.
14. They don't approve….. (us/ our) leaving early.
15. Joe resented …..(Fadi/ Fadi's) losing the match.

Exercise (12)

Complete the following table with the gerund and past form of the following verbs:

Verbs	Gerund	Past form
stop	stopping	stopped
die		
argue		
agree		
enjoy		
fix		

Exercise (13)

Correct the verbs in brackets to fit the meaning of the sentences.

1. Since 1999, I ……….Jerash city. (not/ visit).
2. Two of Aljazeera correspondents…...the news at this minute. (present)
3. After I ………. her, she came to see me. (call)
4. I………..(drive) the lorry for the last six hours. I feel really terrible.
5. A: How long ………..(teach) ?
    B: All my life.
6. As the teacher ……the situation, the student fell down. (figure out)

7.   My child always ……….. milk. (drink)

8.   At 9:00 last night they ……….. (study) English.

9.   Did you ……….. (watch) TV last night?

10.   When my parents ……….. (have) breakfast, the phone rang.

11.   My favourite sport ……….. (be) jumping. I usually do it once a week.

12.   What are you doing right now? I ……….. (run) round the sport field.

13.   Do you often……….. (walk) or run in the school yard?

14.   Do you go……….. (swim)?

15.   What ……….. you……….. wear) at the moment?

16.   ……….. you ever……….. (see) the pyramids?

17.   I ……….. (observe) the demonstration all the day. That is why I'm a bit tired.

Exercise (14)

Circle the appropriate answer.

1.   It is important………. fit.
   a. to keep   b. keeping   c. kept

2.   ………..fruit and vegetables helps you keep healthy.
   a. Eating   b. To eat   c. Ate

3.   You look tired. What have you ………..doing?
   a. been   b. be   c. were

4.   My friends could be ………about their new century plans.
   a. think   b. thinking   c. thinks

5.   ……. been stealing the farmers' stores. That is why the police are trying to arrest him
   a. He's   b. Hes'   c. Is he

6. Dan ………..gorgeous.
   a. looks   b. look   c. were looking

7. None of the students ………smart enough to win.
   a. is   b. are   c. were

8. A number of cadets ………visiting USMA West Point.
   a. is   b. are   c. was

9. Daily exercises ………good to keep yourself fit
   a. is   b. are   c. have

10. A chair with two arms……..comfortable to sit in.
   a. is   b. are   c. have

11. One million dollars…….the price of this piece.
   a. is   b. are   c. were

12. Neither Ahmad nor I …….. fit to fight.
   a. is   b. are   c. am

Exercise (15)

Choose the suitable items to fill in the blanks.

become	wasn't	weren't	will use

Next year, our college tennis team ……….. new fields and courts for training. They ……….. that professional last year; but now they've ……….. more and more well trained and organized.

Exercise (16)

Study the following pair of sentences and answer the question below.

1. Mrs. Bartlett has read a poem of Blake.
2. Mrs. Bartlett has been reading a poem of Blake for some time.

Which sentence indicates that Mrs. Bartlett has finished reading a poem of Blake?………….

Exercise (17)

What part of the sentence is each underlined phrase? (subject, verb, object, complement or adverbial).

1. Jim had <u>a great time</u>. Object
2. <u>Everybody</u> was brilliant. ………
3. I <u>liked</u> your suggestion. ………
4. I'm <u>happy</u> today. ………
5. She visits her grandmother <u>weekly</u>. ………
6. I love <u>Silvia</u>. ………

Exercise (18)

Make sentences by putting the following words in the correct order. You can refer to the simple sentence forms.

1. is/ people/ Ali/ to/ going/ meet/some
   ……………………………………………
2. have/ I/ 15/ buildings
   ……………………………………………
3. Aaron/ sick/ was/ yesterday
   ……………………………………………
4. is/ looking/ He/ at/ Gabriel
   ……………………………………………
5. gave/ they/ a/ him/ Swiss watch
   ……………………………………………

9. Negation

النفــــي

9.1 Main negative patterns   الأنماط الرئيسة للنفي

We can follow different patterns to change affirmative sentences into negative sentences, as follows:

يمكننا أن نحول الجمل المثبتة إلى منفية وفق أنماط مختلفة، وكالتالي:

a. **First pattern:** To change an affirmative sentence into negative, add '**not**' to the auxiliary and modal verbs: is, was, are, were, am, has, have, had, must, should, etc., as in:

النمط الأول: لتحويل الجملة من حالة الإثبات إلى حالة النفي أضف كلمة not بعد الفعل المساعد، كما في الأمثلة التالية.

- Sami **is** sleeping.   (affirmative)
  Sami **is not** sleeping. (negative)
- Suha **can** play well. (affirmative)
  Suha **cannot** play well. (negative)
- Khadija **was lying** in her bed. (affirmative)
  Khadija **was not lying** in her bed. (negative)
- George and Sara **were** rich. (affirmative)
  George and Sara **were not** rich. (negative)
- Sandra **is going to** Japan. (affirmative)
  Sandra **is not going to** Japan. (negative)
- Mark **has** seen the accident. (affirmative)
  Mark **has not** seen the accident. (negative)
- I **must** go to Petra. (affirmative)
  I **must not** go to Petra. (negative)
- She **had** visited Petra. (affirmative)
  She **had not** visited Petra. (negative)

Second pattern: When the verb is in the simple present tense and the subject is plural, put (do not) before the verb. But, when the subject is singular, put (does not) before the main verb and omit the (s/es). When (has) is used as the main verb, it becomes (have) as a main verb- in this pattern.

من النمط الثاني: حين يكون الفعل في الزمن المضارع البسيط والفاعل جمع أضف قبل الفعل do not أما اذا كان الفاعل مفردا فأضف does not قبل الفعل واحذف es/ آخر الفعل الرئيس، واذا كان الفعل الرئيس المستخدم هو has فأضف does not وحول has الى have ، و كما في الأمثلة التالية:

Examples:

- Rashad **speaks** English fluently. (affirmative)
  Rashad **does not speak** English fluently. (negative)
- They **live** in Jordan. (affirmative)

They **do not live** in Jordan. (negative)

- She **has** two kids. (affirmative)

  She **does not have** two kids. (negative)

- They **have** two kids. (affirmative)

  They **do not have** two kids. (negative)

c. Third pattern: If the verb is in the past simple, use (did not) before the infinitive form of the verb. When (had) is used as a main verb, it becomes (have) as a main verb preceded by (did not).

النمط الثالث: اذا كان الفعل في الزمن الماضي البسيط، استخدم مصدر الفعل بدلا منه وأضف: وتضيف قبله did not قبل الفعل المجرد، أما اذا كان الفعل الرئيسي هو had فتبدله بـ have . كما في الأمثلة التالية.

Examples:

- Rashad **watched** a comedy film. (affirmative)

  Rashad **did not watch** a comedy film. (negative)

- They **wrote** a short story. (affirmative)

  They **did not write** a short story. (negative)

- She **had** two children. (affirmative)

  She **did not have** two children. (negative)

9.2   Negative Prefixes (un-, il-, im-, dis-, ir-, in-):

They all mean 'not' or 'do the opposite of'. They can be used with verbs, adverbs, nouns and adjectives.

un, il, im, in, ir, and كل منها بادئة للكلمة وتستخدم لتفيد النفي أو الضد. ويمكن استخدامها مع الأفعال dis

والظروف والأسماء والصفات أيضا.

Un- is the most common negative prefix

un وهي الأكثر شيوعا واستخداما.

Dis- is used with some adjectives

dis وتستخدم هذه مع بعض الصفات وعدد هذه الصفات قليل.

Il- is used with some adjectives beginning with 'l'

il تستخدم مع بعض الصفات التي تبدأ بحرف (l) .

Im- is used with some adjectives beginning with 'm' or 'p'

im تستخدم مع بعض الصفات التي تبدأ بحرف (m / p) .

Ir- is used with some adjectives beginning with 'r'

ir تستخدم مع بعض الصفات التي تبدأ بحرف (r) .

In- is used with many adjectives

in تستخدم مع عدد كبير من الصفات.

Examples:

Word		**Negative/ opposite**	
aware	مدرك	**un**aware	غير مدرك
employment	توظيف	**un**employment	بطالة
important	مهم	**un**important	غير مهم
common	شائع	**un**common	غير شائع
comfortable	مريح	**un**comfortable	غير مريح

clear	واضح	unclear	غير واضح
likely	محتمل	unlikely	غير محتمل
limited	محدود	unlimited	غير محدود
familiar	مألوف	unfamiliar	غير مألوف
friendly	ودي	unfriendly	غير ودي
tidy	مرتب	untidy	غير مرتب

Word		Negative/ opposite	
polite	مؤدب	impolite	غير مؤدب
moral	أخلاقي	immoral	لا أخلاقي
possible	ممكن	impossible	غير ممكن
partial	منحاز	impartial	محايد
mortal	فاني	immortal	خالد
perfect	تام	imperfect	غير تام
probable	محتمل	improbable	غير محتمل
pure	طاهر/غير نقي	impure	ملوث/غير نقي
patient	صبور	impatient	غير صبور

Word		Negative/ opposite	
accurate	دقيق	inaccurate	غير دقيق
complete	كامل	incomplete	غير كامل
active	نشط/ فعال	inactive	غير فعال
separable	قابل للفصل	inseparable	غير قابل للفصل
convenient	مريح/مناسب	inconvenient	غير مريح
credible	مصدق/معقول	incredible	غير معقول
direct	مباشر	indirect	غير مباشر
visible	مرئي	invisible	غير مرئي
human	إنساني	inhuman	لا إنساني
correct	صحيح	incorrect	غير صحيح
formal	رسمي	informal	غير رسمي
sufficient	كافٍ	insufficient	غير كافٍ

Word		Negative/ opposite	
appear(ed)	يظهر /ظاهر	disappear(ed)	يختفي/ مختفي
order	يرتب/ ينظم	disorder	يخل بالنظام
approve(d)	يثبت/ مثبت	disapprove(d)	ينفي/ منفي
connect(ed)	يصل/ يربط -موصول	disconnect(ed)	يفصل/ مفصول
like	يحب	dislike	لا يحب
advantage	حسنة	disadvantage	سيئة
obey	يطيع	disobey	يعصي
agreement	اتفاق	disagreement	اختلاف
honest	أمين	dishonest	غير أمين

Word		Negative/ opposite	
recoverable	يمكن إصلاحه	irrecoverable	لا يمكن إصلاحه أو استرداده
resistible	يمكن مقاومته	irresistible	لا يقاوم
regular	منتظم	irregular	غير منتظم
responsible	مسؤول	irresponsible	غير مسؤول
reducible	يمكن إنقاصه	irreducible	متعذر إنقاصه
replaceable	يمكن استبداله	irreplaceable	لا يمكن استبداله
responsive	مستجيب	irresponsive	غير مستجيب
relevant	متصل بالموضوع	irrelevant	غير متصل بالموضوع
religious	ديني	irreligious	مارق/ زنديق

Word		Negative/ opposite	
legal	شرعي	illegal	غير شرعي
logical	منطقي	illogical	غير منطقي
legitimate	شرعي	illegitimate	غير شرعي
liberal	متحرر	illiberal	متعصب/ جلف

Consider the following examples:

If you are **inexperienced**, you shouldn't apply for this teaching vacancy.

Everybody thinks that Sami and his sons are **unpleasant** people.

It's quite **impossible** to meet all the requirements.

Last meeting was one of the most **disorganized** meetings I've ever participated in.

Haifa and Sadeq are **inseparable** couple.

Du'a was fired because she was **inefficient**.

I feel awful every time **unexpected** visitors come to meet me.

9.3 Hardly, rarely, seldom, etc.

It is incorrect to have two negatives together in an English sentence (double negation). Thus, words of negative meaning must be used with a positive verb. When a sentence begins with a negative word, the subject and the verb are inverted, as in:

إن من غير الصحيح أن يكون في الجملة الانجليزية نفيان. لذا يجب استخدام الكلمات التي تعطي معنى النفي مع الأفعال المثبتة. وفي حال بدء الجملة بإحدى الكلمات التي تعطي معنى النفي يجب قلب ترتيب الفاعل والفعل المساعد في الجملة، وكما في الأمثلة التالية:

a.   I will **never** _do_ this again.

Never _will I_ do this again.

    b. <u>I have **rarely** *drunk*</u> coffee.

       Rarely *have I* drunk coffee.

    c. <u>He **hardly** *comes*</u> to the meeting on time.

       Hardly *does he* come to the meeting on time.

    d. <u>He not only broke</u> the window but also damaged the car.

       Not only *did he* break the window but also damaged the car.

    e. <u>You **seldom** see</u> photos of jaguars.

       Seldom *do you* see photos of jaguars.

    f. <u>She **scarcely** remembers</u> the events.

       Scarcely *does she* remember the events.

    g. <u>Ali **barely** arrived</u> in time.

       Barely *did Ali* arrive in time.

    h. Babies **no sooner** learn to crawl than they start walking.

       No sooner *do babies* learn to crawl than they start walking.

    i. I **little** thought that I would be visiting Tokyo for work.

       Little *did I* think that I would be visiting Tokyo for work.

9.4 Contracted forms of auxiliary verbs with not

The following are short/ contracted forms of auxiliary and modal verbs with 'not' as used in written texts. It is key to know which letters are dropped and where to put the apostrophe.

تاليا الشكل المختصر للأفعال المساعدة في حالة النفي (من الأهمية بمكان أن تلاحظ وتعرف الحرف الذي يتم حذفه ومكان رسم الفاصلة العلوية).

Full form	Short form	Full form	Short form
is not	isn't	may not	mayn't
are not	aren't	ought not	oughtn't
cannot	can't	need not	needn't
could not	couldn't	dare not	daren't
did not	didn't	shall not	shan't
does not	doesn't	would not	wouldn't
do not	don't	am not	aren't
has not	hasn't	should not	shouldn't
have not	haven't	was not	wasn't
had not	hadn't	were not	weren't
must not	mustn't	will not	won't

9.5 Imperative and negative imperative

We usually use the imperative to give instructions and to give orders/ or commands. It is important to know how to make positive and negative imperatives. Commands and instructions can be preceded by *'please'*.

عادة ما نستخدم صيغة الأمر لإعطاء الإرشادات والتعليمات وإصدار الأوامر، وما ينبغي معرفته هنا هو كيف تصيغ أمرا بالإثبات (افعل) وأمرا بالنفي (لا تفعل). ويمكن أن تبدأ الأمر بكلمة:please.

Fundamental English Grammar Review

a. Use the base form of the verb to form an affirmative imperative sentence meaning (**Do**).

استخدم مصدر الفعل لتشكل جملة أمرية، حيث يوضع الفعل المجرد في البداية، وكما في الأمثلة التالية:

Please, *turn off* the lights.

Listen to your teacher.

Close the window.

Tell the truth.

Ali, *speak* **up**.

Press the 'enter' button.

Ahmed, *turn* the radio *on*.

Be quiet.

Pay your rent.

b. To form a negative imperative sentence you should begin with (**Don't**) then add the base form of the verb, as in:

Don't run in the corridor.

Don't upset your wife.

Don't smoke cigarettes in this area.

Don't work for long hours.

Don't think deep.

Don't count your money.

لصياغة جملة أمرية منفية ابدأ جملتك بـ:
Don't يليه فعل مجرد، كما في الأمثلة أعلاه.

Note: In indirect command, the verbs of command are followed by (to- infinitive). To make a negative indirect command, add (not) before the to- infinitive (following this pattern: **subject+ verb+ object+ not+ to-infinitive**).

في الأمر غير المباشر يأتي بعد الأفعال التمهيدية التي تفيد الأمر infinitive to. ولنفي
الأمر غير المباشر أضف not قبل infinitive to . كما في المثال التالي:

-    Hussein **told me <u>to close</u>** the door.

Hussein **told me <u>not to close</u>** the door.

Exercise (19)

A: Choose the right answer.

1.   Where was George born?

He …….. in Yemen.

   a. was   b. is born   c. was born   d. were born

2.   What does your cat drink?

It ……..milk.

   a. drink   b. drank   c. drinks   d. was drinking

3.   What will you study in Harvard?

I …….. applied linguistics.

   a. study   b. will study   c. I'm studying   d. studied

4.   When do your brothers usually take new courses?

They usually ……. new courses in summer.

   a. takes   b. is taking   c. take   d. took

5.   How did Hanan go to London?

She…….to London by air.

   a. goes   b. went   c. is going   d. go

6.   How old are you?

I…….. 28 years old.

   a. was   b. is   c. am   d. are

7.   He …….millions of money.

   a. has   b. have   c. am   d. do

8.   …… you go to school by bus?

   a. Do   b. Does   c. Is   d. Were

Exercise (20)

Change the sentences into negative.

1.   I'm going to see my friend.

2.   My father will come back soon.

3.   I want to sell my apartment.

4.   These shirts cost too much, so that I don't want to buy them.

5.   My T-shirt cost a lot of money.

6.   She shook hands with me.

7.   Put this letter in the envelope.

8.   He could leave early.

9.   She has two daughters.

10.   You had to come by ship.

11. Rice is grown in Egypt.

Exercise (21)

Select the appropriate verb form.

1. Maha (buy/ bought/ has bought) a new watch last week.

2. My father (leave/ will leave/ left) for Cairo next week.

3. It (be/ is/ are) hot in summer.

4. October, November and December (is/ were/ are/ have) the last three months of the year.

5. My mother (already buys/ has already bought/ will already buy) some fish.

6. A couple of days ago we (have/ had/ do/were) a wonderful party.

7. He has ..... for Moscow. (leave/ left)

8. Don't .... (eat/ to eat/eating/ ate) too many sweets.

Exercise (22)

Which sentence means 'that Ali's residence in Amman is permanent'?

1. Ali lives in Amman.   2. Ali is living in Amman.

Exercise (23):

Change the following affirmative sentences into negative.

1. Jack lives in Barcelona.

....

2. Hitler lived in Germany.

....

3. Steve and Ross prefer pop music.

....

4. Mrs. Obama has two daughters.

....

5. We are close friends.

....

10.   Derivation and order of nouns, verbs, adjectives, and adverbs

إشتقاق وترتيب كل من (الإسم والفعل والصفة والظرف) في الجملة

It is vital to know the main affixes that are used to form the noun, verb, adjective and adverb. It is also important to learn where they usually are in a sentence.

انه لمن الضروري أن تعرف وتلم بالإضافات (اللواحق والتوابع) التي تستخدم لتشكيل وصياغة الاسم والفعل والصفة والظرف. و من المهم أيضا أن تتعلم أين يأتي كل منها في ترتيب الجملة.

10.1   Word affixes. The following are the common affixes used to form nouns, verbs, adjectives or adverbs:

<u>Verbs</u>   fy (justify), ize (organize), ate (relate), en (strengthen

<u>Nouns</u>   ness (sleeplessness), ity (popularity), ment (development)

ing (running), sion (decision), tion (production), ture (culture)

ade (lemonade), age (advantage), ance (significance), ence (confidence),

ism (professionalism), ian (Jordanian), er (player)

or (actor), ist (typist) ship (friendship), ism (marxism), hood (neighborhood)

<u>Adjectives</u>   ed (developed), ing (exciting), ous (famous), ive (impressive)

ful (helpful), ible (visible), able (reliable), ic (forensic), ical (musical), ly (lovely), y (cloudy), en (golden), some (handsome)

less (sleepless)

<u>adverbs</u>   regular adverbs ending in '**ly**': (quick**ly**, fantastic**ly**)

there are some adverbs not ending in 'ly' (e.g. **hard, fast, well**)

10.2   General guideline of where nouns, verbs, adjectives, and adverbs usually come in the sentence.

دليل عام يحدد المواضع التي عادة ما يأتي بها الاسم، والفعل و الصفة والظرف.

- **The noun is usually used as follows:** عادة ما يستخدم الاسم كما يلي
  a.   As a *subject* of a sentence, e.g.   كفاعل للجملة

  <u>Visiting</u> relatives is a good thing to do

  b.   As an *object*, e.g.   كمفعول به في الجملة

  I had good <u>expectations.</u>

  c.   After the definite and indefinite *articles*, e.g. *The*بعد أدوات التعريف والتنكير.

  <u>improvement</u> of food quality is good for our health.

  d.   After the *adjectives*, e.g.   بعد الصفات

  That's a *good* <u>explanation</u>.

  e. After *determiners/ quantifiers* (this, these, few, some, no, etc), e.g.

بعد المحددات الكمية وأسماء الاشارة

  This <u>punishment</u> is just fair.

  f. After *possessives*, e.g.   بعد صفات و الملكية

  His <u>loyalty</u> was for a foreign country

  g. After *prepositions*, e.g.   بعد حروف الجر

  This exercise is perfect *for* <u>revision and meeting</u> your needs.

● **The verb is usually used as follows:عادة ما يستخدم الفعل كما يلي**

  a. After *modals*, e.g.   بعد الأفعال الشكلية

  I *can* <u>rely</u> on you.

  b. After *to* (to-infinitive), e.g.   بعد to

  I work *to* <u>earn</u> more money.

  c. After *(do)* verbs, e.g.   بعد أفعال do التي تستخدم كفعل مساعد

  Do you <u>drive</u> cars?

  d. To form *imperatives*, e.g.   لصياغة الأمر واعطاء الارشادات

  <u>Listen</u> to your teacher attentively.

  e. A verb of a sentence (after the subject) بعد الفاعل كفعل للجملة

  e.g. John <u>passed</u> the exam.

● **The adjective is usually used as follows:عادة ما تستخدم الصفة كما يلي**

  a. Before *nouns*, e.g.   قبل الأسماء

  He is a <u>brave</u> man.

  b. In *comparatives* and *superlatives*, e.g. في المقارنة والتفضيل

  Mary is *more* <u>beautiful</u> *than* Sue.

  Mary is *the most* <u>beautiful</u> girl in town.

  c. After *linking verbs* (seem, sound, taste, look,etc.) and *be* (is, are, am, was, were) as a complement, e.g.

بعد أفعال الربط كتكملة للجملة

  That building *looks* <u>nice</u>.

  She *is* <u>stunning</u>.

  d.After *adverbs and some intensifiers* (so, very, quite), e.g.

بعد الظروف ومشدات الصفة

  It is *so* <u>hot</u>.

  He is *very* <u>enthusiastic</u>.

● **The adverb is usually used as follows:عادة ما يستخدم الظرف كما يلي**

  a. At the beginning of the sentence, e.g. في بداية الجملة فاصلة

  Serien fell off her bike. <u>Consequently</u>, her arm was broken.

  b. At the end of the sentence, e.g. في نهاية الجملة

  She moved <u>slowly</u>.

  c. Before the verb, e.g.   قبل الفعل

  Peter <u>regularly</u> meets his friend.

    d.   Before adjectives, e.g.   قبل الصفات

        The show is <u>absolutely</u> great.

    e. Before another adverb, e.g.   قبل ظرف اخر

        Shoroq has worked <u>very</u> hard.

The following is a list of adjectives and adverbs:

Adjectives	Adverbs	Adjectives	Adverbs
happy	happily	fast	fast
strong	strongly	straight	straight
repeated	repeatedly	deep	deeply
real	really	low	low
absolute	absolutely	little	little
obvious	obviously	hard	hard
slow	slowly	friendly	friendly
beautiful	beautifully	daily	daily
regular	regularly	high	high/ highly
			(He jumped high. It's highly recommended.)
certain	certainly	late	late/ lately
			(He came late. He's been ill lately.)
loud	loudly	remarkable	remarkably
much	much	quick	quickly

The following are derivation of some words :

Verb	**Noun**	**Adjective**	**Adverb**
care	care	careful	carefully
repeat	repetition	repeated	repeatedly
---------	happiness	happy	happily
---------	carelessness	careless	carelessly
confide	confidence	confident	confidently
perform	performance	performed	------------
differ	difference	different	differently
annoy	annoyance	annoying	annoyingly
deploy	deployment	deployed	------------
endanger	danger	dangerous	dangerously
act	action	active	actively
depend	dependence	dependent	dependently
attract	attraction	attractive	attractively
excite	excitement	exciting; excited	excitingly
comprehend	comprehension	comprehensive	comprehensively
signify	significance	significant	significantly

strengthen	strength	strong	strongly
-------------	fluency	fluent	fluently
educate	education	educational	educationally
vary	variety	various	variously
produce	production	productive	productively

- Consider the following:

Using the dictionary entry below, choose the correct form of the word to fill in the blanks.

1. Nadia did ………….well in the last English exam. She got 98%.

2. Sara's performance was………… Everyone loved her afterwards.

3. My brother's coming home tomorrow. Let's prepare something special that may…….. him.

---

amaze (v): to astonish by making something special or new.
amazing (adj): to make others feel astonished.
amazingly(adv): to do something in a way that pleases others.

(Answers: 1. amazingly, 2. amazing, 3. amaze)

Using the dictionary entry below, choose the correct form of the word to fill in the blanks.

1. In your interview, make sure to leave a good ………in your examiners.

2. Nadia's performance was really ……...

3. Ibrahi dresses like that to……people.

---

impress (v): to make someone admire someone or something
impression (n): idea, feeling and thought
impressive (adj): remarkable, inspiring, etc.
(answers: impression, impressive, impress)

Using the dictionary entry below, choose the correct form of the word to fill in the blanks.

1. Sara is hard-working and can also ………other people.

2. Salam was highly….….before acting on the stage. She was so thrilled.

3. Workers need……… to carry out their tasks.

---

motivate (v): to encourage someone to do somthing
motivation (n): encouragement, drive, etc.
motivated (adj): being stimulated or encouraged to do something
(answers: motivate, motivated, motivate)

10.3   Parallel Structure

When information in a sentence is given in the form of a list all components must be grammatically parallel/ equal. If the first is, for example, a noun, the rest must also be nouns. Consider the following sentences.

حين تكون المعلومات الواردة في الجملة واردة على شكل سلسلة من الكلمات أو أشباه الجمل فيجب أن تكون تلك الكلمات متوازنة قواعديا (من حيث نوع وأقسام الكلمة). فإذا كانت مثلا الكلمة الأولى اسما فيجب أن تكون بقية الكلمات/ الأسماء المعطوفة بصيغة الإسم وهكذا. تأمل الأمثلة التالية:

- John is <u>rich</u>, <u>clever</u> and <u>popular</u>.

        adj   adj   adj

- John is a <u>doctor</u>, a <u>lawyer</u> and a <u>teacher</u>.

        n   n   n

- The friendly troops approached the camp <u>silently</u> and <u>slowly</u>.

                adv   adv

- She likes <u>swimming</u>, <u>fishing</u> and <u>running</u>.

        n   n   n

Exercise (24)

Use the following dictionary entry to fill in the blanks in the following sentences:

(1)   The project we have is very...............

(2)   The boss told me that it was so important to….. in the test.

(3)   What a great ....!

Succeed (v): have success, prosper

Success (n): accomplishment of what was aimed at

Successful (adj): prosperous

Exercise (25)

Using the dictionary entry below, choose the correct form of the word to fill in the blanks.

Advertisement (n): public notice offering/ asking for good, services,....etc.

Advertise (v): to describe a product publicly

---

(1)   Henry decided to visit Petra after reading an ......about it.

(2)   It isn't cheap to ......on TV.

Exercise (26)

Choose the correct word.

1. Please keep ……. (quiet/ quietly)
2. You should do it with …..... (care/ carefully)
3. You can …… do the task. (easy/ easily)
4. His success is a ……. (certain/ certainty)
5. A cut causes an …….pain. (immediately/ immediate)
6. Ali ran so……in the log race. (fast/ fasten)
7. Sami's show was …... (wonderful/ wonderfully)
8. Suzan's project was …...planned. (perfect/ perfectly)

Exercise (27)

A   Identify the underlined word or phrase that is unacceptable in standard English in each sentence:

1. The study of wild animals **are** interesting, and many books **have** been written about **them**.
2. **Buying** clothes **are** a very time- consuming **practice**.
3. I spent **too many** time **checking the** new files.
4. Flat T.V **is** too expensive for **I** to buy **these** days.
5. After **to take** the vaccine, the old **man** became much **better**.

B   Change the following sentences so that they are parallel.

1.   Melissa is a scholar, an athlete, and artistic.
2.   Children love playing in the mud, running in streets, and they get very dirty.

11. Subject- Verb Agreement

التوافق بين الفعل والفاعل

The most common form of agreement in English language is that between subject and verb. The following are the main points that you should take into consideration:

a. Singular nouns are usually accompanied by singular verbs, as in:
- _Sam   looks_ better.

  Sing. n sing. v
- My *car works* properly.

الأسماء المفردة تأخذ أفعالا مفردة، كما في المثال أعلاه.

b. Plural nouns are usually accompanied by plural verbs, as in:
- _They   look_ better.

  pl. n   pl. v
- The *employees are* working so hard.
- The old *women have* arrived.

الأسماء الجمع عادة ما تأخذ أفعالا بحالة جمع، كما في الأمثلة أعلاه.

c. When the noun can be either singular or plural, it takes a singular verb when regarding the people/items referred to by the noun as a group, as in:

    (1)   The *Committee is* changing the rules.

        The *family is* watching T.V.

(The committee and the family are considered as one body)

(or it takes a plural verb) if the user is regarding the   individuals, as in:

    (2)   The *committee are* changing the rules.

        The *family are* watching T.V.

(The committee and the family's individuals/ members are considered)

اذا كان الاسم يحتمل أن يكون مفردا وجمعا فان الاسم يأخذ فعلا مفردا إذا اعتبرت الأشخاص أو المواد التي يشير لها الاسم كجسم واحد كما في الأمثلة في المجموعة الأولى أعلاه(1)، أما إذا تعاملت مع الاسم وقصدت أفراد المجموعة أحاداً وأفراداً فان الاسم يأخذ بحالة الجمع كما في أمثلة المجموعة (2) أعلاه.

d. Two or more nouns acting as the subject connected by 'and', take a plural verb, as in:

    '*Dan and Robert are* leaving tomorrow.'

اذا كان هناك اسمان مربوطان بأداة الربط And فإنهما يأخذان فعل جمع كما في المثال أعلاه.

e. Indefinite pronouns such as, **anyone, anything, anywhere, everyone, everybody, everything, nobody, nothing,** and **nowhere** are singular; therefore, they are followed by singular verbs, for example:
-    *Everyone is* welcome.
-    *Everybody has* got a name.
-    *Is anyone* here?

No, nobody is here.

الضمائر غير المعرفة تأخذ فعلا مفرداً كما في الأمثلة أعلاه.

f. When the subject is singular separated from the verb by a number of plural names, its verb is in the singular, as in:

'*A list* of men's and women's names *is* ready to copy.'

'A list' is singular noun separated by 'men's and women's names'- a number of plural names.

إذا كان الفاعل مفردا ومفصول عن الفعل بعدد من الأسماء الجمع فان الفاعل يأخذ فعلا مفردا.

g. '**A** number of+ plural noun' pattern takes plural verb, as in (a number of+ new roads):

' *A number of* new *roads* **are** under construction'

عبارة (a number of + اسم جمع معدود) تأخذ فعلاً جمعاً كما في المثال أعلاه.

h. '**The** number of+ plural noun' pattern takes singular verb, as in (The number of+ new roads):

'The number of new roads, that are under construction, **is** ten'

عبارة (the number of+ اسم جمع) تأخذ فعلاً مفرداً كما في المثال أعلاه.

i. '**None**+ of the+ mass noun+ singular verb', as in:

اذا جاء بعد none of the اسم غير معدود فيأخذ حينها فعلاً مفرداً، كما في المثال التالي:

'None of the money you gave me was found.'

'**None**+ of the+ plural count noun+ plural verb', as in:

اذا جاء بعد none of the اسم معدود جمع فيأخذ حينها فعلاً جمعاً، كما في المثال التالي:

'None of the students have finished the test yet.

j. The following expressions have no effect on the verb:

التعابير التالية ليس لها تأثير على حال الفعل واتفاقه مع الفاعل.

together with   along with   accompanied by   as well as

As in:

- *A boy* as well as a girl *is* coming.
- *A boy* with two adults *is* coming.

فإذا كان الفعل الذي يأتي قبل هذه التعابير مفرداً فيأخذ فعلاً مفرداً، واذا كان جمع يأخذ فعلاً جمعاً .

k. The noun preceded by (each, every) is singular, so the verb is singular, as in:

- *Each pilot is* wearing a cap.
- *Every cadet deserves* a medal.

الاسم المسبوق بـ every/ each يكون مفرداً لذا يأخذ فعلاً مفرداً، كما في المثالين أعلاه.

l. Names of books are singular and take singular verbs, as in:

Romeo and Juliet was written by Shakespeare.

Binoculars is written by A. S. Etaywe.

أسماء الكتب تعامل كأسماء مفردة وتأخذ فعلاً مفرداً ولو كان صيغة العنوان بالجمع كما في المثال أعلاه.

m. A sum of money is singular, as in:

'*Thirty dollars is* the salary you deserve.'

مبلغ من المال يعامل معاملة المفرد.

n. In **not only...but also, either...or, neither...nor**, the verb agrees with the nearest subject, as in:

مع أدوات الربط هذه فان الفعل يتفق مع حالة الفاعل أو الاسم الأقرب له كما في الأمثلة التالية:

- Either Josef or *his mates* have gone.
- Either Ali or *his brothers* are studying.
- Neither Sam's friends nor *he is* coming.
- Not only my relatives but also **my friend, Ali, is** coming tonight.

ففي الأمثلة الأول والثاني فان الاسم brothers جمع وهو الأقرب للفعل لذا فإن الفعل جمع.
اما في المثال الثالث فان الضمير heمفرد وهو الأقرب للفعل لذا فأن الفعل مفرد، وكذلك في
المثال الرابع حيث أن الفاعل الأقرب للفعل هو my friend Ali وهو مفرد أخذ فعلاً مفرداً.

o. **'All'** takes a plural verb when followed by a plural countable noun, as in:

all تأخذ فعلا جمع اذا سبقت إسما معدودا بحالة الجمع، كما في:

All the company men are to be considered for the new post.

p. Some nouns have a plural form and take a plural verb, as in:

بعض الأسماء لها صيغة الجمع وتأخذ أفعالا بصيغة الجمع كالاتية:

(clothes, belongings, goods, surroundings, troops, customs, remains, thanks, and congratulations), as in:

The *goods were* sent to Paris.

Your *belongings are* packed up in boxes.

The *troops have* forced the enemy to surrender.

q. Some nouns have a plural form but take a singular verb, as in

بعض الأسماء لها شكل وصيغة الجمع حيث تنتهي بـ sوالا أنها تأخذ فعلا مفردا، كما في:

- Subjects المواضيع: *politics, statistics, physics, etc.*

- Activities الأنشطة: *athletics, gymnastics,* etc.

- Illnesses الأمراض: *measles, numps, AIDS,* etc.

- Games الألعاب: *billiards, dominoes,* etc.

As in:

Politics is an interesting field of study.

Billiards is my favourite game.

Measles is awful.

r. A pair noun is plural and takes a plural verb. We use a pair noun for things made of two parts which are the same, as in:

أسماء الأشياء التي تتألف من جزئين متماثلين تأخذ فعل جمع، كما في:

trousers, shorts, pants, binoculars and *glasses.* We say example, *'My trousers need washing'*; *'These glasses are cheap'*.

s. If the subject and the verb are separated by a prepositional phrase, the prepositional phrase has no effect on the verb.

Subject+ (Prepositional phrase)+ verb

اذا وقع بين الفاعل والفعل شبه جملة جار ومجرور يحتوي على اسم جمع أو مفرد فإنها لا تؤثر على حالة الفعل، فالذي يحدد صيغة الفعل وشكله هو الفاعل.

- **The study** *of languages* **is** very interesting.
- **The view** *of these courses* **varies** from time to another.
- **The effects** *of that crime* **are** terrible.
- **The fear** *of money and power* **has caused** me to leave the country.

t. If a sentence begins with a gerund (verb+ ing), the verb must be singular.

اذا بدأت الجملة بفعل بصيغة اسم فاعل كفاعل للجملة فانه يأخذ فعلا مفردا، كما في الأمثلة التالية:

- **Knowing** him **has** made me rich.
- **Dieting is** important for athletes.
- **Writing** letters **is** my favourite habit.

Exercise (28)

Choose the correct form of the verb in brackets in the following sentences.

1. Hassan along with thirty friends (is/ are) planning a party.
2. The picture of the students (bring/ brings) back many memories.
3. If the duties of the commanders (isn't/ aren't) reduced, many of the subordinates will leave the service.
4. Advertisements on radios (is/ are) getting more competitive than a few years ago.
5. Non of the examples (is/ are) relative to this project.
6. Neither my relatives nor Hussein (is/ are) going to the country this weekend.
7. Neither Maria nor her friends (is/ are) bringing the car.

12. Pronouns and Nouns

الضمائر والأسماء

12.1   Personal Pronouns   الضمائر الشخصية

	(1) 1st person	(2) 2nd person	(3) 3rd person
<u>Singular</u>			
Subject فاعل	I	you	he , she , it
....	....	....	....
Objectمفعول به	me	you	him, her, it
....	....	....	....
*Possessive*ملكية	*my/mine*	*your/yours*	*his/his;her/hers;its/its*
....	....	....	....
<u>Plural</u>			
Subject فاعل	we	you	they
....	....	....	....
Objectمفعول به	us	you	them
....	....	....	....
*Possessive*ملكية	*our/ours*	*your/yours*	*their/theirs*

a.   The subject forms are used when the pronoun is the subject and it has a verb,
صيغ الفاعل تستخدم حين يحل الضمير فاعلا للجملة كما في الأمثلة التالية: as in

- **She** is fine.
- **I** like Ali.
- **He** will go for a trip.
- **You** have to take the wings off.
- **We** must stick to the rules.
- **They** are meeting their parents tonight.

b.   The object forms are used when the pronoun is the object of a verb or preposition, as in:
صيغ المفعول به تستخدم حين يحل الضمير مفعولا به للفعل المتعدي أو لحرف الجر كما في الأمثلة التالية:

- I have met **her**.
- She has gone with **him**.
- Sue invited **me** to the party.
- I'll kill **you** if you don't give me the money I need.
- I invited **them** to the party.
- The police warned **us** to drive carefully.

c.   Possessive forms are used to indicate that something belongs to somebody or to imply the possession of something, as in:

صيغ الملكية تستخدم لتشير إلى أن شيئاً ما تعود ملكيته لشخص أو شيء بعينه- دون سواه.

- I saw **my** bag.   (رأيت حقيبتي)
- This bag is **mine**.   (هذه الحقيبة لي/ ملكي)

d.   The **first person pronouns** refer to the person who is speaking or writing. These include "I, me, my (self), mine, we, us, our (selves) and ours".

ان الضمائر الواردة في العمود الأول (1) تعود للمتكلم.

e.   The **second person pronouns** refer to the thing/ person to whom one is talking.

ان الضمائر الواردة في العمود الثاني (2) تعود للمخاطب.

f.   The **third person pronouns** refer to a third party, not the speaker or the person/ thing being spoken to.

ان الضمائر الواردة في العمود الثالث (3) تعود للغائب (ليس للمتكلم ولا المخاطب)

12.2   Possessive Pronouns   ضمائر الملكية

Group A Possessive adjectives	Group B Possessive pronouns
my	mine
your	yours
his	his
her	hers
our	ours
their	theirs
its	its

تستخدم القائمة (أ) والتي تسمى صفات الملكية حين يكون في الجملة اسما أو ضميرا ورد سابقا وتعود ملكية her الشيء الموصوف بصفة الملكية في الجملة إليه. ففي الجملة الأولى التالية هناك اسم وهو رانيا ولها تعود ملكية وارتباط daughter فيسبقها صفة الملكية:

Examples include:

1.   Rania met *her* daughter.
2.   I saw *my* cat.

وفي المثال الثاني فإن الضمير I تعود ملكية القطة له فنستخدم صفة الملكية my قبل الاسم cat لتصفه وتحدد لمن تعود ملكيته.

غالبا ما تستخدم القائمة (ب) والتي تسمى **ضمائر الملكية** حين تبدأ الجملة باسم اشارة أو محدد يتبعه اسم الشيء الذي هو مدار الحديث ثم فعل كينونه أو فعل ربط ثم ضمير الملكية المناسب، وكما يلي:

(ضمير اشارة+ اسم المادة +is, are, was, were + ضمير الملكية)

Examples:

1. This house is *mine*.

(ضمير اشارة this + اسم المادة house + فعل الكينونة is + ضمير الملكية mine)

2. That room is *hers*.

(ضمير اشارة that + اسم المادة room + فعل الكينونة is + ضمير الملكية hers)

Note: Possessive adjectives modify nouns while Possessive pronouns replace nouns.

ملاحظة: صفات الملكية تصف وتحدد الاسم ولا تستبدل به، بينما ضمائر الملكية تحل محل الاسم ولا تصفه:

My book= my+ book (my= possessive adjective)

Mine= my+ book (mine= possessive pronoun)

- **This is my book.**

This is mine.

- **Our books are heavy.**

Ours are heavy.

| **Reflexive Pronouns** | | **الضمائر الانعكاسية** |

(ملاحظة: تشتق الضمائر الانعكاسية باضافة self للمفرد و selves للجمع)

15	Reflexive pronoun	
I	myself	مـع المـتكلم المفـرد
you (singular)	yourself	مع الاسم المخاطب المفرد
he/ or singular masculine noun: (the man, Ali, etc.)	himself	مع الاسم المذكر الغائب المفرد
she/ or singular feminine noun: (the lady, Asma, etc.)	herself	مع الاسم المؤنث الغائب المفرد
it	itself	مع الجماد/ وغير العاقل
we	ourselves	مع المتكلم الجمع
you (plural)	yourselves	مع المخاطب الجمع
they	themselves	مـع الغـائب الجمـع
one	oneself	مع المفرد النكرة

We use reflexive pronouns in the following situations:

تستخدم الضمائر الانعكاسية في المواقف التالية:

1. **When it refers to the subject.** حين تشير الى الفاعل، كما في:

 - *I prepared the meal myself.*

 'Myself' refers to the subject 'I'. حيث myself تشير للفاعل I

 - Hold the dagger firmly or *you* will hurt *yourself.*

 'Yourself' refers to the subject 'You'.

 حيث yourself تشير للفاعل you

 - *Rana* is tall enough to catch the ball *herself.*

 'Herself' refers to the subject 'Rana'.

 حيث herself تشير للفاعل Rana

More examples include:

 - **I hurt myself.**
 - **You'll cut yourself.**
 - **Khalil injured himself.**
 - **Sumaia burnt herself.**
 - **You two behave yourselves.**
 - **Samir and Sue hurt themselves.**

2. **After prepositions.** بعد حروف الجر، كما في الأمثلة التالية

 - Sadeq is old enough to take care **of** *himself.*

 - You know that you should look **after** *yourself.*

Note: We use object pronouns (me, him, etc) after prepositions of place, e.g. behind, next to, and with. As in:

ملاحظة: نستخدم الضمائر الشخصية (في حالة المفعول به) مثل me, him, her بعد حروف الجر الدالة على المكان مثل behind, next to, with.

3. **To refer to idiomatic meanings.** As in: لتشير الى معنى اصطلاحي، كما في:

 - Last night my friends really *enjoyed themselves.*

 'Enjoyed themselves' means '**had a good time**'. (امضوا وقتا ممتعا)

 - Your classmates should *behave themselves.*

 'Behave themselves' means '**behave well**'. (بمعنى:يسلك سلوكا حسنا)

 - I don't want to stay **by myself.** (alone, on my own -وحيداً)

4. **Used as emphatic pronouns, as in:** كضمائر تفيد معنى التوكيد

 - The brigadier general *welcomed me himself.*

'Welcomed me himself' means 'not someone else'.

بمعنى: ذاته ليس أحدا اخر

 - I *did the homework myself.* (It means '**without help**')

بمعنى: بنفسي دون مساعدة الغير

12.4   Nouns: Types of Nouns   الأسماء- أنواعها

a.   Abstract Nouns

An abstract noun is the name of a thing that is immaterial/cannot be touched but refers to a quality, concept or idea– like *anger*, *beauty*, *fear*, *ignorance*, *loyalty*, *pain*, *observation* and *comment*.

الأسماء المجردة/ المعنوية: ويقصد بها تلك الأسماء التي تشير لأشياء غير ملموسة فتعبر عن فكرة أو مفهوم أو قيمة كما في معنى: غضب، جمال، خوف، جهل، ولاء، ألم، مراقبة، تعليق، الخ.

b.   Proper Nouns

Proper nouns are nouns with unique reference. They include:

    (1)   Names of people like *Asma* and *Hassan*.

    (2)   Names of places like *Hyde Park* and *Arizona*.

    (3)   Names of countries like *Egypt* and *Qatar*.

    (4)   Names of days, holidays and months like *Sunday*, *Christmas* and *February*.

أسماء العلم/ أسماء المعرفة المميزة: و يشير كل منها الى دلالة محددة ومميزة - وكما في الأمثلة أعلاه- حيث تشير الى أسماء الأشخاص مثل(حسن) وأسماء الأماكن المحددة مثل (اريزونا) وأسماء الدول مثل (مصر) وأسماء الأيام (الأحد) و الشهور (شباط) والمناسبات الرسمية مثل (عيد ميلاد المسيح).

c.   Common Nouns

Common nouns name things or persons in a general way, e.g. *tree*, *city*, *manager*, *mother* and *student*.

الأسماء العامة والمشتركة: وهي أسماء تشير لأشخاص وأشياء بشكل عام دون تحديد مثل: شجره، مدينة، مدير، أم، طالب.

d.   Collective Nouns

Collective nouns refer to a group of things or people. It can be treated as singular, when the whole group is being considered, or as plural when looking to the individuals.

أسماء الجمع: وتشير الى مجموعة من الأشياء أو الأشخاص، ويمكن التعامل معها كأسماء مفردة اذا ما تم النظر اليها كمجموعة متكاملة أو كجسم واحد، ويمكن اعتبارها أسماء جمع عند النظر الى أفرادها المكونين لها، كما في الأمثلة التالية:

Examples include: *'family*عائلة *', government* حكومة *', 'army*جيش *', 'crew* طـاقـم *', 'staff* قطيع أو مجموعـة مـن *gaggle of geese', جماعة* من الأسود *pride of lions', 'team'* فريق *'*,هيئة *'herd of cattle*الماشية من قطيع *', and 'shoal of herring* السردين/السمك من فوج *'*,الأوز *'*.

e.   Compound Nouns

A compound noun is the noun that is made up of two words or more that function as a single part of speech.

الأسماء المركبة: هي تلك التي تتكون من كلمتين وأكثر الا أنها تعمل كأسم مكون من كلمة واحدة..

A compound noun can follow many different patterns, such as:

ومكن أن يأتي الاسم المركب وفق أنماط مختلفة مثل:

Patterns	Examples
noun+ noun اسم + اسم	football+ pitch = football pitch sales+ man = salesman grammar+ book = grammar book bicycle+ wheels = bicycle wheels medal+ parade = medal parade fitness+ test = fitness test tennis+ court = tennis court
adjective+ noun صفة + اسم	common+ sense = common sense physical+ training = physical training
gerund+ noun اسم فاعل+ اسم	sitting+ room = sitting room dining+ hall = dining hall
noun+ prepositional phrase اسم+ شبه جملة جار ومجرور	mother+ in law = mother-in-law sister+ in law = sister- in- law
possessive noun+ noun اسم بصيغة ملكية+ اسم	women's+ talk = women's talk men's+ toilet = men's toilet
verb+ preposition فعل+ حرف جر	make+ up = make up warm+ up = warm up
verb+ adverb فعل+ ظرف	cool+ down = cool down break+ down= break down

12.5 Count and Mass; Singular and Plural

الإسم المعدود وغير المعدود، المفرد والجمع

12.5.1 Count and mass nouns   الأسماء المعدودة وغير المعدودة

Nouns can be either countable- الأسماء اما أن تكون معدودة: أي لها صيغة جمع ومفرد (they've
singular and plural forms and can be counted as in: *one book and two books; one table and
two tables; one child and two children, one woman and two women*) or uncountable (things
that are literally uncountable), for example:

أو أن تكون غير معدودة: أي يتعذر عدها حرفيا، كما في:

water, gas, love, traffic, pollution, and *air* or things that are extremely difficult to count, e.g.
sugar, hair, salt, rice, and *sand*).

Mass nouns include: الأسماء غير المعدودة تشمل

   a.   Abstract nouns, as in:

الأسماء المجردة، كما في:

'courage', 'innocence', 'beauty', evidence', 'proof', 'time'
'information', 'energy', 'vocabulary', 'fun', 'knowledge', 'advice',
'luck', 'health' and 'grammar'.

   b.   Liquids السوائل, e.g. tea, blood, water, and milk.

   c.   Materials which consist of particles, مواد تتكون من جزيئات صغيرة e.g. sugar,
flour, sand, dust, corn, dirt, salt, pepper, and wheat.

d. Weather and natural phenomena الظـواهر الطبيعيـة, as in (ice, snow, rain, hail, fog, heat, cold, gravity, humidity, lightening, wind, sleet, thunder, and fire)

e. Languages اللغات: English, Spanish, Arabic, etc.

f. Recreationالرياضات ووسائل الترفيه: soccer, tennis, chess, etc.

g. Gases الغازات, as in: air, oxygen, smog, pollution, etc.

h. Groups made of similar items مجموعات مكونة من أجسام مماثلة e.g. baggage, luggage, furniture, meet, food, fruit, hardware, software, mail, money, change and traffic.

i. Miscellaneous: gold, silver, iron, paper, wood, bread, cotton, news, homework, work, traffic, laughter, scenery accommodation, and travel.

12.5.2 Singular and Plural Nouns الاسم المفرد والاسم الجمع

A plural noun is a noun that refers to more than one thing. Singular nouns refer to one thing and they form plural forms in different ways:

الاسم الجمع هو الاسم الذي يشير لأكثر من واحد، بينما يشير الاسم المفرد الى واحد. ويتم صياغة الجمع من الاسم المفرد بطرق مختلفة:

a. Most singular nouns add *'s'*, as in:

معظم الأسماء المفردة يضاف لها s لتشكل الجمع منها كما في:

Singular	Plural
bat	bats
table	tables
pen	pens

And they add *'es'* to singular nouns ending in (x,ch,sh,s,ss), as in:

ويضاف للأسماء المفردة es لتشكل الجمع اذا كانت تنتهي بـ (x,ch,sh,s,ss) كما في:

Singular	Plural
church	churches
box	boxes

b. Singular nouns ending in a consonant followed by ' y' add 'ies' as in: story/ stories, baby/ babies, lady/ ladies. If (y) is preceded by a vowel, you only add (s). Examples include: (key= keys, day= days, and boy= boys).

الأسماء التي تنتهي بـy يسبقه حرف صحيح/ ليس علة تحذف منها y ويضاف ies كما في story/ stories, baby/ babies, lady/ ladies
اما اذا كان حرف y مسبوق بحرف علة فنبقي على هذا الحرف ونضيف له s فقط كما في الأمثلة التالية: key= keys, day= days, and boy= boys

c. Some nouns are already in the plural form as in:

بعض الاسماء بصيغة جمع أصلا لذا لا يطرأ عليها أية تغيير، كما في:
('scissors', 'trousers', 'police', 'pants', etc.)

d. Some plural forms are ***different in form*** from the singular forms and don't simply add an ending. Examples:

بعض صيغ الأسماء المفردة تختلف عن صيغ الجمع ولها شكل خاص ليس بزيادة S كما مر انفا، وإنما كما يلي:

Singular	Plural
man	men
woman	women
mouse	mice
louse	lice

e. Some irregular plurals are formed by ***changing the vowel*** of the singular forms.

بعض الجمع غير المنتظم يتم صياغته بتغيير شكل حرف العلة كما في:

Singular	Plural
foot	feet
goose	geese
tooth	teeth

f. Some irregular plural forms are formed by ***adding – 'en/ren'***. Examples:

بعض الجمع غير المنتظم يتم صياغته باضافة ren /en للإسم المفرد، كما في:

'*oxen*' from 'ox'

and '*children*' from 'child'.

g. Some irregular plurals forms are ***originally Latin*** plural forms.

بعض أشكال الجمع غير المنتظمة أصلها لاتيني كما في الأمثلة التالية:

Singular	Plural
stimulus	stimuli
phenomenon	phenomena
criterion	criteria
larva	larvae
formula	formulae
index	indices/ indexes

h. Some nouns have ***the same form*** for the singular and the plural. فان بعض الأسماء شكل المفرد لها هو نفس شكل الجمع كما في:

sheep, *salmon*, *deer* and *fish*.

i. Some nouns ending in '-*f*' or '*fe*' form plurals in '-*ves*'.

بعض الأسماء التي تنتهي بـ fe /f يصاغ الجمع منها باستبدال f/fe بـ ves :

Examples:

Singular	Plural
loaf	loaves
half	halves
wife	wives
thief	thieves

But, the following names do not follow the same pattern:

ولكن الأسماء التالية تشذ عن هذه القاعدة:

Singular	Plural
handkerchief	handkerchiefs
chief	chiefs
dwarf	dwarfs
roof	roofs
safe	safes
gulf	gulfs

i. Compound nouns: In two-word nouns we pluralize the last word. في الأسماء المركبة والمكونة من كلمتين فاننا نجمع الكلمة الأخيرة منها

Examples:

'travel agent'= *'travel agents'*,

'football pitch'= *'football pitches'*,

'basketball net'= *'basketball nets'*,

'tennis racket'= *'tennis rackets'*,

'basketball bat'= *'basketball bats'*,

'tennis court'= *'tennis courts'*.

In three-word nouns we pluralize the first word, as in:

وفي الأسماء المركبة التي تتألف من ثلاث كلمات فإننا نجمع الكلمة الأولى، كما في:

'brother-in-law'= *'brothers*-in-law',

'mother-in-law'= *mothers*- in-law'.

j. If the singular noun ends in (o) preceded by a vowel, you add (s) to the noun to become plural, as in:

اذا كان الاسم المفرد ينتهي بـ o مسبوقة بحرف علة أضف s ليصبح جمع، كما يلي:

radio= *radios*,

zoo= *zoos*.

If the noun ends in (o) preceded by a consonant we usually add (es), but not always.

اذاكان الاسم المفرد ينتهي بـ o مسبوقة بحرف صحيح أضف es ليس دائما هذه هي الحال، فمنها ما يأخذ s فقط أو الحالتين معا، لاحظ الأمثلة التالية:

Examples:

cargo= *cargoes (or cargos)*, commando= *commandoes (or commandos)*,

hero= *heroes*, negro= *negroes*, potato= *potatoes*, tomato= *tomatoes*, volcano= *volcanoes*, motto= *mottos (or mottoes)*, zero= *zeroes*,

mosquito= *mosquitoes (or mosquitos)*.

The following words take only (s): casino= *casinos*, piano= *pianos*, kilo= *kilos*,

photo= *photos* and rhino= *rhinos*.

k. Some nouns ending in *'is'* form plurals in*'es.*

بعض الأسماء التي تنتهي بـ is يصاغ الجمع منها باستبدال is بـ es :

Examples:

Singular	Plural
crisis	crises
axis	axes
basis	bases
thesis	theses

l. We can't use *'a'* or a number before a mass/ uncountable noun. We can't say 'a petrol' or 'two rice'. However, we can use **a/number+ count noun+ of+ mass noun**, as follows:

لا نستطيع استخدام a او رقم يسبق الاسم غير المعدود مباشرة

لكن نستخدم القاعدة التالية: a/ رقم +اسم معدود+of + الاسم غير المعدود

كما في المثالين التاليين:

- A cup of tea
- Two cups of tea

tea	a cup of tea	lemon	a slice of lemon
water	a glass of water	bread	a loaf of bread
chips	a bag of chips	chocolate	a bar of chocolate
paper	a sheet of paper	tooth paste	a tube of tooth paste
rice	a kilo of rice	jam	a jar of jam
coke	a can of coke	soup	a tin of soup
cheese	a piece of cheese	ice cream	a scoop of ice cream
biscuits	a packet of biscuits	lettuce	a head of lettuce

12.6 Possessive Nouns

We use possessive nouns to show possession. We use the following techniques to imply how things belong to people/ or things:

أسماء الملكية: تستخدم لتبين ملكية وارتباط شيء ما باسم ما، وتستخدم الطرق التالية لنبين ارتباط الأشياء

بالأشخاص أو بأشياء أخرى:

a. Add an apostrophe (') and (- s) as follows ('s) to a singular noun, as in:

أضف (s ') للاسم المفرد، كما في الأمثلة التالية:

Noun	Possessive noun	Examples
boy	boy's	This is the boy's ball.
girl	girl's	That is the little girl's bag.
husband	husband's	My husband's house is in Amman.

If a singular noun ends in (s), you can either add ('s), or add only an apostrophe ('), as in:

أضف فقط الفاصلة العلوية (') أو ('s) للاسم المفرد المنتهي بـ s للاسم المفرد:

Noun	Possessive noun	Examples
Thomas	Thomas's/ Thomas'	'Thomas's house is spectacular', or 'Thomas' house is spectacular'.

b. Add only an apostrophe to a plural noun which ends in (s), for example:

أضف فقط الفاصلة العلوية (') للاسم الجمع الذي ينتهي بـ s كما في الأمثلة التالية::

Noun	Possessive noun	Examples
boys	boys'	The *boys' school* is over there.
wives	wives'	The *wives' ball* is blue.
husbands	husbands'	The *husbands' best perfume* is Dunhill'.

c. Add an ('s) to plural nouns that don't end in (s), for example:

أضف (s') للاسم الجمع غيرالمنتهي بـ s وكما يلي:

Noun	Possessive noun	Examples
women	women's	Those are the women's shirts.
men	men's	These are the men's neck ties.

12.7   There + be

When 'there' is used, the subject follows 'be', and the subject determines the correct form of 'be' which you should use.

عند استخدام There فان الفاعل يأتي بعد فعل (كينونة) والفاعل هو الذي يحدد شكل الفعل (مفرد أو جمع) وكما يلي:

a.   Use a singular form of 'be' when the subject is singular, as in:

استخدم فعل بصيغة المفرد من أفعال الكينونة اذا كان الفاعل مفرد وكما في المثال التالي:

There *is* a *table* over there. The subject is 'table' which is singular.

الفاعل هو the table وهي مفرد.

b.   Use a plural form of 'be' when the subject is plural, as in:

استخدم فعل بصيغة الجمع من أفعال الكينونة اذا كان الفاعل جمع وكما في المثال التالي:

'There are some tables in that class. (The subject is 'tables')

الفاعل هو tables وهي جمع.

12.8   Indefinite Pronouns   ضمائر النكرة/ غير المعرفة

Pronouns	Usage	Example
Somebody, Someone شخص ما	Used in affirmative sentences, and in questions when a yes- answer is expected. تستخدم في الجمل المثبتة، وفي الأسئلة المتوقع اجابتها بالاثبات/ بنعم.	-There is *somebody/ someone* sitting in the garden. -A: I hear some voice inside. Is there someone in the house? B: Yes, she is my mother.
Anybody, Anyone أي أحد	Used in negative sentences, and questions تستخدم في الجمل المنفية، وفي الأسئلة.	There *isn't anybody/ anyone* at home. Is there *anyone?*
Nobody, No one لا أحد	Used after the answer 'No' تستخدم بعد الجواب بلا.	A: Is there anybody/ anyone here? B: No, there is *nobody/ no one* here.

Exercise (29)

A: Circle the correct form of pronoun or possessive adjective to complete the following sentences.

1.   (I, my, myself)….. will visit Abdelrahman tomorrow.
2.   They called….. (we, us, our) on the phone.
3.   Johnson told….. (herself, she, her) a story.
4.   Alfred will make his presentation after…..(his, him, he) finishes his exercise.
5.   Mugabi is eating ….. (himself, him, he, his) dinner.
6.   …..(My, Mine, Me) sitting room is freezing.
7.   I go to the school with …..(he, him, himself) every day.
8.   She speaks to…..(we, us) every day.
9.   I hurt …..(my, mine) leg.
10.   John …..(he, himself) went to the meeting.
11.   Hussein and…..(my, me, I) would go to Essex.
12.   …..(Her, Hers) car didn't go as fast as …..(our, ours)

B: Which of the following nouns are countable or mass nouns?

television   car   news   furniture   person   water   tooth
money minute cup   information   economics

Countable nouns	Mass nouns

13.	Premodifiers: Quantifiers, Articles, and Demonstrative Pronouns

المحددات القبلية:المحددات الكمية، أدوات التعريف والتنكير، وضمائر الإشارة

## 13.1	Quantifiers	المحددات الكمية

Some phrases of quantities are used with countable nouns while others are only used with mass nouns. However, there are some of them you can use with both mass and countable nouns. The table below shows quantifiers.

تستخدم بعض أشباه الجمل والعبارات التي تدل عل الكمية مع الأسماء المعدودة بينما تستخدم أخرى مع غير المعدودة منها، ومع هذا فان هناك بعض المحددات هذه ما يمكن استخدامه مع أي من الأسماء سواء كان مفردا أو جمعاً. والجدول التالي يبين تلك المحددات:

With Plural Countable Nouns مع الأسماء المعدودة	With Mass/uncountable Nouns مع الأسماء غير المعدودة	With Countable/Mass Nouns' مع الأسماء المعدودة وغير المعدودة
many, few, a few, a large number of, a great number of, too many, several, fewer...than, (one, two, three, etc.)	a great deal of, little, a little, much, too much, a large amount of, less...than	a lot of, lots of, plenty of, some, enough, any, no, all, none

Examples:

1.	*Many people* supported the principal.

2.	*A few dictionaries* are necessary for English language learners.

3.	*A large number of car accidents* take place every year.

4.	*Too many bikes* are used nowadays on London's streets.

5.	*Several topics* are to be discussed in today's conference.

6.	You should keep in touch with *a few* of your *friends*.

7.	You have to provide me with *a great deal of information* about Ali in five days.

8.	I have *little coffee* left. I'm afraid the amount is not enough to prepare a cup for each of you.

9.	The cake tastes sweet. I think you added *too much sugar* to the mix.

10.	I saw *a lot of children* gathering outside the UN building.

11.	I stored *a lot of food* in the grand store.

12.	Do you have *enough rice* for tonight's party?

13.	Are there *enough people* to vote for the decision?

14.	Can you give me *some advice* before I begin the tournament?

15.	Do you have *any* coffee? I have *no* coffee.

16.	Do you have *any* pens? I have *no* pens.

13.1.1 Using 'few', 'a few', 'little' and 'a little'.

● **Note:** 'few' and 'a few' are used with countable nouns;
'little' and 'a little' are used with mass nouns.

ملاحظة: تستخدم few/ a few مع الأسماء المعدودة أما little/ a little فمع غير المعدود منها.

a. 'few' and 'little' give a negative idea of something or something is largely absent, for example:

few/ little يستخدمان ليعطيا معنًى سلبي، أو أن شيئا ما غير متوفر بما يكفي، لاحظ الأمثلة:

- Ali has *few friends* because he has a lot of problems with people.
- Ali has *little information* about the thief. That is why he couldn't find him.

b. 'a few' and 'a little' give a positive idea of something, for example:

a few/ a little يعطيان معنى ايجابي أو أن شيئا ما متوفر بما يكفي، وكما في الأمثلة التالية:

- *A few students* answered the questions due to the lecturer's clear explanation of the book.
- Let me give you *a little advice*. I think you can use my Laptop.

'Few' means 'not many', whereas 'little' means 'not much'.

13.1.2 'Too' and 'Enough'

'Too' precedes an adjective- and we usually use infinitives with 'to'- to imply a negative result or **more than the right amount**, as in:

Too تسبق الصفة وتفيد معنى سلبيا (أكبر من المحتمل) وعادة ما نستخدم بعدها أيضا مصدر يسبقه to لتفيد نتيجة سلبية، ففي المثال التالي (فان الصندوق ثقيل جدا لدرجة أنني لا أقدر على حمله)

-        The box is *too heavy* for me <u>to carry</u>.

(This means that it is impossible for me to carry that box)

'Enough' follows an adjective, and it precedes a noun. It means the **right amount**, as in:

Enough تأتي بعد الصفة وقبل الاسم وتفيد معنى (مقدار صحيح / الكمية المقبولة).

Jim is <u>*brave*</u> *enough* to talk to his boss.

Adjective

The president has *enough* <u>*courage*</u> to wage a war

Noun

13.2 Demonstrative Pronouns   ضمائر الإشارة

A demonstrative pronoun is used to indicate things or people in relationship to the speaker/ writer in space or time. The following table shows how we use (this, these, that, and those).

ضمائر الإشارة: وتستخدم لتشير إلى العلاقة بين الأشياء أو الأشخاص وبين المتكلم من حيث البعد أو القرب في الزمان أو المكان. والجدول التالي يبين كيفية استخدامها.

Demonstrative	Position	Examples
This هذا	It comes before singular nouns (it indicates nearness) تأتي قبل الأسماء المفردة وتحمل دلالة القرب	Take this book.
These هؤلاء	It comes before plural nouns (it indicates nearness) تأتي قبل الأسماء الجمع وتحمل دلالة القرب	These flowers are yours.
That ذلك/ تلك	It comes before singular nouns (it refers to distant thing/ person) تأتي قبل الأسماء المفردة وتشير للبعيد	That is my brother.
Those أولئك	It comes before plural nouns (it refers to far people/ things) تأتي قبل الأسماء الجمع وتشير للبعيد	Those shirts are not mine.

This and *that* are used with both countable and mass nouns. *These* and *those* are used only with countable nouns.

this, that يستخدمان مع الأسماء المعدودة وغير المعدودة أما these, those مع المعدودة فقط.

- This/ That boy is handsome. (√)
- This/ That rice is delicious. (√)
- These/ Those boys are kind. (√)
- These/ Those rice are delicious. (x) This/ That rice is delicious. (√)

13.3   Articles   الأدوات

13.3.1 Definite Article أداة التعريف

Definite article is a term for ' *the*' which is used before nouns, as follows:

أداة التعريف the وتستخدم قبل الاسم، وكما يلي:

a.   Before names of a thing that has already been mentioned, As in قبل أسم شيء

ورد ذكره في النص أو السياق من قبل، كما في المثال التالي :

'Jack built a **model**. **The model** was of a plane'.

b.   To make a general statement about all things of a particular type, as in: لعمل

تعميم حول مجموعة أشياء/ أ أشخاص من نفس الفئة

'**The car** has caused damage to the environment'. (which means all cars)

c.   Before a name of a whole group, as in: ' **The younger generations'**, and '**The rich** should donate to **poor elderly people'**.

قبل الاسم الذي يشير إلى مجموعة أو فئة كاملة، كما في معنى "الشباب" ونقصد كل شاب وكذلك "الأغنياء" ونقصد كل غني.

d.   Before a name that refers to services or systems, as in 'They are on **the phone'**.   قبل الاسم الذي يشير إلى نظام خدمة معينة

e.   Before a person/ or thing which is the only one of its kind (unique), as in: مع أسم الشيء الوحيد في العالم من نوعه-فريد

'the Bible', 'the White House', 'the president of the USA', 'the sun', and 'the Earth'.

The sun sets in the west.

The earth is not straight.

f.		In front of superlative adjectives, as in:

قبل صفات المفاضلة، كما في الأمثلة

' *the largest* building', *'the most beautiful* woman'.

g.		Instead of a possessive determiner to refer to parts of the body, بـدلا مـن

ضمير ملكية لتشير إلى أجزاء من الجسم، وكما في المثال التالي

'She took him by *the arm'*.

h.		Before the names of kingdoms, states, republics and unions, as in: قبل أسماء

الممالك والولايات والجمهوريات والاتحادات، كما في الأمثلة التالية

'The USA', 'The UK', 'The Soviet Union', 'The Republic of Ireland', etc.

i.		With the nationality to mean the people of a country, as in:

مع الجنسية لتعني الناس وشعوب تلك البلد المشار لها بالجنسية

The British are so punctual.

j.		Before the names of oceans, rivers, seas and canals, as in *'the Red Sea', 'the Nile', the Suez canal, the Pacific ocean'.*

قبل أسماء المحيطات والأنهار والبحار والقنوات.

k.		Before the directions (the west, the east, etc.) قبل الاتجاهات

l.		With the plural names of countries, as in 'The Philippines'.

مع أسماء الدول التي بصيغة جمع.

m.		With mountain ranges, as in 'The Alps'. مع سلاسل الجبال

n.		With groups of islands, as in' The Canaries'. مع مجموعات الجزر.

o.		With names of musical instruments (The piano, the violin).

مع أسماء الالات الموسيقية.

p.		In the main parts of the day:		مع أجزاء اليوم الرئيسية

in the morning, in the evening, and **in the afternoon.**

q.		To indicate something that we know about as in:

عند الحديث عن شيء نعلمه تماما

'The boy in *the corner is my brother.*'

r.		With schools, colleges, and universities when the phrase begins with (school, college, university), as in:

مع أسماء المدارس والكليات والجامعةالتي تبدأ بـكلمة university /college /school

	- I'm teaching at **the University of Jordan.**

	- **The University of Exeter** is universally admired.

s.		With ordinal numbers (first, second, third) as in: the first world war, the second chapter.

مع الأرقام الترتيبية (الأول، الثاني...الخ).

Note: We do not use *'the'*: لا نستخدم أداة التعريف في الحالات التالية

1. With titles, as in: Mr., Mrs., and Doctor/Dr. مع الألقاب

2. Before names of meals that aren't preceded by adjectives (dinner,   breakfast, etc.). قبل أسماء الوجبات غير المسبوقة بصفة

3. Individual mountains, as in (Everest). مع الجبال المنفردة

4. Continents, as in (Europe, Asia, Africa). مع أسماء القارات

5. Cities and states, (Amman, Cairo, Florida). مع أسماء المدن والولايات

6. Countries with only one word (France, Jordan). مع اسم الدولة المكون من كلمة واحدة

7. Means of transport (bus, train). مع وسائل المواصلات

8. Time of day/night (at night, at dawn, at noon). مع مواقيت الليل والنهار

9. Sports (baseball, basketball) أسماء الرياضات

10. Fields of study, or areas of subject matter as in mathematics. حقول الدراسة.

11. With holidays as in: Christmas, Thanksgiving مع أسماء العطل الرسمية

* With uncountable nouns you use the article "the" if speaking is in specific terms, but use "no article" if speaking is in general as in:

مع الأسماء غير المعدودة تستخدم أداة التعريف عند الحديث عن شيء ما بالتحديد مثال(2)، ولا تستخدمها عند الحديث عن الشيء ذاته ولكن بصورة عامة مثال(1).

1. Honey is sweet.   (general- all honey)

2. The honey on the table is from Yemen. (specific- that is on the table)

* Plural nouns are not preceded by "the" when they mean everything within a certain class, as in:

الاسم الجمع لا يسبقه أداة التعريف عندما يشير الى كل ما يقع ضمن تصنيف ذلك الاسم.

   - Oranges are green until they are ripe. (all oranges)

* We don't use "the" with schools, colleges, and universities when the phrase begins with a proper noun as in:

لا نستخدم أداة التعريف مع أسماء المدارس والكليات والجامعات التي تبدأ باسم علم.

- Gerorge University.

- Ibn Khaldoon College.

- Exeter University.

13.3.2   Indefinite Articles (*'a'* and *'an'*)   أدوات التنكير

(A):

   a.   The form *'a'* is used before words which begin with a consonant sound, as (*a box, a road, a book*).

تستخدم a قبل الأسماء التي تبدأ بحرف صحيح.

   b.   *'A'* is used before singular countable nouns not mentioned before, as in:

تستخدم قبل الأسماء المعدودة المفردة التي تذكر لأول مرة في النص أو السياق

'There are seven men and *a lady* in the house.'

'I saw *a girl* in the street.' (We don't know which girl)

c.   'A' can be used with words of quantity: *a few, a lot of, a good deal of.*

تستخدم مع عبارات المحددات الكمية

d.   ' A' can be used in exclamation, as in ' what *a great* idea!'.

تستخدم في جمل التعبير عن التعجب

e.   ' A' can be used instead of per, as in 'I have two tests *a week*'   أي بمعنى

تستخدم بدلا عن كلمة per(كل) كأن نقول (كل ساعة/ كل أسبوع)

f.   'A' is used with a noun complement, as in 'Jessica *is a teacher*', and 'Simpson *is a doctor*'.

تستخدم مع الاسم كتتمة للفعل.

(*An*):   The form 'an' is used before words that begin with a vowel sound, as in '*an a*pple', '*an ostrich*', '*an hour*', '*an honest* man'.

ويستخدم An قبل الكلمات التي تبدأ بصوت متحرك-علة.

Hour/ honest كل منها لا يبدأ بحرف علة الا أن الصوت متحرك-علة.

The following words begin with a consonant sound and thus must be preceded by 'a':

الكلمات التالية تبدأ بصوت ساكن/ صحيح لذا يجب أن يسبقها A

a home	a European…	a half	a house	a heavy…
a union	a uniform	a university		
a universal…				

The following words begin with a vowel sound and thus must be preceded by 'an':

الكلمات التالية تبدأ بصوت علة/ متحرك لذا يجب أن يسبقها An

an hour	an hier	an herbal	an honor
an uncle	an umbrella	an understanding	an unnatural

Note: We don't use a/an: لا نستخدم أدوات التنكير في المواقف التالية

- Before plural nouns, e.g. boys not a boys.

قبل الأسماء الجمع

- Before uncountable nouns, e.g. news, furniture, wood, stone, and beauty.   قبل الأسماء غير المعدودة

- With meals, unless preceded by adjectives,

مع الوجبات الا اذا كانت مسبوقة بصفة كما في:

-    You should have your dinner.

-    I had a good dinner.

Exercise (30)

Choose (a), (b), or (c) to complete the following sentences.

1. I feel sorry for her. She has .... friends.

   a. little   b. much   c. few

2. I have ...... apple trees.

   a. a lot of   b. too much   c. a great deal of

3. The .... house is there.

   a. boie's   b. boys'   c. boys's

4. The ...... coach is that one.

   a. mens'   b. men's   c. mans'

5. Aseel met three......

   a. childs   b. children   c. childrens

6. Tonight I'm going to tell you two short......

   a. stories   b. storys   c. storieis

7. I sold five......of bread.

   a. loafs   b. loaves   c. loves

8. Alzarqa city has....... air pollution.

   a. too much   b. too many   c. a few

9. He was lucky to have ......knowledge about the issue.

   a. enough   b. a few   c. a little

10. Politics....... not good to study.

    a. is   b. are   c. have

11. Let me give you ....advice.

    a. an   b. some   c. few

12. There seemed to be a lot of.......on the road.

    a. traffic   b. traffics   c. trafficing

13. My parents left me alone at home. So that I had to make a sandwich........

    a. my   b. myself   c. mine

Exercise (31)

Select the correct answer.

1. Nadia usually takes .... apple before she goes to her office.

   a . an   b. a   c. the   d. x

2. I saw a girl with a dog. .... girl was very beautiful.

   a . the   c. an   b. a   d. x

3. What....... nice car!

   a. a   b. an   c. the   d. x

4. Sue had .... dinner with her brother.

   a. a   b. an   c. the   d. x

5. I can see many planes in .... sky.

   a. a   b. an   c. the   d. x

6. Anna is .... most beautiful girl I've ever seen.

      a. a   b. an   c. the   d. x

7. I hate .... rich.

      a. a   b. the   c. an   d. x

8. .... house looks awful.

      a. These   b. Those   c. This   d. theese

9. .... are my chairs.

      a. This   b. That   c. These   d. thats

10. There is .... sitting by the lake.

      a. somebody   b. anybody   c. nowhere   d. somewhere

11. A: Is Rakan coming to the party?

    B: I think so, I've invited ....

      a. he   b. him   c. his   d. she

12. You and I work well together. ....are an excellent team.

      a. we   b. our   c. us   d. your

13. On our trip to.....Spain, we crossed ....Atlantic Ocean.

      a. a/an   b. an/the   c. x/the   d. x/x

14. Rita plays ......violin and her sister plays ....guitar.

      a. a/the   b. an/a   c. the/the   d. x/x

15. Kazim attended...... Princeton University.

      a. a   b. an   c. the   d. x

16. Henry was admitted to....School of Medicine.

      a. a   b. an   c. the   d. x

Exercise (32)

Supply (a, an, the, or nothing) in gabs.

1. Ali crossed....... Mississippi.
2. Mount Rum is one of....... highest mountains in Jordan.
3. .... Alps lies in....... Europe.
4. The shepard gave me .... animal.
5. You need ....pen and ....exercise book to practice well.
6. ......million people received my text message at Christmas Eve.
7. ....few people were fortunate to escape the fire.
8. French is .... easy language to learn.
9. My father is....... honorable man.
10. ....gold is very precious metal.

Exercise (33)

Make sentences by putting the following words in the correct order.

1. old/ sick/ was/ the/ man ....
2. my/ finished/ ago/ I/ task/ years/ three ....
3. parents/ have/ into/ my/ apartment/ a/ new/ moved...........
4. Alia/ well/ English/ speaks ....

5. you/ tell/ I / did/ job/ about/ the/ new? ....

6. met/ few/ I/ a/ people/ school/ in/ the..................

7. better/ is/ cure/ than/ prevention ....

Exercise (34)

Choose the correct reflexive pronoun, possessive adjectives or possessive pronoun.

1. Mary hurt (himself/ yourself/ herself).
2. We helped the old woman (himself/ ourselves/ themselves).
3. Did you see Alison (himself/ yourself/ themselves)?
4. Alia's coat is red; (my/ mine) is brown.
5. Lucy is preparing (hers/ her) clothes.
6. Is that (your/ yours/ yourself) motor cycle?

14. Modal Verbs

الأفعال الشكليـــة

14.1 Modals and Uses

الأفعال الشكلية واستخداماتها

Remember that modals must be followed by the base form of a verb. The following table shows the modals and their uses:

الأفعال الشكلية واستخداماتها: تذكر أن الأفعال الشكلية هي أفعال -ذات معانٍ- يتبعها فعل رئيسي مجرد، إلا أنها لا تعطي معنى تام إذا ما ذكرت وحدها. والجدول التالي يعرض أبرز هذه الأفعال واستخداماتها.

Auxiliary	Uses	Examples
May	(1) polite request <div dir="rtl">طلب/ استئذان بأسلوب لبق</div>	A: May I use your car? B: Yes, certainly.
	(2) formal permission <div dir="rtl">السماح بأسلوب رسمي</div>	You may leave the office.
	(3) (less than) 50% certainty "possibility/probability" <div dir="rtl">الاحتماليـة والإمكانيـة/ درجـة تأكيـد تساوي أو تقل عن 50% إلا أن نسبة التأكد هنا تكون أعلى منها في might</div>	Where's Timor? He may be at the library. ('may' gives the meaning of being slightly more certain than what 'might' does)
Might	less than 50% certainty "possibility/probability" <div dir="rtl">الاحتماليـة والإمكانيـة/ درجـة تأكيـد أقل من 50%</div>	Where's Timor? He might be at the library.
	(2) polite request <div dir="rtl">طلـب أو استئذان بأسـلوب لبـق أو مؤدب</div>	Might I borrow your pencil? Yes, of course.
Should	advisability <div dir="rtl">تقديم النصيحة</div>	You should see the dentist.
	(2) 90 % certainty <div dir="rtl">درجـة عاليـة مـن الاحتماليـة تـصل لـ90%</div>	She should do well in the final exam. She studied so hard. (future)
	(3) internal motive to do something- personal <div dir="rtl">حافز داخلي للقيـام بـأمر معـين إيمانا بضرورته ورغبة به</div>	I should study hard tonight as I have exam tomorrow.
Ought to	(1) advisability <div dir="rtl">تقديم النصيحة</div>	I ought to study hard.
	(2) 90 % certainty <div dir="rtl">درجـة عاليـة مـن الاحتماليـة تـصل لـ90%</div>	She ought to do well on the test.(future)

	(3) external motive to do something- impersonal دافع خارجي للقيام بأمر معين تفيد عدم الرغبة الحقيقية للقيام به	I ought to study tonight. I'm really fed up of studying.
Must	(1) strong obligation حاجة ملحة	I must leave tonight by 7 o'clock.
	(2) prohibition (negative) تعطي معنى المنع والتحريم	You must not disobey your father.
	(3) certain/ or strong deduction استنتاج قوي أو مؤكد	Fredrick isn't at school. He never misses a class. He must be sick.
	(4) external obligation (by the law, etc...) الزام مصدره خارجي	In hospitals you must switch your phone off.
Will	(1) 100% certainty 100% تأكد	He will join our league. (future only)
	willingness الرغبة والطواعية في أداء عمل ما	The phone's ringing. I'll answer it.
	(3) Decision or offer made at this moment قرار أو عرض يقدم هذه اللحظة (أثناء الحديث)	- I'm bored. I'll go out. - A: I can't lift the box. It's too heavy B: I'll help you.
	(4) polite request طلب لبق/ مؤدب	Will you please close the door?
	(5) for prediction للتنبؤ بحدوث شيء	It will rain tomorrow.
Shall	(1) polite question to make a suggestion سؤال بقصد تقديم عرض /اقتراح	Shall I open the store?
Can	(1) ability/ inability/ possibility المقدرة/ عدم المقدرة/ الإمكانية	- I can('t) jump high/ I can wait for a while. (ability/ inability) - Computers can crash. (possibility) ('can' is more general than 'may' and 'might'/ theoretical possibility)
	(2) informal permission السماح بشكل رسمي	You can use my computer tonight.
	(3) informal polite request طلب مؤدب غير رسمي	A: Can I use your car? B: Sure.
	(4) impossibility (negative only) الاستحالة	Your plan can't be valid.

Could	(1) past ability قدرة في الماضي	I could run ten miles a day when I was young.
	(2) polite request طلب لبق/ مؤدب	Could I use your phone? Could you support me? Yes, of course.
	(3) suggestion تقديم اقتراح	A: I need help in IELTS. B:You could talk to your teacher.
	(4) less than 50% certainty "possibility/probability" احتمالية درجتها أقل من 50%	Where's Sal ? She could be at home.
	(5) impossibility استحالة (negative only)	That plan couldn't be valid.
Would	polite request طلب لبق/ مؤدب	Would you please keep me posted? Yes, I'd be glad to.
	(2) preference للتفضيل	I would rather join the navy than stay unemployed.
	repeated action in the past أحداث متكررة في الماضي (لا تعبر عن حالة)	When I was young, I would meet my folks weekly.
Would you mind	(1) polite request طلب لبق/ مؤدب	A: Would you mind if I paint the bedroom? B: No, not at all A: Would you mind painting the sitting room? B: No, of course not
Dare	to mean 'have the courage' تستخدم بمعنى "يجرؤ"	-I dare not speak loudly. -Dare you talk to Rashid?
Need	to mean 'necessitate, require, should, and want' تستخدم بمعنى "يريد، يتطلب الأمر، يحتاج"	- I need not speak to Sam. - Need I speak to Sam?

* Prohibition and lack of necessity (must / have to):

التعبير عن المنع والتحريم، وغياب الضرورة باستخدام Must/ have to

Must not	- You *must not smoke in the office*. يمنع التدخين في المكتب. - You *must not kill* wild animals. يحرم عليك صيد الحيوانات البرية	- It is **prohibited** to smoke in the office. - killing wild animal is **unlawful**.
Not have to (not modal)	- You *don't have to* leave home these days. ليس عليك أن تغادرالبيت هذه الأيام	- It is **not necessary** for you to leave home these days.

14.2   Degrees of Certainty درجات التأكد

You can use modals to express how certain you are about something. The following tables show the degree of certainty that some modals convey.

يمكنك استخدام الأفعال الشكلية للتعبير عن مدى تأكدك من أمر ما، والجداول التالية تعرض ذلك.

Present positive: التعبير عن مدى التأكد في الزمن الحاضر(بالإثبات)

Why is Ali absent?   لتوضيح ذلك نطرح سؤالا: لماذا علي متغيب (عن الصف) ؟

Modals	Degree of Certainty	Examples
May be, might be, could be	- less than 50 % sure (weak degree of certainty) تستخدم للتعبير عن درجة منخفضة من التأكد، بنسبة تقل عن 50%	- He may/ might be/ could be sick. ربما يكون مريضا، يحتمل أن يكون مريضا.
Must be	- almost sure (strong degree of certainty) تستخدم للتعبير عن درجة تأكد مرتفعة، تصلالى 95% / استنتاج We know that Ali is a good student. He usually attends the lessons. He wasn't feeling good over the last two days.	- He must be sick. **لا بد أنه مريض.** وعادة ما يكون هناك إمارات تقود للتوصل لهذا التوقع المرتفع، ففي هذا المثال: عندما نعلم أن علي طالب مجتهد ولم يتغيب عن الصف وكان يشعر بالإجهاد في اليومين السابقين وهو في غرفة الصف فكل هذا يقودنا لاستنتاج هذا التوقع المرتفع سقفه الذي قد يصل حد التأكد التام.
Be (is, are) (not modals) لا تصنف هذه الصيغة مع الأفعال الشكلية ولكن وردت ههنا لتبيان الفرق في المعنى	- 100 % sure تأكد تام	He is sick. انه مريض

Present egative: التعبير عن مدى التأكد في الزمن الحاضر (بالنفي)

Why isn't Ali drinking water?   سؤال للتوضيح: لماذا لا يشرب علي الماء؟

Modals	Degree of Certainty	Examples
May not be, might not be	- less than 50 % sure (to mention possibilities) تستخدم للتعبير عن درجة تأكد تقـل عـن 50%، لإمكانيـة وجـود أكـثر مـن احتمال	- He may/ might not be thirsty. Maybe he doesn't see the water bottle. Or perhaps, he drank earlier. ربما لا يكون عطشانا. أو لا يرى مطرة الماء. أو لربما قد شرب من قبل.
Must not be	- 95% sure تستخدم للتعبير عـن درجـة تأكد مرتفعة، تصل الى 95% (بمعنى: لا بد)	- He mustn't be thirsty. لا بد أنه ليس عطشانا.
Can't be/ couldn't be	- sure	- He can't/ couldn't be thirsty.

		That is impossible. I just saw him drinking water. مــن المــستحيل أن يكــون عطــشانا لقــد شاهدته يشرب الماء للتو.

Past positive التعبير عن مدى التأكد في الزمن الماضي (بالإثبات)

Why was Ali absent? ؟ لتوضيح ذلك نطرح سؤالا: لماذا تغيب علي (عن الصف)

Modals	Degree of certainty/ past time	Examples
May/might/could have been	- less than 50% sure درجة منخفضة من التأكد حول أمر ما، بنسبة تقل عن 50%	- He may/ might/ could have been sick. لربما كان مريضا
Must have been	- sure تأكد ناجم عن استنتاج منطقي	- He must have been sick. لا بد أنه كان مريضا
Was, were (not modals)	- 100% sure التأكد التام	- He was sick. لقد كان مريضا

14.3 Past forms of modals: صيغ الماضي من الأفعال الشكلية

Modals	Past forms	Remarks/ Examples
Should	Should have+ p.p (Negative form: should not have+ p.p كان ينبغي أن لا)	Used for late advice; to express lost opportunity and criticism تعبر عن نصيحة متأخرة أو ندم على فرصة قد فاتت ولتوجيه الإنتقاد وتستخدم بمعنى: **كان ينبغي** - Ali should have gone to the meeting. **كان ينبغي** أن يذهب أحمد للاجتماع
Ought to	Ought to have+ p.p (Negative form: ought not to have+ p.p كان ينبغي أن لا)	For late advice لنصيحة متأخرة أو فرصة قد فاتت ومعنى: **كان ينبغي** - Ali ought to have gone to the meeting.
Can	Could تمكن، استطاع	- I could lift that heavy box.
Could	Could have+ p.p بمعنى لعل/ كان بالامكان	To express that something was possible to happen للتعبير عن شيء كان ممكن أن يحدث. - Musa could have gone to school. **لعل** موسى **ذهب** الى المدرسة.

		- You could have asked her to help you. **كان بإمكانك** أن تطلب المساعدة منها
May/ might	May/ might have+ p.p	For something probably/ possibly happened للتعبير عن شيء ممكن أو من المحتمل أن قد حدث في الماضي - Mosa may have gone to school.
Must	had to	- Sam had to leave early.

14.4 Probability الاحتمالية

You can use the following ways to express probability:

يمكنك استخدام أيا من الطرق التالية للتعبير عن الاحتمالية:

1. Using (can, could, may, might, must)   استخدام الأفعال الشكلية التالية

    For example:

    - Britney sings beautifully. She **could** be a great singer.
    - Sonia speaks French fluently. She **may** be French.
    - Michelle looks stunning. She **might** win the celebrity prize.
    - Asma speaks Arabic well. She **must** be living in an Arabic   speaking country.

2. Using the introducing statements: استخدام عبارة تمهيدية تتبع النمط التالي

(it is+ likely/ unlikely/ probable/ improbable/ possible/ impossible/ definite+ that clause), e.g.

    - It is likely that it rains today.

    - It is possible that he becomes a brigadier. Things happen.

    - It is probable that he is waiting for her at the roundabout.

3. Using adverbs استخدام الظروف such as: **possibly, probably**, and **definitely**.

    - The enemy forces *possibly* surrender.

    - That little girl *definitely* lives in Oslo.

    - She is *possibly* a French singer.

14.5   Would rather/ prefer

'Would rather' means the same as 'prefer'. However, 'would rather' must be followed by a verb, whereas 'prefer' may/ may not be followed be a verb.

Would rather تعني "يفضل" كما في الفعل Prefer الا أن الأولى يجب أن يتبعها فعل أما الثانية (Prefer) قد يتبعها وقد لا يتبعها فعل، وكما في الأمثلة التالية:

-   Suha **would rather eat** apples **than** carrots.
-   Suha **prefers eating** apples **to eating** carrots.
-   Suha **prefers** apples **to** carrots.

لاحظ أن would rather يتبعها than بينما prefer يتبعها to.

14.6 had better, be supposed to, be to, have to, have got to, be going to, be able to, and used to.

(إن الأفعال وصيغ المعاني هذه ليست أفعالاً شكلية -رغم سردها في الغالب تحت نفس الباب- ويتبعها فعل مجرد)

	Uses	Examples
Had better	(1) advisability with threat of bad result النصيحة ويرافقها تخويف من عاقبة ما	You had better get dressed a bit early, or we will leave without you.
Be supposed to	(1) expectation توقع حدوث شيء	The session is supposed to begin at 17:00 hrs.
Be to	(1) formal order أمر رسمي	You are to attend the meeting at 13:00 hrs.
Have to	necessity ضرورة أو إلزام مصدره ذاتي داخلي (تستخدم باللغة الرسمية)	I have to leave Paris tonight.
	(2) lack of necessity (in negative) عدم وجود داع أو ضرورة	I don't have to visit Jordan this summer.
Have got to	(1) necessity ضرورة (تستخدم بسياق غير رسمي)	I have got to meet her today.
Be going to	(1) planned, and pre-intended action/ or with future results of a present situation حدث مخطط له، منويُ القيام به	I'm going to build a new house. (future only)
Be able to	(1) للتعبير عن القدرة ability	She is able to help Rami.
Used to (to mean accustomed to)	(1) repeated action in the past. حدث متكرر في الماضي، وتستخدم بمعنى "معتاد على"	I used to smoke cigarettes when I was a child.

	Past forms	Examples
Be supposed to	Was/ were supposed to	-I *was supposed to join* you.
Be to	Was/ were to	-He *was to listen* carefully.
Has to/ have to	Had to	-I *had to run* fast to catch the train.
Have got to	Had got to	-I *had got to run* fast to catch the train.
Be going to	Was/ were going to	-She *was going to kill* her husband.
Would rather	Would rather+ have+ p.p (contrary to the fact)	- I *would rather have* prepared myself for the party.

Exercise (35)

Correct the underlined errors to give the right form in the following sentences:

1.   Jima <u>can to dance</u> perfectly.
2.   Rose <u>wills</u> join us today.
3.   Rashid <u>should had</u> played better.
4.   May Fatima <u>to play</u> well?
5.   <u>I'm able</u> jump higher than the Kangaroo.

Exercise (36)

Rewrite the following sentences, so that the new sentences give the same meaning - probability. (You can do that in different ways)

1.   **Beethoven may be English**.
     - It is possible that Beethoven is English.
     Or - Beethoven is possibly English.
2.   **Mills will probably leave this summer**.
     -..
3.   **It is likely that Rashid flies tomorrow morning**.
     - ....

Exercise (37)

Choose the meaning of the underlined verbs/ phrases in the following sentences:

1.   I **could** climb mountains when I was young.
         a. Ability   b. Request   c. Will
2.   She **should** have called me.
         a. Ought to   b. Have to   c. Could
3.   I **can** penetrate the international borders easily.
         a. Be able to   b. Should   c. Had better
4.   **Would you mind** calling me after midnight?
         a. Ability   b. Request   c. Obligation
5.   You **mustn't** drive when you have had a drink.
         a. Necessity   b. Advisability   c. Prohibition
6.   You **don't have to** work till midnight.
         a. Necessity   b. Lack of necessity   c. Prohibition
7.   **I have to** study tonight.
         a. Internal obligation b. External obligation c. advisability

15.   Phrasal Verbs أشباه الأفعال

(Verb+ particle: preposition/ adverb)

A phrasal verb is a simple verb combines with a preposition, as in 'call up' , with adverb, as in 'go forward' or with both as in 'look forward to'. Some phrasal verbs are intransitive, as in 'get ahead' in "She will get a head", and 'blow up' which means 'suddenly become very angry', as in 'When I told jerry the solid proof, he blew up', while others are transitive, as in 'get back'.

ويقصد بهذا المصطلح الفعل المركب من فعل+ حرف جر Call up وكذلك فعل+ ظرف مثل Go forward أو كليها (فعل+ ظرف+ حرف جر) كما في Look forward to . وبعض هذه الأفعال يكون لازما مثل Get ahead أو متعديا مثل Get back.

- I will **get** my car **back**.
- She will **get a head**.

The transitive phrasal verbs are classified into:

و المتعدية منها تقسم إلى قسمين: الأولى <u>يمكن فصل فعلها عن الأداة</u> إذ يأتي المفعول به بين الفعل والأداة (حرف الجر أو الظرف) <u>وأخرى لا يمكن فصل فعلها عن الأداة</u> وكما يلي:

15.1   Separable phrasal verbs: With separable phrasal verbs a noun may come between the verb and the particle or after the particle, whereas the pronoun comes only between the verb and the particle. If the object is short, it can come between the verb and the particle. The short object is made of two words or less.

If the object of the separable phrasal verbs is long, the   object   will come only after the phrasal verb, as in *'I can get back many of my objects.' 'Many of my objects'* isn't short to come between the verb and the particle.

أشباه الأفعال القابلة للفصل: يمكن للمفعول به القصير- أي الذي لا يزيد عن كلمتين- أن يأتي بين الفعل والأداة بالاضافة الى أنه يمكن أن يأتي بعد الأداة، واذا كان المفعول به أطول من ذلك فلا يتم الفصل بل يجب أن يأتي بعد الأداة (سواء كانت الأداة حرف جر أو ظرفاً). أما إذا كان المفعول به ضميراً فيجب أن ياتي بين الفعل والأداة ولا يمكن أن نؤخره بعد الأداء، وكما في الأمثلة التالية حيث وضع خط تحت المفعول به.

Examples:

- We will *get **it** back*.
- My teacher gave me a few hints. I need to *write **them** down*   before I forget.
- I *wrote* <u>the number</u> *down*. (short object)

(Or) I *wrote down* <u>the number</u>.

- *Put* <u>your hands</u> *up*. (Or) *Put up* <u>your hands</u>.
- I can't *get back* <u>any of my objects</u>. (long object)
- I'll *try on* <u>the dress in that room</u>. (long object)
- I'll *carry out* <u>a number of physical exercises</u>. (long object)
- We will *get* <u>our car</u> *back*. (Or) We will *get back* <u>our car</u>.

15.2 **Non-separable phrasal verbs** with which a noun or a pronoun must follow the particle, as in *'feel over'* in 'He *felt over* the rocks'.

أشباه الأفعال غير القابلة للفصل: هي تلك التي يجب أن يأتي المفعول به سواء كان أسما أو ضميرا بعد الأداة، وكما في المثال التالي:

'He *felt over* the rocks'

15.3 **The following is a list of separable phrasal verbs:**

قائمة أفعال قابلة للفصل

call up يتصل	hand in يسلم	hold back يكبح	set back يعيق، يـؤخر عقارب الساعة
make out يكتشف	put off يؤجل	write down يدون	break down يعطل،يدمر
get back يسترجع	get down ينزل	bring back يعيد	set out يعلن
get over يتغلب على	pass on ينتقل	back up يـدعم (confirm fact)	switch off يطفئ، يغلق
figure out يحسب، يفهم، يحل	count in يدخل في الحساب	bring down يصرع، يذل، ينزل من	cut down يقطع، يخفض
cut off يعزل، يقطع	cut out يقطع (تسلل)	leave out يهمل	blow up ينفجر،ينفخ
let in يضيق ثوبا	get out يخرج	turn on يشغل	
let out يوسع ثوبا	look over يفحص	mix up يخلط	
make up يكمل، يخترع	put up يغمدسيفا، يحيط فلان يلعب علما	break up يقتحم (بنـاء) عنـوة، يقطـع الحـديث	throw away يطرح، يبـدد، يـضيع فرصة
turn down يخفض صوتا	ring up يتصل	bring up يربي	carry out ينجز، ينفذ
run down ـ يصطدم بـ يخفض عدد المستخدمين	Set up يرسم خطة،ينصب	cross out يشطب	hand over يسلم
turn over يقلب،يسلم الى	Do over يعمـل أمـرا مـن جديد،يعيده	turn off يطفئ	try on يقيس (ثوبا)، يختار

The following is a list of inseparable phrasal verbs:

قائمة أفعال غير قابلة للفصل

get away ينصرف	get by يمر، يتجنب اخفاقا	get in يدخل	get over يتعافى من
get together يصل الى اتفاق	come up with يدرك	fall out ينصرف	care about يهـــــــتم ب
call for يقتضي	hang up ينهي مكالمة	cut down يخفض	send for يستدعي
get up يتسلق	pull in يكبح	pull out يرحل، ينجو	clear up يصحو
look after يعتني بـ	look for يتطلع الى	look through يفحص بعناية	look forward to يتطلع إلى
lang about يتسكع	hold on يستمر	call in يستدعي	stick to ـ يلتزم ب
go on يواصل	go out يرحل	go down ينزل	give in يستسلم
brush up on (review) يراجع	bone up on (review) يراجع	get off يترجل، يبدأ	get on يركب،يعتلي

15.3.1 Phrasal verbs with (up) and their meaning.

ring up=	phone	يتصل
give up=	stop doing something	يترك، يتخلى عن
back up=	make a copy of something	يدعم بنسخ احتياط
set up=	establish	يؤسس
bring up=	start to talk about something	يقدم قضية ما
speak up=	speak more loudly	يتكلم بصوت عالي
eat up=	eat all the food	يأكل كل الطعام
make up=	invent	يبتكر، يخترع
hold up=	delay	يؤجل
turn up=	arrive	يصل

(See appendix (5) for more examples of phrasal verbs/ multi-part verbs.)

Exercise (38)

Select the correct answer.

1. The King Abdullah canal ....
    a. holds 30 cubic meters of water back.
    b. holds back 30 cubic meters of water.

2. Janet smokes a lot. She should ....
    (give it up/ give up it)

3. I think I'll ....my coat ....It is too hot here.
    (turn on/ take off)

4. I will ....over there.
    a. put up the picture you bought to me
    b. put the picture you bought to me up

5. Those two words are so similar. They ....
    a. mix me up.
    b. mix up me.

6. You need to ....
    a. look after your child.
    b. look your child after.

7. You still have some weaknesses. I think you will ....soon.
    a. get over them
    b. get them over

16.   The Adjectives

الصفـــــــات

An adjective is a word that describes a noun or pronoun. It is said to make a noun or pronoun more specific as it limits the word it describes in some way. Adjectives tell us something about the colour, size, quantity, quality, origin, material, number, distance, possession or classification of a noun or pronoun, as in:

الصفة هي كلمة تصف الاسم أو الضمير لتجعل منه أكثر تحديدا وتعريفا، والصفة تخبرنا شيئا عن الموصوف (لونه، حجمه، كميته، جودته، منشأه وأصله، مادته، وطرازه...الخ) كما في الأسماء الموصوفة التالية:

red book, *large* house, *spacious* room, *tiny* can, *five* children, *delicious* food, *modern* languages, *little* baby, *large* houses, *Indian* food, *rich* people and *carton* box.

The adjectives could be **predicate** (that comes after the noun/ or pronoun), as in:

والصفة قد تكون **اسنادية** تأتي بعد الاسم أو الضمير، كما في المثالين التاليين حيث جاءت الصفة في المثال الأول أدناه بعد الاسم الموصوف وهو "علي" وفي المثال الثاني كذلك.

1.   **Ali** is *kind*. 'Ali' precedes the adjective 'kind".

2.   **Ali** is *clever*. 'Ali' precedes the adjective 'clever'.

In addition, the adjective could be **attributive** (that comes before the noun/ or pronoun), as in:

والصفة قد تكون **وصفية**، تأتي قبل الاسم أو الضمير، كما في المثال التالي حيث جاءت الصفة friends قبل الاسم الموصوف .

Ali and Ahmad are *close friends*. The adjective 'close' precedes 'friends'.

16.1   Order of Adjectives   ترتيب الصفات

We usually describe nouns with one or two adjectives, as in:

1. A *spacious* room.
2. A *big white* building.
3. A *delicious Chinese* food'.

Interestingly, several adjectives may modify one noun or pronoun, as in:

4. The *small black Chinese cat* bit me'.

- عادة ما نصف الاسم بصفة واحدة كما في المثال (1) أو بصفتين كما في المثالين (2، 3).

ويجدر بالذكر أنه يمكن وصف أسم واحد بعدة صفات كما في المثال (4) اذ أن Cat وصفت بصفة لون و حجم وصفة أصل تدل على البلد الذي تنحدر منه تلك القطط.

Fundamental English Grammar Review

This calls for an order in which the adjectives appear. The table below shows the order of adjectives you should follow:

هذا يستدعي وجود ترتيب معين تظهر به الصفات، والجدول التالي يعرض الترتيب الذي يمكنك اتباعه:

Opinion	Size	Age	Shape	Color	Origin Nationality	Material	Noun
nice	large	old	rounded	green	Egyptian	wooden	villa

Note: Adjectives don't change their form. They remain the same whether the noun to which they refer is singular or plural.

ملاحظة: الصفات لا يتغير شكلها سواء كان الاسم الموصوف مفرد أو جمع.

Many adjectives are formed from either the **past participles** of verbs, or from the **present participles** and so end in (ing), as in:

بعض الصفات تتشكل من التصريف الثالث للفعل، وهي تعرف بصفات اسم المفعول وبعضها ا لاخر   للفعل يعرف بصفات إسم الفاعل وتصاغ باضافة ing للمجرد. ومن الأمثلة عليها:

Past participles adjectives		**Present participles adjectives**	
صفات اسم المفعول		صفات اسم الفاعل	
annoyed	منزعج	annoying	مزعج
damaged	معطّل	damaging	معطِل، مخرِب
imported	مستورَد	importing	مستورِد
refused	مرفوض	refusing	رافض
used	مستعمَل	used	مستعمِل
bored	مال، ضجر	boring	ممل
captivated	مأسور	captivating	اسر، يأسر الاخرين
satisfied	مشبَع، مَرضي	satisfying	مُرضي
worried	قلق	worrying	مقلق
excited	مثار، مبتهج	exciting	مثير
washed	مغسول	washing	غاسل، منظف
invited	مدعو	inviting	داعي
occupied	محتل، وقع عليه الإحتلال	occupying	محتل، الذي يقوم بالاحتلال

Some adjectives end in (ical) or (al), particularly nouns ending in (ic).

بعض الصفات تنتهي بـ ical/ al خاصة التي تصاغ من الأسماء التي تنتهي بـ ic مثل:

Examples include: 'comical' from comic, 'fanatical' from fanatic, 'musical' from misic, and 'skeptical' from skeptic.

Sometime the adjectives ending in (ical) are formed from nouns that end in (ics).

وبعض الصفات التي تنتهي بـ ical تصاغ من الأسماء التي تنتهي بـ ics مثل:

These include: 'ethical' from ethics, 'tactical' from tactics, and 'statistical' from statistics.

Some adjectives end in (ic). Those are formed from nouns end in (ics), as in 'electronic' from electronics.

وبعض الصفات التي تنتهي بـ ic تصاغ من الأسماء التي تنتهي بـ ics كما في:
'electronic' from electronics .

Other common adjective endings include:

ومن النهايات الشائعة و التي تضاف للإسم لصياغة الصفة ما يلي:

'**ful**' as in 'beautiful' and 'useful'

'**less**' as in 'graceless' and 'meaningless'

'**able**' as in 'acceptable' and 'agreeable'

'**ible**' as in 'accessible' and 'visible'

'**ive**' as in 'active' and 'impressive'

16.2   Present and Past Participle Adjectives:

صفات اسم الفاعل واسم المفعول

Some adjectives end in (ing) and some others end in (ed) and the difference in meaning between the two forms of adjectives is as follows:

a.   The present participle adjectives, that end in (ing), describe what effect they have on others. A present participle adjective describes the source of the effect, as in 'exciting', 'disappointing', and 'boring' in examples below:

1. The programme was *exciting*.

2. The proposal was *disappointing*.

3. The party was *boring*.

ان صفات اسم الفاعل التي تنتهي بـ ing تصف مصدر ومُسبب الحدث والتأثير الذي
يحمله معنى الصفة، كما في الصفات الواردة في الأمثلة الثلاثة أعلاه، اذ أن سبب الاستياء the
the programme هو مصدر الاثارة والبهجة و proposal
the party الحفلة هي سبب ومصدر الملل فهي "مُمِلة".

b.   The **Past Participle** adjectives, that end in (ed) describe, how we feel, and describe the recipient of the action, as in 'excited', disappointed, and 'bored' (in examples bellow):

1. I am really *excited* now. I liked that programme.

2. She is really *disappointed* as she goes against the proposal.

3. I didn't like her birthday party. I felt just *bored*.

ان صفات اسم المفعول التي تنتهي بـ ed تصف مستقبِل الحدث والذي وقع عليه تأثير
الحدث وكيف يشعر تجاه الحدث، ففي الأمثلة أعلاه (1-3) فإن الضمائر I, she, he
هي التي وقع عليها تأثير الحدث فهم من يشعرون بالإثارة والإستياء والملل على التوالي.

More examples of present and past participle adjectives include:

Present participle adjectives	Past participle adjectives
producing	produced
arresting	arrested
carrying	carried
exporting	exported
warning	warned

16.3 Compound Adjectives الصفات المركبــة

Compound adjectives are adjectives made up of two words or more. The following are the most common forms of compound adjectives:

الصفات المركبة هي الصفات التي تتكون من كلمتين أو أكثر وفيما يلي الأنماط الأكثر شيوعا في صياغة الصفات المركبة:

a. **Present participle**: (adjective+ **verb**+ **ing**+ noun), as in:

'a good- *looking* woman'

'a Spanish- *speaking* teacher'

'a gas producing country'

صفات اسم الفاعل: (صفة + فعل+ing+ اسم)

Meaning	Compound adjectives
a company that *publishes Irish novels*	an Irish novels **publishing** company
a woman who looks good	a good- *looking* woman'
a teacher who speaks Spanish	a Spanish- *speaking* teacher
a country which produces gas	a gas- **producing** country

b. **Past participle**: (adjective+ **past participle**+ noun), as in:

صفات اسم المفعول: (صفة+ اسم مفعول+ اسم)

'ready- *made* shirt'

'newly- *published* book'

c. (ed) added to the nouns: (adjective+ **noun**+ **ed** + noun), as   in: اسم موصوف

يضاف **ed**للاسم: صفة+ اسم +**ed** +

Meaning	Compound adjectives
a girl with blue eyes	a blue- *eyed* girl
a man with a good temper	a good- *tempered* man
a shirt with long sleeves	a long- **sleeved** shirt
a man who has a red face	a red- **faced** man

d. When talking about measurements, the compound adjective can either come after the described noun as in 'a man two meters high', or before the noun, as in:

عند الحديث عن المقاييس فان الصفة المركبة يمكن أن تأتي بعد الاسم الموصوف مثل:

'a man *two meters high*' أو قبل الاسم: كما في الأمثلة التالية وهذا ما يهمنا هنا:

n   *compound* adj.

Meaning	Compound adjectives
a hotel that is a hundred feet high	**a hundred- foot high hotel**
a man who is 20 years old	**a twenty- year- old man**
a building with 15 stories	**a 15-storey building**
a woman who is 30 years old	**a 30-year- old woman**

a ring that costs 30 dollars | **a 30- dollar ring**

Note: In this form of compound adjectives you bring the plural into singular, as in (foot not feet, storey not stories, year not years, and dollar not dollars).

لاحظ أن في هذا النمط من الصفات المركبة فانك تحول الاسم الجمع الذي يلي الرقم الى مفرد   بدلا

فنقول foot بدل feet و storey بدل stories و year بدل years و dollar منdollars .

Don't forget to: لا تنسى ما يلي

1. Put a/ an initially when making compound adjectives.

ابدأ الصفة المركبة بـ a/an .

2. Put a hyphen (-) between the adjective and (past participle/ present participle/ noun+ ed).

ضع (-) بين الصفة التي هي جزء من الصفة المركبة وبين الاسم المفعول/ او الفاعل أو الاسم + ed في الأنماط الثلاثة الأولى.

3. In measurements, put a hyphen (-) between the number and the following name except for the ages and when you talk about years as you put a hyphen (-) before and after the word 'year'.

في النمط الرابع حيث نتعامل مع المقاييس فتضع (-) بين الرقم وبين الاسم الذي يليه. ما year

عدا حين تتكلم عن العمر أو عدد السنين فتضع (-) قبل وبعد كلمة

لاحظ أن كلمة year تكون مفردة في الصفة المركبة.

16.4   Comparative and Superlative: المقارنة والمفاضلة

Comparative degree is used to compare two persons or things whereas superlative degree is used when more than two persons or things are compared.

ان المقارنة كأحد درجات الصفات تستخدم للمقارنة بين شيئين أو شخصين اثنين.اما المفاضلة (وهي اقصى درجة في الصفة) تستخدم عند اجراء مفاضلة بين أكثر من اثنين (بين مجموعة).

16.4.1 Comparative degree: درجة المقارنة

To simplify the way you form comparatives, adjectives can be classified into 'one syllable adjectives', 'two syllable adjectives', and 'three or more syllable adjectives'.

لنيسر طريقة صياغة الصفات في درجة المقارنة فانه يمكن تصنيف الصفات الى **صفات ذات المقطع الواحد وأخرى ذات المقطعين وأخرى ذات الثلاث مقاطع وأكثر.**

a. One-syllable adjectives form their comparatives by adding (er), as in:

الصفات ذات المقطع الواحد تتشكل صفة المقارنة فيها باضافة er للصفة، مثال:

large   larger (than)

big   bigger (than)

short   shorter (than)

brave   braver (than)

dry   drier

(subject+ verb+ adjective-er/ adverb-er+ than+ noun/ pronoun)

- Rami is shorter than Sami.

Note: In adjectives that end in (y) we change (y) into (i) before adding (er).

في الصفات التي تنتهي بـ y فيبدل هذا الحرف ليصبح i ثم نضيف er كما في dry=drier.

b. Two -syllable adjectives that end in (er), (y), or (le) form their comparatives by adding (er), otherwise, they take (more), as in:

الصفات ذات المقطعين المنتهية بـ er/ y/ le يضاف er للصفة، اما اذا لم تنتهي باحدى هذه النهايات فتأخذ الصفة قبلها كلمة more .

clever	clever**er** (than)
pretty	pretti**er** than
gentle	gentl**er** than

- Rami is cleverer than Sami.

c. Adjectives with three or more syllables form their comparatives by using 'more' before them, as in:

الصفات ذات الثلاث مقاطع وأكثر يأتي قبلها كلمة more ، وكما في الأمثلة التالية:

beautiful	**more** beautiful
realistic	**more** realistic
sophisticated	**more** sophisticated

(subject+ verb+ more adjective/ adverb+ than+ noun/ pronoun)

- Joe drives more cautiously than Bob.
- Joe is more cautious than Bob.
- I behave more carelessly than Ali.

d. Some adjectives are irregular in their comparative forms, as in:

بعض الصفات شاذة ولا تتبع أيا مما ذكر أعلاه لتشكل صفات المقارنة، ومنها:

good	better
bad	worse
many	more
little	less
far	further/farther

- My car is better than yours.

Note: 'er' means exactly the same as 'more'. Therefore, they aren't used together. It isn't correct to say "more better"

ملاحظة: er تفيد معنى More تماما، لذا فانه من غير الصحيح أن يستخدما معا فلكل منها استخدامه. تستخدم than بعد الصفة أو الظرف بصيغة المقارنة ولا تستخدم في المفاضلة.

16.4.2 Superlative degree: درجة المفاضلة

It is the form of an adjective that expresses the highest or utmost degree of the quality or manner of the word.

المفاضلة تعبر عن اقصى درجة في الصفة.

a. The one -syllable adjectives end in (est), as in:

الصفات ذات المقطع الواحد تتشكل صفة المفاضلة فيها باضافة est للصفة، كما في:

large	the larg**est**
big	the bigg**est**
short	the short**est**
brave	the brav**est**

(subject+ verb+ the+ adjective+ est+....)

- Hassan is the shortest boy in my family.

b. The longer adjectives use (most), as in:

الصفات الطويلة (أكثر من مقطع) يأتي قبلها كلمة most، وكما في الأمثلة التالية:

beautiful	the **most** beautiful
realistic	the **most** realistic
sophisticated	the **most** sophisticated

(subject+ verb+ the+ most adjective/ adverb....)

- This computer is the most sophisticated of all.

c. Some adjectives have irregular superlative forms, as in:

بعض الصفات شاذة ولا تتبع أيا مما ذكر أعلاه لتشكل صفات المقارنة، ومنها:

good	the **best**
bad	the **worst**
many	the **most**
little	the **least**
far	the **furthest/ farthest**

- This test is the worst.

16.4.3 Steady/ unsteady degree (equal/ unequal degree)

درجة الثبات والتباين (التساوي والاختلاف)

■ An equal comparison indicates that the two entities are exactly the same. To express the equal comparison degree in an adjective that two things or people share, we usually use the following pattern (**subject+ verb+ as+ adjective/ adverb+ as+ noun/ pronoun**).

للتعبير عن درجة المساواة في الصفة الواحدة بين شخصين أو شيئين يشتركان في الصفة ذاتها عادة ما نستخدم النمط التالي: (as + الصفة + as)، دون اجراء تغيير على الصفة الأصلية (أي لا نجعلها بصيغة المقارنة ولا المفاضلة):

Examples:

- Shawkat is **as tall as** she.

- This building is **as high as** the other one.

However, we can use the following words and phrases to show steadiness in the degree of the adjective:

ومع هذا فانه ميكننا استخدام الكلمات وأشباه الجمل التالية لنبين التساوي في الصفة الواحدة:

1. **Similar to:**   Shawkat's house is **similar to** Ramzi's.
2. **Like:**   My car is **like** yours.
3. **So +adj+ as:**   Hala is **so nice as** Rami.
4. **The same:**   My wallet and hers are **the same.**
5. **The same+ noun+ as:**   My house is **the same height as** his.
6. **Look alike:**   Those two girls **look alike.**
7. **Very +adj+ as:**   It is **very quick as** the BMW.
8. **As+ adj+ as:**   Shawkat is **as tall as** Sami.

Note: The subject form of the pronoun will always be used after 'as'.

ملاحظة: بعد as نستخدم دامئا صيغة الفاعل من الضمير.

- To express the unequal/ unsteady degree in an adjective we usually use the following pattern (**not+ as+ adjective+ as**).

للتعبير عن درجة عدم المساواة في الصفة ذاتها ، عادة ما نستخدم النمط التالي:

(as + الصفة + not as)،دون اجراء تغيير على الصفة الأصلية، كما في:

- Shawkat is **not as tall as** Ramzi.

- This building is **not as high as** the other one.

However, we can use the following words and phrases to show unsteadiness in the degree of adjectives:

ومع هذا فانه ميكننا استخدام الكلمات التالية لنبين عدم التساوي في الصفة الواحدة:

1. **Different from:**   My watch is **different from** his.
2. **Not+ so+ adjective+ as:** Fadi is**n't so strong as** Kareem.
3. **Not like:**   The weather in Irbid is**n't like** the weather in Madaba.
4. **Not the same:**   This chair is**n't the same** as that one.
5. **Not similar to:**   My husband is **not similar to** yours.
6. **Not as tall as:**   Shawkat is **not as tall as** Ramzi.

16.5   The Functions of the Adjectives and Adverbs

وظيفة و عمل الصفات والظروف:

c. An adjective describes a noun/ pronoun, as in:

الصفة تصف الاسم أو الضمير، كما في املثال التالي:

I bought *expensive* <u>clothes</u>.

       Adjective   noun

(*'expensive'* describes *'clothes'*)

b. An adverb describes a verb, as in: الظرف يصف الفعل، كما في

We _regularly_ meet the boss.

        Adverb verb

('_regularly_' describes '_meet_')

c.   an adverb can also describe an adjective/ or another adverb, as in: ويمكـن

للظرف أن يصف الصفة ويصف ظرفا اخر، كما في المثالين التاليين

The weather is _really_ hot. ('_really_' describes '_hot_')

        Adv.   Adj.

She crossed the road _very_ slowly. ('_very_' describes '_slowly_').

        Adv Adv

Note: We usually form adverbs of manner by adding (ly) to the adjective,i.e. **adjectives+ ly**, as follows:

عادة ما نصيغ الظرف باضافة ly للصفة كالاتي:

Interesting= interestingly; brave= bravely; happy= happily

a.   When **'y'** comes after a consonant in an adjective, you add **'ily'**, as in:

اذا جاء في نهاية الصفة حرف y مسبوق بحرف صحيح فتحذف وتضيف ily للصفة:

- easy =   easily

Otherwise, you only add 'ly', as in "quick= quickly"

b.   You don't omit 'e' from the adjective, as in:

لا تحذف حرف e من نهاية الصفة، كما في:

nice =   nicely.

باستثناء بعض الصفات مثل:

Except for: (**true**= truly, and **whole**= wholly)

16.6   Much more comfortable

We can put the following words before a **comparative** to say how much (comfortable, for instance) something is.

يمكن وضع الكلمات التالية قبل صفة المقارنة لتبين مقدار الصفة ودرجتها:

(**much, a lot, far, rather, slightly, a bit, a little, any, no**)

متبعين أحد الأنماط التالية في صياغة الجملة:

- (Subject+ verb+ far/ much...+ adjective/ adverb+ er+ than+ noun/ pronoun)
- (Subject+ verb+ far/ much...+ more+ adjective/ adverb+ than+ noun/ pronoun)
- (Subject+ verb+ far/ much...+ more+ noun...)

Examples:

-   A paper bag is **much better than** a plastic bag.

كيس الورق **أفضل بكثير** من كيس البلاستيك.

-   Modern cars are **far more comfortable than** old cars.

السيارات الحديثة **أكثر راحة بكثير** من السيارت القديمة.

-   My house is **a bit more spacious than** yours.

منزلي **أكثر اتساعا من** منزلك بقليل.

- I slept **a little earlier than** the day before yesterday.

نمت **أبكر بقليل من** يوم أول أمس.

- This shop is **slightly bigger than** mine.

هذا الدكان **أكبر بقليل من** دكاني.

- You need to spend **a lot more time** on studying English.

أنت بحاجة لأن تمضي **المزيد المزيد** من الوقت على دراسة الانجليزية.

- He speaks English **much more rapidly than** he does French.

- Your second wife was **no better than** your first one.

زوجتك الثانية **لم تكن بأحسن** حال من الأولى.

'**No**' has a negative meaning: أي لها معنى سلبي

'**Any**' is used in negative statements and in questions.

'Any' تستخدم في الجمل المنفية وفي الأسئلة.

- This building **isn't any higher than** Sami's.
- Are you playing **any better**?

16.7   better and better/ more and more difficult

We use expressions like (better and better, higher and higher, shorter and shorter, faster and faster, longer and longer, more and more valuable, more and more expensive, more and more childeren etc.) to say that something is increasing all the time. It also makes the meaning more emphatic.

نستخدم هذه الصيغة من الصفات لنظهر أن أمرا ما بازدياد وتكاثر. لاحظ أننا نضيف للصفة القصيرة   وكما كما ورد سابقا er ونضيف قبل الصفة الطويلةmore في الصيغ التالية الموضحة بالأمثلة:

- (صفة قصيرة + and + صفة قصيرة)
- (more and more+ صفة طويلة)

- The economy was developing **faster and faster** in Jordan.
- The queue of the soldiers is getting **longer and longer**.
- Cotton is getting **more and more expensive**.
- Jordan government is losing **more and more skilled** people.

16.8   Comparison of nouns

Nouns can also be used in comparisons. You can use the following patterns for guidance:

- (subject+ verb+ as+ **many/ much/ little/ few**+ noun+ as+ noun/ pronoun)
- (subject+ verb+ **more/ fewer/ less**+ noun+ than+ noun/ pronoun)

Examples:

- I have more houses than she.
- They have as few classes as we.
- January has more days than February.
- Sandra has as much information as my sister.

16.9 Double comparatives   المقارنة المضاعفة

We can begin a sentence with a comparative construction, and consequently the second clause must begin with a comparative, as well.

Try to use the following patterns:

نستطيع أن نبدأ الجملة بصيغة المفاضلة وبناء عليه يجب أن تبدأ العبارة الثانية من الجملة بتركيب المفاضلة ذلك more/ er. أيضا، مع الانتباه الى حقيقة اذا ما كانت الصفة من مقطع أو للصفة أو أكثر لتحدد بناء على اذا ما كنت تحتاج لاضافة

حاول اتباع الصيغتين التاليتين وهما الأكثر استخداما في هذا السياق:

- the+ comparative+ subject+ verb+ the comparative+ subject+ verb
- the more+ subject+ verb+ the+ comparative+ subject+ verb

For example:

- The higher you fly, the worse you feel.
- The bigger the house is, the harder to clean.
- The hotter it is, the more miserable you feel.
- The more you practice, the more fluent you'll be.
- The more she studies, the more intelligent she becomes.

16.10 Adjectives with linking verbs

الأفعال التالية تعرف بأفعال الربط وتربط الفاعل بالصفة، ويتبع هذه الأفعال صفات.

Linking verbs, as mentioned earliear, don't show action. They link the subject with its complement. Those verbs must be modified by adjectives, and they include:

Be   stay   appear feel   look   smell
Taste   seem sound   become remain

Examples:

- Hamad **feels bad** about his result.
- Ibrahim **becomes tired** quikly.
- Lucy will **look attractive** in her new dress.
- Jasmin **smells sweet.**
- This food **tastes delicious.**
- She **remained sad.**
- This music **sounds lovely.**

Exercise (39)

Select the appropriate answer

1. The sea food seems............
   a. deliciously   b. delicious   c. deliciousness

2. Areej is............ than Sali.
   a. fitter   b. fittest   c. more fit

3. This blueprint is the .... ever.
   a. good   b. best   c. better

4. She is the............ lady in town.
   a. gorgeous   b. most gorgeous   c. gorgeousest

5. This line of seats has............ arm chairs than ours.
   a. much   b. more   c. the most

6. The game was............ I really loved it.
   a. interested   b. interesting   c. interestingly

7. Rania is as .... as Sylvia.
   a. healthy   b. healthier   c. the healthiest

9. Ali walks ....
   a. slow   b. slowly   c. slower

10. He drives ....
   a. fast   b. fastingly   c. fastly

11. My brother has brown eyes. He is.............
   a.brown-eyes   b.brown-eyed   c.eyes-browned

Exercise (40)

Correct the adjectives in brackets to fit the sentences.

1. This film is the ....I have ever seen. (interesting)
2. This test is..........than the previous one. (easy)
3. What is .... river in Europe? (long)
4. This case is ....that one. (bad)
5. My earache is..........than it was yesterday. (painful)
6. Cairo is........than Amman. (large)
7. This armchair is ....than mine. (comfortable)
8. This is .... hotel in Jordan. (high)
9. My vase is..........(not/ good) yours. Your vase is well decorated.
10. Ali is ....(strong) a horse. He looks much better today.

Exercise (41)

Circle the correct phrase that has the appropriate compound adjective.

1. 'A hotel with seven stars' is called
   a. a seven-star hotel   b. a seven- stars hotel

2. 'A house with five bed rooms' is called:
   a. a five-bedroom house   b. a five-bedroom- house

3. 'A word with ten letters' is called:

   a. a ten- lettered word   b. a ten-letter word

4. 'A mother who has dark hair' is called:

   a. a dark-haired mother b. a dark- hairing mother

5. 'A man who is at the age of 110' is called:

   a. a 110-year-old man   b. a-110 year old man

Exercise (42)

Complete the following table with the correct forms of adjectives. Remember to add only 'r' or 'st' when the adjective ends in 'e'; if the one syllable adjective ends in a vowel, double the last consonant before you ad 'er' or 'est' :

Adjective	Comparative	Superlative
fine		the finest
short		the shortest
few		
exciting		
nice	nicer	
fat		
difficult		
dim	dimmer	
	uglier	
early		
dry		
young		
		the narrowest
much/ many		most
little	less	
far		

Exercise (43)

Complete each sentence with the correct form of the adjective:

1. I feel ……today. (a bit, good)

2. The shop is …….than the mall. (much, expensive)

3. The missile went……into the sky. (high, high)

Exercise (44)

Supply the correct form of the adjectives and adverbs in brackets.

1. Dove is……..(talented) than Maccaine.

2. This month is …….(hot) as last month.

3. A new apartment is much……(expensive) than an old one.

4. A new apartment is much….(good) than an old one.

5. My dog runs……(fast) than yours.

Exercise (45)

Select the correct form in brackets in the following sentences.

1. Salma is .....(happier/ the happiest) person we know.
2. Ben's car is .....(faster/ the fastest) than Dan's.
3. This picture is.....(colourfuller/ more colourful) than the old one.
4. Hamad is .....(less/ the least) athletic of all men.
5. Ahmad has .....(little/ few) opportunities to join the team.

17. Adverbs and Adverbial Clauses
الظروف والجمل الظرفية

17.1 Adverbs. الظروف

Adverb is a word that modifies or adds information about a verb, as in 'He *works rapidly'*; about an adjective, as in 'She is an ***extremely*** *beautiful* young lady', or about another adverb, as in 'He is sleeping ***very soundly'***. There are different kinds of adverbs that include:

الظرف وكما مر سابقا فانه يصف ويضيف معلومات عن فعل، أو صفة أو ظرف آخر. وهناك أنواع مختلفة للظروف وتشمل:

a.   Adverbs of place: They tell us where something happened; and they include such words as:

ظروف المكان: وهي تخبرنا عن مكان وقوع حدث ما، وهي كثيرة منها:

(*here, there, somewhere, outdoor, underground,* and *abroad*).

Examples:

- His family lives *abroad.*
- I left the keys *somewhere* in the house.
- The new lorry is *there.*
- The train is *underground.*

b.   Adverbs of time: They tell us when something happened, and they include such words as:

ظروف الزمان: تخبرنا عن وقت وزمن وقوع الحدث وتشمل كلمات مثل:

(*now, then, later, soon,* and *yesterday*).

Examples:

- My friends left *yesterday.*
- Salim is listening to the music *now.*
- I will see him *later.*
- I did my homework, *then* I watched my favourite film.

c.   Adverbs of manner tell us how something happens and they include such words as:

ظروف الحال: تخبرنا عن كيفية وقوع الحدث، وتشمل كلمات مثل:

(*badly, cautiously, hotly, fearlessly,* fast, hard, straight, dangerously, and wrong).

Examples:

- Don't get me *wrong.*
- Rula ran *fast.*
- I walked *straight* until I came to a roundabout.
- I met the enemy *fearlessly.*

d. **Adverbs of degrees** tell us the degree, extent or intensity of something that happens. They include such words as:

ظروف الدرجة: تخبرنا عن درجة قوة وشدة الحدث أو الصفة أو الظرف، كما في:

(*immensely, adequately, partially,* and *virtually*).

Examples:

- They are *virtually* penniless.
- The two companies are *partially* separated.
- The tank is *adequately* full of water.

e. **Adverbs of frequency** are used to tell how often something happens, and they include:

ظروف التكرار: تخبرنا عن مدى تكرار حدوث أمر ما، كما في:

(*never, rarely, seldom, occasionally, sometimes, often, frequently, always, regularly, constantly, continually,* and *intermittently*).

Examples:

- She *never* eats breakfast.
- He goes to the dentist *regularly*.
- *Sometimes* I meet my famil members in Cyprus.
- I *rarely* eat noodles.

f. **Adverbs of duration** tell us how long something takes, and they include:

ظروف الاستمرارية: تخبرنا عن المدة التي استغرقها حدوث أمر ما، كما في:

(*briefly, long, indefinitely, always, forever, permanently,* and *temporarily*).

Examples:

- We stopped *briefly* for some coffee.
- They have gone *forever*.
- Asma is living in Damascus *temporarily*.

g. **Adverbs of emphasis** add emphasis to the action described by the verb, and they include:

ظروف التوكيد: وتضيف توكيدا على وصف الفعل، كما في:

(*absolutely, certainly, quite, definitely, really, simply, and just*).

Examples:

- I *simply* must go now.
- Your parents *certainly* detest each other.
- I'm *just* happy.

h. **Adverbs of probability**. They are used to tell us how sure something will happen, and they include:

ظروف الاحتمالية: وتخبرنا عن مدى التأكد من أن أمرا ما سيقع، كما في:

(*probably, possibly, perhaps, maybe, presumably, hopefully, definitely, certainly,* and *conceivably*).

Examples:

- You will *probably* see them there.
- I'm *definitely* in the competition.

  i. **Interrogative adverbs** ask questions, and they include (where, when, how, why, what, etc.), as in:

ظروف استجوابية/ استفهامية: وهي تطرح أسئلة حول أمر ما، وتشمل أدوات السؤال:

- *Where* are you going?
- *What* is Sam doing tonight?
- *How* old are you?

17.2 Adverbial clauses   الجمل الظرفية

An adverbial clause is a subordinate clause that modifies the main clause by adding information about time, place, concession, condition, manner, purpose, reason and result, etc.

الجملة الظرفية جملة تابعة (أي ليس لها معنى تام اذا ما ذكرت وحدها) وهي تضيف معلومات للجملة الرئيسة حول زمن أو مكان أو تحمل فكرة متناقضة أو تكون جملة شرطية أو تعبر عن غاية أو سبب أو نتيجة، الخ. والجملة الظرفية أنواع مختلفة تشمل ما يلي:

a. **An adverbial clause of time** indicates the time of an event, and is introduced by a conjunction such as (after, as, before, the moment, until, when, as soon as, and whilst) e.g.:

الجملة الظرفية الزمانية: وتدل على وقت وزمن وقوع حدث ما ويتم تقديم هذه الجملة بأدوات ربط مثل:

(after, as, before, the moment, until, when, as soon as, and whilst)

Examples:

- He left <u>*after the meal was served*</u>.

     Adverbial clause of time

- The thief ran away <u>*when he saw the police patrol*</u>.

     Adverbial clause of time

- <u>*As soon as I get my certificate*</u>, I will travel to Paris.

   Adverbial clause of time

b. **An adverbial clause of place** indicates the location of an event, and is introduced by a conjunction such as: 'where', and 'everywhere'.

الجملة الظرفية المكانية: تشير الى مكان وقوع حدث ما ويتم تقديمها بأدوات ربط مثل:

where, everywhere وكما في المثال التالي:

"They left the keys <u>*where they found them*</u>".

    Adverbial clause of place

c. **An adverbial clause of concession** contains a fact that contrasts in some way with the main clause, and is introduced by a conjunction such as (although, despite, in spite of, even though, while, whilst, and whereas).

الجملة الظرفية التعارضية: وتحتوي على حقيقة ما تتعارض بشكل ما مع ما جاء بالجملة الرئيسية، ويتم تقديمها بأدوات ربط مثل:

(although, despite, in spiteof , even though, while, whilst, and whereas)

Examples:

- He did so well in the math test *although he isn't clever*.

          Adverbial clause of concession

- Russel went to school *in spite of her illness*.

          Adverbial clause of concession

- I'm busy *whereas Mohammad is free*.

          Adverbial clause of concession

d. **An adverbial clause of condition** deals with possible situation, and is introduced by conjunctions:

الجملة الظرفية الشرطية: ويتم تقديمها بأدوات ربط مثل:

(if, only if, unless, providing, as long as,and provided),as in:

- We can't get in *unless we get permission*.

          Adverbial clause of conditions

- *If you are thirsty*, drink water.

          Adverbial clause of condition

- *As long as you are busy*, I'll not disturb you.

          Adverbial clause of condition

e. **An adverbial clause of manner** describes the way that someone behaves or the way in which something is done, and is introduced by a conjunction such as (as, as if, like, the way), e.g:

        He looked at Sherrie *as if he hated her*.

الجملة الظرفية الواصفة للحال: وتصف الطريقة التي يتصرف بها شخص ما أو الطريقة التي تم بيه أمر ما، ويتم تقديمها بأدوات ربط مثل:

as, as if, like, the way كما في المثال أعلاه .

f. **An adverbial clause of purpose** indicates the intention someone has when doing something and is introduced by a conjunction such as (to, in order to, so, so as to, so that, for), e.g.:

- He kicked the child just *to upset his mother*.
- He works hard *to earn more money*.

الجملة الظرفية الغائية: وتشير للغاية أو القصد من عمل ما، ويتم تقديمها بأدوات ربط مثل:

to, in order to, so, so as to, so that, for كما في الأمثلة أعلاه.

g. **An adverbial clause of reason** explains why something happens, and is introduced by a conjunction such as (because, since, because of, and as), as in:

- We didn't visit my cousin *because the car broke down*.
- *As the weather is cold*, we are not going out tonight.

الجملة الظرفية السببية: وتشير لسبب حدوث أمر ما، ويتم تقديمها بأدوات ربط مثل:
because, since, because of, as كما في الامثلة أعلاه .

h. **An adverbial clause of result** indicates the result of an event, and is introduced by a conjunction such as (so, so that), as in:

جملة النتيجة الظرفية: وتشير لنتيجة حدث ما، ويتم تقديمها بأدوات ربط مثل:so, so that

- She fell off the bike *so that she broke her leg*.
- Liza arrived a bit late *so she was punished*.

18. Conditional Clauses
الجمل الشرطية

18.1 Types of conditional clauses
أنواع الجمل الشرطية

There are four types of conditional clauses, each of them consists of two parts: the 'if clause' and the 'main clause'. The following table helps you get familiar with those types easily.

هناك أربعة أنواع للجمل الشرطية ويتكون كل نوع من (جملة الشرط وتبدأ بـ If و أخرى جملة رئيسية- جواب الشرط). والجدول التالي يمكنك من الإلمام بهذه الأنواع بسهولة.

Type	Meaning	Forms and Examples
1st conditional (Type 1)	Used to mean that the action: is probable/ possible/ or likely to happen in the future. يستخدم حين يكون الحدث محتملاً أو ممكن أن يقع مستقبلا.	(If+ present simple, will/ shall/ can/ may/ must/ should/ have to+ bare infinitive): - If you run fast, you will catch the train. اذا ركضت بسرعة فستدرك القطار. - If you obey the orders, you can succeed. اذا تطع الأوامر فسوف تنجح. - If you want to do well in the IELTS test, you should work hard. * The verb in the 'if clause' could be 'present progressive', as in: يمكن أن يكون زمن الفعل في الـ If clause مضارعاً مستمراً، كما في المثال التالي: - If you are studying hard, you may find it easy to pass.
2nd conditional (Type 2)	Used when the action is not true now or improbable/ unlikely to happen; when we talk about unreal or hypothetical situations. يستخدم حين يكون الحدث غير محتمل أو غير ممكن الحدوث، أو للحديث عن أمر افتراضي أو غير حقيقي.	(If+ past simple, would/ could/ might + bare infinitive) Examples: - If you solved the puzzle, you would win the game. (You probably won't solve the puzzle, so it is unlikely to win the game) لو كنت حللت اللغز لفزت بالمباراة.(هذا يعني أنه قد لاتحل اللغز بالتالي فانه ليس من الممكن أن تفوز). - If you played well, you would win. (You probably won't play well) "If I were you"-تستخدم لتقديم للنصيحة "We usually use 'were' with all nouns and pronouns in type 2"; and we use this pattern to give advice, as in: تستخدمWere مع كل الأسماء والضمائر الجمع والمفردة - If I were you, I would go to the dentist. لو كنت مكانك لذهبت الى طبيب الأسنان. (بمعنى:أنصحك بالذهاب لطبيب الأسنان)

3rd conditional (Type 3)	Used when the action is impossible to happen, and when a past action didn't happen يستخدم حين يكون الحدث مستحيل الوقوع، أو أنه لم يقع فعلا في السابق	(If+ past perfect, would/ could/ might + have + p.p.) - If she had married early, she would have had a baby. (She didn't marry early. She didn't have a baby.) لو أنها قد تزوجت باكراً لأنجبت أطفالاً. (الا أنها تزوجت متأخرة وبالتالي فمن المستحيل أن تنجب أطفالا لأن الوقت فاتها ومن المستحيل أن تعيد الزمن لتتزوج باكرا) -If he had had enough time, he could have visited you.
General/ Zero conditional	Used to describe rules and something that is always true/ or it regularly happens. It has general meaning, and it doesn't refer to the future. هذا النوع من الجمل الشرطية لا يشير الى المستقبل. وهو يستخدم لوصف قواعد وأشياء غالبا ما تكون صحيحة	(if+ present simple, present simple) In zero conditional we don't use modals. لا نستخدم الأفعال الشكلية في هذا النوع من الجمل الشرطية Examples: - If I feel thirsty, I drink water. اذا كنت عطشانا، اشرب الماء. - If you boil water, it evaporates. اذا غليت الماء، سيتبخر. - If you stop smoking, you save money. اذا توقفت عن التدخين فستوفر المال.

Note: 'Open conditional' is a type of conditional sentences. In this type 'present tense' is used in the conditional clause and 'imperative' is used in the main clause, for example:

- **If you need** any help, **give** me a call.

الجمل الشرطية "المفتوحة" أحد أنواع الجمل الشرطية، وبها يستخدم **الزمن المضارع** في العبارة الشرطية أما في العبارة الرئيسية/ جملة جواب الشرط فتستخدم **صيغة الأمر** وكما في المثال أعلاه.

Note: The 'if clause' can start or end a conditional sentence. When the 'if clause' starts a sentence, we use a comma after the 'if clause'.

عبارة الـ If clause يمكن أن تأتي في أول أو آخر الجملة، اذا جاءت في البداية فضع بعدها فاصلة، أما اذا جاءت في النهاية فلا تستخدم الفاصلة، مثال:

- If I *were* you, I *would go* to the dentist.
- I *would go* to the dentist if I *were* you.

More examples:

First conditional	- If I'm late, I will phone the supervisor. - If I go shopping, I'll buy some pens. - How will you get home if you miss the bus? - If the tickets are too expensive, I won't be able to get one. - If Mary doesn't feel well, she won't go to school. - If it doesn't stop raining, our house will be flooded. - If I have the money, I'll buy a new car. - If you want to pick up some food, you should use the upper chopstick.
Second conditional	- If I were you, I'd get the right shirt. - If I were you, I wouldn't run in the dark. - If I were you, I'd wear comfortable clothing. - What would you do if you found some money? - I would buy a new camera if I had more money. - If you told me a secret, I wouldn't tell anyone. - If I missed the train, I would walk to school. - If I had the time, I'd go to the beach this weekend. - If he were here, he would tell you about the case. - If he didn't speak so loudly, you could understand him. - If people swithed to chopsticks, eating on the move would be useless.
Third conditional	- If I had known that you were in Qatar, I'd have written you a letter. - If Alia had found the right agent, she would have sold the old boat. - If we hadn't lost our way, we would have arrived a bit earlier. - If pressure had been put on resources, people could have forced the authorities to conserve fuel.
General conditional	- If I'm hungry, I eat some food. - If you feel cold, wear some warm clothes. - If you are tired, go to bed. - If you turn off extra lights, you save energy. - If my doctor has free time, he visits his patients in the hospital. - If Ali has enough time, he usually walks to school.

18.2   'If ' and 'Unless'   "إذا" و" إذا لم"

'Unless' means 'if not'. Sometimes you are asked to rewrite a sentence that uses 'if' to another using unless. The following are the way of doing that:

عادة ما يطلب منك أن تعيد كتابة الجملة الشرطية باستخدام Unless ، تاليا كيفية عمل ذلك:

If the verb in the 'if clause' is negative   إذا كانت جملة if منفية

a.   You omit *'if'* and *'don't'* and leave what is left in the sentences as it is, then use 'unless' instead of 'if '.

احذف if و don't واستبدل if بـ unless :

If you **don't come**, you will suffer.

Unless you **come**, you will suffer.

b.   Omit *'if'* and *'doesn't'* from the sentence and add 's' or 'es' to the   verb that comes after 'doesn't', then use 'unless' instead of 'if '.

احذف if و doesn't وأضف es/s للفعل الرئيس واستبدل if بـ unless :

If she **doesn't drink** water, she will die.

Unless she **drinks** water, she will die.

- **If** Sue **doesn't have** a car, she can't come.

Unless she **has** a car, she can't come.

c.   Omit *'If'* and *'didn't'* and write the past form of the verb that comes after 'didn't', then use 'unless' instead of 'if '.

احذف if و didn't واكتب التصريف الثاني للفعل الرئيس واستبدل if بـ unless :

If he **didn't write** a letter, he would be fired.

Unless he **wrote** a letter, he would be fired.

d.   Omit only *'if'* and *'not'* if be, have or modals are used in the sentence and use *'unless'*.

احذف if و not اذا كان هناك احد أفعال الكينونة أو التملك واستبدل if بـ unless :

- **If** she **is not** good at physics, she can't pass.

Unless she **is** good at physics, she can't pass.

- **If** she **hasn't** money, she can't join us.

Unless she **has** money, she can't join us.

e.   Add 'not' to the main clause when you use ' unless' in case the sentence with 'if' was affirmative.

اضف not لجملة جواب الشرط اذا كانت جملة if مثبتة واستخدم unless بدلا من if .

If he plays well, he will win.

Unless he plays well, he will **not** win.

If the 'if clause' is affirmative and the main clause is negative:

إذا كانت جملة if مثبتة وجملة جواب الشرط منفية

f.   If the 'if clause' is affirmative and the 'main clause' is negative, omit 'not'/ the negation from the main clause and use 'unless' instead of 'if'.

احذف not من جملة جواب الشرط اذا كانت جملة if مثبتة واستخدم unless بدلا من if .

If the weather is cold, we **won't go** swimming.

Unless the weather is cold, we **'ll go** swimming.

18.3   Wish   التمني

'Wish' mustn't be followed by any present tense verb or auxiliary.

الفعل Wish يجب أن لا يتبعه فعل أو فعل مساعد بالزمن المضارع على الاطلاق.

18.3.1   Wish...would/ could (future wish)

'Wish...would' expresses a **wish for a change in behaviour**, as in:

في جملة wish نستخدم Would للتعبير عن تمني لأن يصبح تغير في سلوك ما، مثال:

- I **wish** you **would** be more patient with your boss.

(you probably won't be)

أتمنى أن تصبح أكثر صبرا في تعاملك مع مسؤولك.

- I **wish** you **wouldn't** fight with your parents anymore.

أتمنى أن لا تتشاجر مع والديك مجددا.

Besides, 'wish...would' expresses **a wish for something to happen**, as in:

جملة التي فيها wish...would تستخدم كذلك للتعبير عن تمني حدوث أمر ما، مثال:

- I **wish** you **would** find a real value out of 'The Binos' dictionary of military terms- by Etaywe Awni.

أتمنى أن تجد قيمة حقيقية بعد قراءتك لقاموس (المنظار للمصطلحات العسكرية- اعداد عوني العطيوي).

- I **wish** your car **would** work properly.

أتمنى أن تعمل سيارتك جيدا.

- جملة التي فيها wish...could تستخدم كذلك للتعبير عن عدم المقدرة على فعل ما، مثال:

- I **wish** you **could** come to the party. (it means I can't)

أتمنى أن تأتي للحفلة.

18.3.2   Wish.... Simple past tense verb (present wish)

'Wish' with 'a past tense verb' express a **wish for the present situation to be different**, as in:

جملة wish المستخدم معها فعل ماضٍ بسيط تستخدم للتعبير عن تمني تغير أمر قائم، مثال:

-     This villa isn't big enough. I **wish** it **was** much bigger.

(it is not big enough)

الفيلا ليست كبيرة بما يكفي. أتمنى لو كانت أكبر بكثير مما هي عليه.

-     I can't afford a Mercedes car. I **wish** I **had** a better income.

لا أقدر على شراء سيارة مرسيدس. أتمنى لو كان لي دخل أفضل .

18.3.3   Wish.... past perfect

We use Wish and past perfect to **express a past wish**, as in:

جملة wish و فعل بالزمن الماضي التام تستخدم للتعبير عن تمني في الماضي، مثال:

- I **wish** I **had told** the judge the truth. I'm in jail now for not telling the truth. (This means 'I didn't tell the judge the truth')

أتمنى لو أنني أخبرت القاضي بالحقيقة. أنا الان في السجن لعدم ذكري الحقيقة. (أنا لم أقل الحقيقة)

- I **wish** I **hadn't got rid** of the governor's phone number. I really need him. (This means 'I already got rid of the number')

أتمنى لو أنني لم أتخلص من رقم هاتف الحاكم. أنا بحاجته حقا. (لقد تخلصت من الرقم من قبل)

- I ate too many sweet cakes. I don't feel well. **I wish I hadn't eaten too many sweet cakes.** (It means that I shouldn't have eaten too many sweet cakes)

- I didn't do enough work when I was at scool. **I wish I had done enough work when I was at school.**

18.4 Hope

Hope and **wish** are similar in meaning but different in grammar. 'Hope' indicates something which possibly happened or will possibly happen. 'Hope' can be followed by any tense. As in:

- I **hope** that **you'll** come tonight.

(I don't know if you're coming)

- I **hope** that they **came** last night.

(I don't know if they came)

18. 5 As if/ as though

As if, and **as though** indicate something unreal/ or contrary to the fact. The verb that follows these conjunctions must be in the past tense or past perfect.

تستخدم as if/ as though لنشير الى شيء غير حقيقي أو يخالف الحقيقة. والفعل الذي يأتي بعد هذه أدوات الربط يجب أن يأتي بصيغة الزمن الماضي أو الماضي التام. وحسب الأنماط التالية:

-"Subject+ verb (present)+ as if/ as though+ subject+ verb (past simple)"

-"Subject+ verb (past)+ as if/ as though+ subject+ verb (past perfect)"

لاحظ أنه اذا كان الفعل بالشق الأول من الجملة مضارعاً فإن الفعل الذي يأتي بعد أدوات الربط هذه يكون بصيغة الماضي البسيط، أما اذا كان الفعل بالشق الأول الذي يأتي بعد هذه الأدوات يكون بصيغة الماضي التام، وكما في الأمثلة التالية:

- The lady **treats** me <u>**as if she were**</u> my mother.

(She is not my mother)

- Asma **walks** <u>**as though she studied**</u> fashion.

(She didn't study fashion)

- Rasmi **looked** <u>**as if he had seen**</u> a monster.

(He didn't see a monster)

- Majed **looked** <u>**as though he had run**</u> ten kilometers.

(He didn't run ten k.m)

لاحظ أننا نستخدم were مع الفاعل المفرد (والجمع) كما في الجملة الأولى.

Exercise (46)

Correct the verbs in brackets.

1. If I were you, I ……. to Spain. (travel)
2. If you jump a bit higher, you ……. the record. (break)
3. If she had had an extra payment, she ……. the project. (finish)
4. Unless you ……. (keep) your voice down, you will be dismissed.
5. If you freeze the water in that bottle, the water……. (expand)
6. If I knew the answer, I ……. (tell) you.
7. If you take cannabis, you……. (be) an addict.
8. If she……. (listen) to my advice, she wouldn't have made a mistake.
9. Unless he pays attention, he ……. (get) high score this term.
10. I would be surprised if Sami……. Alia. (marry)
11. If I get the award, I ……. it to my chief.(give)
12. If I had seen Lady Macbeth, I ……. with her. (live)
13. If I were a lord, I ……. a castle. (buy)
14. If she is hungry, she……. (eat) a sandwich.
15. If you ……. (be) tired, go to bed early.
16. Asma walks as though she ……. fashion. (study)
17. Rasmi looked as if he ……. a monster. (see)
18. George ……. on a trip to Honolulu if he had had time. (go)
19. If I had a bike, I ……. it every morning. (ride)
20. I wish I ……. A lot of money. You know I'm really poor. (have)

Exercise (47)

Rewrite the following sentences.

1. If I wasn't sick, I would attend the session.

Unless…………………………………………………..

2. If you call her, she will be grateful.

Unless…………………………………………………..

3. Shadi isn't telling me the truth.

I wish …………………………………………………..

4. I can't pay any attention.

I wish…………………………………………………..

5. I woke up late this morning and I missed the flight to Amsterdam.

I wish…………………………………………………..

19.   Conjunctions and Linkers

أدوات الربــــط

There are words in English language you can use to link or connect words, phrases, clauses, and ideas. Those words have particular meanings and some of them convey special relationships between the sentence parts. The following table has a number of those words which are known as conjunctions that are commonly used in English language.

هناك كلمات في اللغة الانجليزية يمكنك استخدامها لربط كلمات أو أشباه جمل أو جمل أ و أفكار بعضها ببعض. وهذه الكلمات لها معاني محددة ومنها ما يعبر عن علاقة خاصة بين أجزاء الجملة. وهذه الكلمات تعرف باسم (أدوات الربط) والجدول التالي يعرض الأكثر شيوعا منها:

19.1   and, and…too, but, or, whereas, while, also, as well, both…and, and not…either.

Words	Use	Examples
and (و)	to connect two affirmative words (verb/ noun/ adjective/ adverb), phrases, and clauses (used to add information) <div dir="rtl">تستخدم لإضافة معلومات، ولربط كلمتين (فعلين/اسمين/صفتين/ظرفين) أو جملتين مثبتتين معا</div>	- *Ahmad* **and** *Ali* are staying home today. - The children *eat* **and** *play* all day. - The test was *long* **and** *difficult*. - John works *carefully* **and** *quietly*. - *David went to eat after class,* **and** *in the evening he went to a movie*
and…too (و...كذلك)	to connect two affirmative sentences but of different subjects. <div dir="rtl">(1) تربط جملتين مثبتتين لكل منها فاعل منفصل. (2) يمكن حذف الفعل من الجملة الثانية إذا كان الفعل مشترك بين الفاعلين. (3) يمكن حذف الفاعل من الجملة الثانية إذا كان نفس الشخص هو فاعل للجملتين.</div>	*(1) I like fish,* **and** *my wife likes fish,* **too**. (2) I will go to Finland, and Fahad, too. (3) I can play football, and go skiing, too.
but (لكن)	to show a contrast between two items, to connect an affirmative sentence with a negative sentence <div dir="rtl">لتبين التناقض، وتربط جملة مثبتة المعنى بأخرى منفية أو تتعارض معها</div>	- *Ali is fat* **but** *his father is thin.* - *Ali likes playing football* **but** *he doesn't like to play basketball.*

	to connect a positive verb/ noun/ adjective/ adverb with a negative one. لربط فعل أو اسم أو صفة أو ظرف ايجابي باخر سلبي	- I don't like *shirts* **but** *T-shirts*. - The team *tried* to score a goal **but** *failed*. - Ali is *fat* **but** *handsome*. - Ali works *hard* **but** *carefully*.
or (أو)	to indicate a choice of two items or an alternative. It connects verbs/ nouns/ adjectives/ adverbs/ or clauses لتشير إلى خيارات، وهي تربط فعلين أو اسمين أو صفتين أو ظرفين أو جملتين معا	- Would you like *tea* **or** *coffee*? - You may *borrow* my car **or** *take* the bus. - She always wears *blue* **or** *white* shoes. - Betty always arrives *too late* **or** *too early*. - *You have to finish your dinner,* **or** *you can't have dessert.*
whereas/ while (بينما)	to compare two things/ or people showing opposition لمقارنة شيئين أو شخصين لاظهار التناقض بينهما	- *Jeffrey is rich* **whereas** *Janet is poor.* - *Qasim is polite* **while** *Sari is impolite.*
also= too أيضا	to add information: it comes after auxiliaries and before the main verb تستخدم لإضافة معلومة وتأتي قبل الفعل المساعد وقبل الفعل الرئيسي	-Husam is a great teacher. He **is also** a good father. - Husam teaches the poor children English language. He **also helps** the elderly.
as well= too أيضا	to add some information لإضافة معلومة وغالبا ما تستخدم في اخر الجملة	-Elizabeth studies French and English, **as well**.
both...and (كل من...و)	to connect two subjects لربط فاعلين	- **Both** Ahmad **and** Sami are leaving tomorrow.
and not either...ولا...حتى	to connect two negative clauses لربط جملتين منفيتين	- *I don't like milk* **and** *Ali doesn't* **either**.
either بمعنى أي/ كلا		- There are palm trees on **either** bank of the Nile river.

19.1.1   'Both...and' follows the following formulas:

يتبع الصيغ التالية عند استخدام Both...and:

a. **(Subject+ verb+ both+ adjective+ and+ adjective)**
   - Robert is *both clever and polite*.

b. **(Subject+ verb+ both+ noun + and + noun)**
   - Bernard plays *both violin and the guitar*.

c. **(Subject+ verb+ both+ adverb+ and+ adverb)**
   - She writes *both quickly and neatly*.

      d. **(Subject+ verb+ both+ prepositional phrase+ and + prepositional phrase)**

         - He excels *both in physics and in literature.*

      e. **(Subject+ not only+ verb+ but also+ verb)**

         - Bernard *both plays* the violin *and writes* stories.

19.2 **After, before, when, while, as, since, until, as soon as, whenever, the first time.**

The following table shows the use of conjunctions which have time relationships in adverbial clauses:

الجدول التالي يبين أدوات الربط التي لها دلالات تعبر عن علاقات زمنية، حيث ترد هنا كجزء من جمل ظرفية زمنية. تذكر أن الجمل الظرفية هذه هي جمل تابعة/ غير مستقلة أو كاملة المعنى.

Words	Examples
After بعد	- *After* she arrived, she joined the NY Police Department (NYPD). - *After* I had read the story, I went to bed.
Before قبل	- *Before* you arrive, I will leave. - You should be there *before* the crowds arrive.
When عندما	- *When* I was in Paris, I met Sam. - Can you tell me *when* lunch is ready?
While بينما	- *While* I was watching T.V, my wife entered.
As بينما	- *As* I was talking to Mary, her father came in.
Since منذ	- I haven't seen Suzan *since* I left the town.
Until حتى	- I stayed at home *until* I did my homework. - I played tennis, *until* it got dark.
As soon as حالما	- *As soon as* the train stops, I will give you a call. - *As soon as* I saw the advertisement, I called my mother.
As long as طالما	- I will never talk to Fahed again *as long as* I live.
Whenever متى ما، حينما	- *Whenever* Rana sees her boss, he shouts at him.
The first time أول مرة	- *The first time* I saw her, we went for a walk.
The last time اخر مرة	- *The last time* I studied French, I realy liked it.

Note: When an adverbial clause comes before an independent clause, a comma (,) is used to separate the clauses. When an adverbial clause comes after an independent clause, no comma is used, as in:

اذا جاءت الجملة الظرفية قبل الجملة الرئيسة فانه يوضع فاصلة بعدها، اما اذا جاءت بعد الجملة الرئيسة فلا تستخدم الفاصلة، كما يلي:

'When I told him the truth, he became angry.'

'He became angry *when I told him the truth.*'

19.3 Because, because of, since, now that, as, due to.

The following table shows the use of conjunctions which have reason/ cause-effect relationship, mentioned in adverbial clauses.

الجدول التالي يبين أدوات الربط التي لها دلالات تعبر عن علاقة السبب/ السبب والنتيجة، حيث ترد هنا كجزء من جمل ظرفية سببية.

Words	Examples
لأن/ بسبب: تستخدم أدوات الربط التالية للتعبير عن سبب أمر ما	
Because	- They're going to put on their jackets *because it is getting cold.*
Because of	- I didn't try to drive his car *because of its bad condition.* - *Because of* the hot weather, I stayed home.
Since	- *Since he's confident*, he decided to meet the crown prince.
Now that	- *Now that I've done my job*, I'm going to take a leave.
As	- *As he made fun of Jim*, he had a problem with Jim's dad.
Due to	- *Due to the windy weather*, I didn't leave my camp.

Note: 'Because', 'since', 'now that', and 'as' are followed by a verb phrase, or a clause. 'Because of' and 'due to' are followed by a noun phrase or noun object.

because, since, now that, as يتبعها شبه جملة فعلية أو جملة
أما because of, due to فيتبعها اسم أو فعل بصيغة اسم فاعل. كما في الأمثلة التالية:

Because it was hot, I took my shirt off.

Since it was hot, I took my shirt off.

Now that it was hot, I took my shirt off.

As it was hot, I took my shirt off.

………………………………………………..

Because of the hot weather, I took my shirt off.

Due to the hot weather, I took my shirt off.

Because of/ Due to Ali, I was blamed.

Because of killing a child, he was sent to jail.

Due to killing a child, he was sent to jail.

19.3.1 'So' and 'Such' can be used to indicate a cause and effect relationship, following these formulas:

such و so يمكن استخدامهما للاشارة الى علاقة السبب والنتيجة، وفق الصيغ التالية:

So:

    a. (Subject+ verb+ so+ adjective/ adverb+ that+ subject+ verb)

As in:

-     Britney sang so well that she received many awards.
-     The sea food tastes so good that I will ask for more.

    b. (Subject+ verb+ so+ many/ few+ plural countable noun+ that+ subject+ verb)

As in:

-     I have so many young sons that they will form my own football team.
-     I had so few options that I could select one easily.

    c. (Subject+ verb+ so+ much/ little+ mass noun+ that+ subject+ verb)

As in:

-     Ramzi gave me so much money that I can buy a new house.
-     I have so little milk that I can't give you some.

    d. (Subject+ verb+ so+ adjective+ a+ singular countable noun+ that+ subject+ verb)

As in:

-     It was so cold a night that I stayed indoors.

Such:

    a. (Subject+ verb+ such+ adjective+ plural count noun/ mass noun+ that+ subject+ verb)

As in:

-     Marwan has such exceptional skills that I'm jealous of him.
-     I have such difficult homework that I won't finish it quickly.

    b. (Subject+ verb+ such+ a+ adjective+ singular countable noun+ that+ subject+ verb)

As in:

-     He is such a bad boy that I don't like him.

19.4   To, in order to, so that, for.

The following table shows the use of conjunctions which have purpose relationships in adverbial clauses:

الجدول التالي يبين أدوات الربط التي لها دلالات تعبر عن علاقة الغائية/ الغاية، حيث ترد هنا كجزء من جمل ظرفية غائية وبمعنى "من أجل/ لـ".

Words	Examples
To	- Sam works *to earn more money.* - I went to the shop *to buy some food.*
In order to	- The staff is working hard *in order to complete the project early.*
so that	- I will give you a map *so that you can get there easily.*

| For + noun phrase | - My wife went *for a bike ride.* |
| | - Sa'ad plays *for fun.* |

Note: 'To' and 'in order to' are followed by (infinitive).

to, in order to يتبعهما فعل مجرد/ مصدر الفعل

'So that' used before a subject and a main verb.

so that تسبق جملة/ عبارة تبدأ بفاعل وفعل

'For' is followed by a noun phrase/ or gerund.

for يتبعها شبه جملة اسمية/ اسم/ أو فعل بصيغة اسم فاعل

19.5   But, although, even though, though, in spite of, despite.

The following are conjunctions used to show a relationship of concession in adverbial clauses:

تاليا هي أدوات ربط تشير الى علاقة التناقض، حيث ترد هنا كجزء من جمل ظرفية وبمعنى "رغم/ على الرغم من ذلك".

Words	Examples
But لكن (used to link two clauses)	- I arrived late, *but I found a seat.*
Although	- *Although I arrived late*, I found a seat.
Even though/Though (means the same as although)	- *Though it was cold*, he wasn't wearing warm clothes.
In spite of/ despite	- I succeeded *in spite of/ despite* the difficult test. - I couldn't run *in spite of/ despite* feeling fitter than before.
However	- Ali is clever. *However*, he didn't achieve good results.
Nevertheless	- It is freezing; *nevertheless*, he'll go out.

Note: 'However' comes in the middle of the sentence followed by a comma and preceded by a full stop, whereas 'nevertheless' is followed by a comma and preceded by a semi-colon (;). They are followed by a clause (V+ S+ Complement).

however, nevertheless يأتي بعدهما جملة كاملة فيها فاعل وفعل وتكملة/ مفعول به، إلا أن However تأتي بوسط الجملة متبوعة بفاصلة ومسبوقة بنقطة، أما بالنسبة لـ Nevertheless فيتبعها فاصلة إلا أنه يسبقها فاصلة منقوطة (;).

'Although', 'though' and 'even though'are followed by verb phrases.

though, although, even though يتبعها شبه جمل فعلية/ فعل

'In spite of' and 'despite' are followed by noun phrases, noun or the 'ing' form of a verb in spite of, despite يتبعها اسم/ شبه جمله اسمية/ اسم فاعل.

19.6 Conjunctions Expressing Results

أدوات ربط للتعبير عن "نتيجة"

So لذا	The T.V didn't work, *so I took it back to the shop.*
Therefore/ consequently/ as a result لذلك/ نتيجةً ذلك	She didn't exercise regularly. *Therefore/* consequently/ as a resul, *she had a sprained ankle.*

Note: 'Therefore', 'consequently', and 'as a result' come in the middle of sentences followed by a comma and preceded by a coma/ or full stop. Besides, they are followed by a clause (V+ S+ Complement).

'Therefore', 'consequently', and 'as a result' تأتي وسط الجملة متبوعة بفاصلة أو نقطة وكلها يتبعها جملة/ عبارة فيها فاعل وفعل وتكملة، وكما في الأمثلة التالية:

The following examples show how we use (so, therefore, consequently, and as a result):

- Alia studied hard, so she succeeded.

- Alia studied hard. Therefore, she succeeded.

- Alia studied hard. Consequently, she succeeded

19.6.1 'So that' is used to show purpose and result. After 'so that' is a result clause with a subject and a verb. As in:

(subject+ verb+ so that+ subject+ verb)

So that تستخدم لتبين الغاية والنتيجة. والعبارة التي يرد فيها أداة الربط هذه يجب أن تحتوي على فاعل و فغل وهي نفسها التي تعبر عن النتيجة أو الغاية، وكما في الأمثلة التالية:

- Osama studied hard so that he could pass the exam.

- Ibrahim is sending the card early so that it will arrive in time for his wife's birthday.

19.7 Not only… but also, Either… or, Neither… nor.

You can connect two subjects by (not only/ but also, either/ or, and neither/ nor). Examples:

يمكن ربط فاعلين ببعضهما باضافة كل منهما للاخر باستخدام أدوات الربط الثنائية التالية:

	Examples
Not only… but also ليس فقط...وانما كذلك	- **Not only** Sami **but also** *Ahmad is* swimming in the pool. <div dir="rtl">ليس سامي فقط وانما كذلك أحمد يسبح في البركة.</div> - **Not only** Rami **but also** his *cousins are* coming tonight. <div dir="rtl">ليس سامي فقط وانما كذلك أبناء عمه قادمون الليلة.</div> <div dir="rtl">لاحظ أن الاسم/ الفاعل الأقرب للفعل هو الذي يحدد صيغة الفعل.</div>

Either... or اما...أو	- **Either** small box **or** *malaria is* a dangerous disease.
	- I can drink **either** Coke **or** orange juice.
	- Your car must be **either** BMW **or** Toyota.
Neither... nor لا... ولا	- **Neither** my relatives **nor** *my wife is* flying to Paris.
	لا أقاربي ولا زوجتي مسافرة الى باريس.

19.7.1 Not only...but also can be used in the following formulas:

يمكنك استخدام Not only...but also وفق الأنماط التالية:

a. (Subject+ verb+ not only + adjective+ but also + adjective)

b. (Subject+ verb+ not only + noun + but also + noun)

c. (Subject+ verb+ not only + adverb+ but also + adverb)

d. (Subject+ verb+ not only + prepositional phrase+ but also + prepositional phrase)

e. (Subject+ not only+ verb+ but also+ verb)

As in:

- Robert is *not only clever but also polite.*
- Bernard plays *not only the violin but also the oud.*
- She writes *not only quickly but also neatly.*
- He excels *not only in physics but also in literature.*
- Bernard *not only plays* the violin *but also writes* stories.

19.8 'as well as' can be used in the following formulas:

يمكنك استخدام as well as وفق الأنماط التالية:

a. (Subject+ verb+ noun+ as well as+ noun)

b. (Subject+ verb+ adjective+ as well as+ adjective)

c. (Subject+ verb+ adverb + as well as+ adverb)

d. (Subject+ verb+ prepositional phrase+ as well as+ prepositional phrase)

e. (Subject+ verb+ as well as+ verb)

As in:

- George plays *the guitar as well as the violin.*
- George is *talented as well as handsome.*
- He writes *quickly as well as neatly.*
- He excels *in physics as well as in maths.*
- Bernard *plays* the violin *as well as composes* music.

Exercise (48)

Select the appropriate answers of the following sentences:

1. ……….. you don't have any question, I will leave.
   a. Provided   b. Because   c. Although

2. I went shopping ……….. the weather was cold.
   a. despite   b. therefore   c. although

3. ……….. The weather was cold she didn't visit her father.
   a. Because   b. Due to   c. But

4. ……….. I was walking down the street, I meet an old friend.
   a. While   b. Before   c. As soon as

5. Both my father and my sister ……….. here.
   a. are   b. is   c. were

6. Not only my brother but also my parents ……….. here.
   a. are   b. is   c. were

7. Neither my children ……….. my brother are here.
   a. nor   b. or   c. and

8. ……….. the restaurant was crowded, I managed to book a table.
   a. But   b. Although   c. Despite

9. The heater is ………..keeping the house warm in winter
   a. for   b. to   c. but

10. A: I'm in a good mood.
    B: …………
    a. so am I   b. neither do I   c. too

11. The clerk stopped……….. I came in.
    a. as soon as   b. during   c. for

12. The bus was late……….. I took a cab.
    a. so   b. because of   c. although

13. The IELTS test seems difficult. ……….., I'll attend it.
    a. But   b. However   c. Therefore

14. The child took the prescribed vaccine; ………….., he got sick.
    a. nevertheless   b. despite   c. for

15. Hani ran not only fast but also ………..
    a. care   b. careful   c. carefully

16. Hani is both kind and ………..
    a. clever   b. cleverness   c. cleverly

Exercise (49)

Rewrite the following sentences so that they have similar meaning.

1. Although I slept early, I couldn't wake up on time.

In spite of………………………………………………….

2.   Ahmad postponed his flight because there is a war in Iraq.

Because of..

Exercise (50)

Supply either 'because' or 'because of' as appropriate.
1.   It isn't easy to send your letter.......you have written the wrong address.
2.   I'll leave early.......the party is very boring.
3.   SOS team arrived late...... the bad weather.
4.   Salman can't join the university team ......his grades.
5.   Many British people died last summer......the heat.

Exercise (51)

Use either 'so' or 'such' in these sentences as appropriate.

1.   The sun is shining ......brightly that I have to put on my sunglasses.
2.   Deema is ......a powerful runner that she always wins the races.

Exercise (52)

A: Supply the missing linkers (not only...but also, both...and) in the following sentences:

1.   Mr. Eyad speaks........ Spanish but also English.
2.   I have villas ....in the country and in the city.

B: Supply the missing word ('so' or 'such') in the following sentences:
1.   We had .... a bad night that we couldn't sleep.
2.   She gave me .... good a stereo that I was very grateful to her.
3.   The day was .... hot that everyone went to the sea.
4.   The motel has .... a comfortable room that I don't want to leave.
5.   It was .... dark that I couldn't see my finger.
6.   That restaurant has .... delicious food that I can't stop eating.

20.   **Interrogatives**

الإستفهــــام

There are several types of questions you can form in English. There are yes/ no questions, Wh- questions, and tag questions. You might have come familiar with yes/no questions as discussed earlier in the 'tenses' section. However, you will learn the rules and steps of how to make those three types of questions.

هناك عدة أنواع للسؤال في اللغة الانجليزية وهي تشمل: أسئلة (نعم/ لا)، أسئلة Wh و How ، وكذلك الأسئلة المذيلة. وآلاتي هي خطوات صياغة كل من الأسئلة التالية:

20.1   Yes/ no questions.

a.   When there is an auxiliary or a modal in the sentence, such as; 'do', 'does', 'did', 'is', 'are', 'am', was', 'were', 'can', 'could', 'must', etc.':

(1)   Put the auxiliary/ helping verb first.

(2)   Put the subject.

(3)   Put the main verb.

(4)   Write the rest of the sentence, finishing with (?).

(Auxiliary/ be/ do, does, did+ subject+ verb...)

أسئلة (نعم/ لا):

أ.   حين يكون في الجملة فعل مساعد:

- ضع الفعل المساعد أولا.

- ضع الفاعل.

- ضع الفعل الرئيس.

- أكتب ما تبقى من الجملة المعطاة وانهي بعلامة استفهام. وكما في الأمثلة التالية:

For example:

- Hani **has** built a new house.

Has Hani built a new house?

 (1) (2) (3)   (4)

- Ali **can** speak English well.

Can Ali speak English well?

 (1) (2) (3)   (4)

- Ali **is** calling his dad on the phone.

Is Ali calling his dad on the phone?

(1) (2) (3)   (4)

-   Raheil **should** leave.

Should Raheil leave?

   (1)   (2)   (3)

More examples:

- They **have** broken the lock.

Have they broken the lock?

- Sally **is** perfect.

Is Sally perfect?

- My ex-wife **is** two- faced.

Is my ex-wife two- faced?

- Rahma **was** lazy.

Was Rahma Lazy?

b. When there is no auxiliary in the sentence, use 'do', 'does', or 'did'. Drop the 's/es' from the present verb of the singular subject when you use 'does' in the question. Then, follow steps 2,3, and 4 mentioned in paragraph (12.1/ a) above. When you use 'do', you don't make any changes to the plural verb; you only follow steps 2,3, and 4 mentioned in paragraph (12.1/ a) above. When you use 'did' for the past verb, use the base form of the main verb in your question.

ب. عندما لا يكون في الجملة فعل مساعد استخدم Do,Does, Did وحسب زمن الفعل.
اذا كان الفعل في الجملة مضارعاً والفاعل مفرداً فتبدأ سؤالك بـ Does وتحذف s/es
من اخر الفعل الرئيس ويتبع الخطوات السابقة الواردة في الفقرة -أ- فقرة(20.1) باستثناء
الخطوة الأولى. واذا كان الفعل مضارعاً والفاعل جمعاً: ابدأبـ do وتكرر ما فعلت في الفقرة
(20.1) -أ- أعلاه باستثناء الخطوة الأولى. أما اذا كان الفعل بالماضي استخدم حينها
Did لتبدأ سؤالك وحول الفعل الرئيسي الماضي الى مصدره/ مجرد، ثم كرر الخطوات
السابقة ذاتها، والأمثلة التالية توضح ذلك:

For example:

- Rami plays football.

Does Rami play football?

- The company employees agree on proposals.

Do the company employees agree on proposals?

- The piano player composed new songs.

Did the player compose new songs?

20.2 Negative interrogative: it means that you can begin your sentence with negative form of auxilliaries to form yes/ no questions. Examples:

ويقصد به أن تبدأ سؤال (نعم/ لا) بغعل مساعد بصيغة النفي، كما في الأمثلة التالية:

- Don't you speak French? (informal style)

   Do you not speak French? (formal style)

      No, I don't. (Or) Yes, I do.

- Doesn't Hayfa look stunning?

      No, she doesn't. (Or) Yes, she does.

- Isn't Issam writing a fairy tale?

      No, he isn't. (Or) Yes, he is.

- Didn't Shadi help Salma?

      No, he didn't. (Or) Yes, he did.

- Wasn't Rania kind with you?

      No, she wasn't. (Or) Yes, she was.

- Weren't the students fighting in the classroom?

      No, they weren't. (Or) Yes, they were.

- Haven't you spoken to your ex-wife?

      No, I haven't. (Or) Yes, I have.

- Mustn't Nizar attend the conference?

         No, he mustn't. (Or) Yes, he must.

20.3 **Wh- questions (information questions)** تستخدم للحصول على معلومة

     a.   There are many words with which you can begin the 'wh-questions', as shown in the table below:

Words	Use	Examples
Who	To ask about a subject (it refers to people) (من) تستخدم للسؤال عن أشخاص، حين يكون الشخص محل السؤال يقع فاعلا للجملة	-*Who* is that? That is *Ahmad*. -*Who* broke the vase? *Ahmad* broke the vase.
Where	To ask about places (أين) للسؤال عن المكان	- *Where* is John? *At home* - *Where* are you? *In Amman*.
What	To ask about subject/ object of the question (it refers to things) (ما/ ماذا) للسؤال عن أشياء ويكون الشي محل السؤال فاعلاً أو مفعولاً به في الجملة	- *What* did he say? He said *nothing*. - *What* caused the disturbance? The *explosion* caused it.
Which	Selection, or pinpointing (أيها/ أيُّ) للاختيار أو التحديد	- *Which* driver came last? *The red car's* driver. - *Which* pen is mine? *The big one*.
Whose	Possession, or relationship (لمن) للسؤال عن ملكية الشيء	- *Whose* house is that? It is *mine*.
When	To ask about time (متى) للسؤال عن الوقت والزمن	- *When* did you go to school? At 7 *o'clock*.
Why	To ask about reasons (لماذا) للسؤال عن السبب	- *Why* does he wake up early? *Because* he respects timing.
Whom	To ask about the object of the verb (من) للسؤال عن شخص حل مفعول به في الجملة	- *Whom* did you give it to? I gave it to *Jeff*.
How	To ask about state/ condition/ the how (كيف) للسؤال عن حال، ظرف، كيفية	- *How* are you? *I'm fine*. - A: *How* do you get your homework done quickly? B: *My father helps me*.
How many	To ask about countable nouns (كم عدد) للسؤال عن أسماء معدودة	- *How many* students answered the question? *Twenty one*. - *How many* sugar *bags* do you need? *Three bags* of sugar.

How much	To ask about mass nouns and money (كم) للسؤال عن أسماء غير معدودة، وعن المال	- *How much* money do you have? I have a lot of money. - *How much salt* do you need? - Bags of *salt*.
How far	To ask about distance (كم يبعد) للسؤال عن المسافة	- *How far* is it from Masawa to Asmara? *20 miles*.
How often	To ask about frequency للسؤال عن مدى تكرار أمر ما	- How often do you visit your grand parents? *Once* a month.
How long	To ask about length/ or duration (كم طول) للسؤال عن طول مدة أو استمرارية أمر ما	- *How long* does the trip take? *25 minutes*. - *How long* have you been in England? For *20 years*.
How old	To ask about age (كم عمر) للسؤال عن العمر	- *How old* is Ali? He is *30 years old*.
How tall	To ask about the height of a person (كم طول) للسؤال عن طول شخص	- *How tall* are you? I'm *177 centimeters tall*.
How wide	To ask about width (كم عرض) للسؤال عن العرض والاتساع	- *How wide* is this road? It is *10 m wide*.
How high	To ask about height (كم ارتفاع) للسؤال عن ارتفاع	- *How high* is that mountain? It is *400 meters high*.
How deep	To ask about the depth (كم عمق) للسؤال عن مدى العمق	- How deep is the Suez canal? It's not less than 30 meters deep.

    b.   Steps of how to form 'wh-questions':

خطوات صياغة السؤال Wh و How

- **(whom/what…+ auxiliary/ do, does, did+ subject+ verb…)**
- **(when/ where/ how/ why+ auxiliary/ do, does, did+ subject+ verb+ object)**

    (1)   **When a sentence has an auxiliary:**

    i.   Select the suitable wh-word.
    ii.   Write the auxiliary.
    iii.   Write the subject.
    iv.   Write the main verb.
    v.   Write the rest of the question.
    vi.   Omit the phrase that you are asking about.
    vii.   Write a question mark (?).

حين يكون في الجمل فعل مساعد فإنك تتبع ما يلي:
- اختر أداة السؤال المناسبة.
- ضع الفعل المساعد.
- ضع الفاعل.
- اكتب الفعل الرئيس

- اكتب ما تبقى من السؤال.
- احذف الجزء الذي تنوي السؤال عنه.
- ضع علامة الاستفهام (؟).

Examples:

Ali will visit Petra tomorrow morning.

- <u>What</u> <u>will</u> <u>Ali</u> <u>visit</u> <u>tomorrow morning</u>? (Petra)
    I   ii iii iv   v

- **When** will Ali visit Petra? (Tomorrow morning)

(2)   **When a sentence has no auxiliary:**
   i.   Select the appropriate wh-word.
  ii.   Use 'do' for the plural subject and 'does' for the singular subject when the main verb tense is simple present. Use 'did' whenever the verb tense is past.
 iii.   Write the subject.
 iv.   Write the main verb (base form).
  v.   Write the rest of the question.
 vi.   Omit the phrase that you are asking about.
vii.   Write a question mark (?).

حين لا يكون في الجملة فعل مساعد:
- اختر أداة السؤال المناسبة.
- استخدم Do للاسم الجمع و Does للاسم المفرد حين يكون الزمن المستخدم في الفعل هو المضارع البسيط واستخدم Did للفعل الماضي البسيط.
- ضع الفاعل.
- اكتب الفعل الرئيس مجردا- بصيغة المصدر.
- اكتب ما تبقى من السؤال.
- احذف الجزء الذي تنوي السؤال عنه.
- ضع علامة الاستفهام (؟).

Examples:

The school boys frequently go to Umm Qais at weekends.

- <u>Where</u> <u>do</u> <u>the school boys</u> usually <u>go</u> <u>at weekends</u>?
    I   ii   iii   iv v
  (To Umm Qais)

- **How often** do the school boys go to Umm Qais?
  (Frequently)

(3)   **To ask about the subject when there is no auxiliary,** use 'who/ what' and omit the phrase of the subject you are asking about.

للسؤال عن الفاعل في الجملة وحين لا يكون في الجملة فعل مساعد فانك تستخدم what أو whoوتحذف الجزء الذي تسأل عنه فقط، إلا أن:

Who تستخدم للشخص العاقل أما What فمع الأحداث ومع غير العاقل.

(who/ what+ verb+ object....)

Examples:

- The policeman assured the kidnapped.

Who assured the kidnapped? (The policeman)

- **Gaza bombardment** forced the Palestinians to leave their shelters.

What forced the Palestinian people to leave their shelters?

(Gaza bombardment)

(4) **(How many, how much, which, and whose)** are followed by the noun you are asking about. The auxiliary verb follows that noun.

وتأتي أدوات السؤال هذه متبوعة بالاسم الذي تستفسر عنه ثم يأتي الفعل، كما في الأمثلة التالية:

- This bag is **mine**.

 Whose bag is this? (It'smine)

-**The red** BMW is Ali's.

 Which BMW is Ali's? (The red)

- Ali gave Hassan a **lot of money**.

 How much money did Ali give to Hassan?

- Sali buys **70 balls** a day.

 How many balls does Sali buy a day?

- I sell **old** coins to the rich people.

 Which coins do you sell to the rich people?

- Ahmad is fighting against **the fat guy?**

 Which guy is Ahmad fighting against?

20.4   **Tag Questions** (الأسئلة المذيلة (تستخدم لتأكيد معلومة أو طلب التحقق من معلومة)

The table below shows the steps you should follow to make tag questions.

الجدول التالي يعرض الخطوات التي ينصح باتباعها لصياغة الأسئلة المذيلة.

Steps
1. **Put a comma** before the tag phrase.   ضع فاصلة قبل البدء بالسؤال المذيل   2. **Place the auxiliary** verb to be/ to have/ to do/ or modals if available in the statement. If the statement is affirmative, the tag is negative and vice versa.   اذا كان في الجملة فعل مساعد ضعه، ولكن بحالة تعاكس الحالة المستخدمة في الجملة الأساسية : اذا كانت الجملة بحالة اثبات فانك تنفي الفعل المساعد أما اذا كان بحالة نفي فانك تثبت الفعل المساعد.   When there is no auxiliary in the statement: اذا لم يكن في الجملة فعلا مساعدا اتبع ما يلي: 3. Use **'does'** if the verb in the statement is present simple tense and it has 's/es', or use **'do'** if the verb is without s/es. Use **'did'** if the verb is simple past.   - اذا كان الفعل المستخدم هو مضارع ودليله انه ينتهي بـ s/es استخدم عندها Does كفعل مساعد.   - واذا كان الفعل لفاعل جمع – أي لا ينتهي الفعل عندها بـs/es استخدم do فعلا مساعدا.   (تذكر أن حالة الفعل المساعد تعاكس حالة الجملة الخبرية التي تسبق السؤال المذيل نفيا وإثباتا)   - اذا كان الفعل في زمن الماضي البسيط استخدم did في السؤال المذيل   4. Use a pronoun not a name.   استخدم ضميرا بعد الفعل المساعد وليس اسماً.   5. With 'someone', 'somebody', 'everyone' and 'everybody' use **'they'**.   استخدم الضمير they اذا كان المسؤول عنه أيا من الاتية: someone, somebody, everyone, everybody.   6. With imperative, use **'will(not) + you'**.   - مع جمل الأمر، تستخدم في السؤال المذيل Will you:اذا كان الأمر بالنهي، أي يبدأ بـ don't   - استخدم won't+ you اذا كان الأمر بالاثبات.   7. (I'm) becomes (aren't I) in tag question.   I'm تصبح aren't I و I'm not تصبح am I في السؤال المذيل.

- **When the statement is negative, the answer is negative. When it is affirmative, the answer is affirmative.**

  اذا كانت الجملة بحالة النفي فان جواب السؤال المذيل يكون بالنفي، واذا كانت الجملة مثبتة فالجواب يكون مثبتا أيضا (أي أن الجواب يتفق مع حالة الجملة وليس مع حالة السؤال المذيل).

- The verb 'have' may be used as a main verb (I have two kids) or it may be used as an auxiliary (Ali has gone to school already). When it functions as a main verb in American English, the auxiliary forms (do, does, did) must be used in the tag.

يمكن أن يأتي الفعل Have في الجملة كفعل رئيسي أو كفعل مساعد. أما اذا جاء كفعل
رئيسي ففي الانجليزية الأمريكية نستخدم وفقا لذلك فعلا مساعدا مناسبا من أفعال العمل
(do, does, did) في الأسئلة المذيلة.

You have two children, don't you?

More examples include:

1. Tom is angry, isn't he?
   Yes, he is.

2. Tom isn't angry, is he?
   No, he isn't.

3. Rula will sit for the test tomorrow, won't she?
   Yes, she'll

4. Rula won't sit for the test tomorrow, will she?
   No, she won't

5. Ali and Shadi played football, didn't they?
   Yes, they did.

6. Ali and Shadi didn't play football, did they?
   No, they didn't.

7. You have to write a future plan essay, don't you?
   Yes, I do.

8. He has to write a future plan essay, doesn't he?
   Yes, he does.

9. You had to take a cap, didn't you?
   Yes, I did.

10. It rains in winter, doesn't it?
    Yes, it does.

11. He must leave, mustn't he?
    Yes, he must.

12. Dan is a good teacher, isn't he?
    Yes, he is.

13. Dan isn't a good teacher, is he?
    No, he isn't.

14. Samia cooks well, doesn't she?
    Yes, she does

15. Everyone laughed at him, didn't they?
    Yes, they did.

16. Don't open the window, will you?
    No, I won't.

17. I'm a teacher, aren't I?
    Yes, you are.

18. I have read well, haven't I?
    Yes, I have.

20.5   Embedded Questions الأسئلة المضمنة: كجزء من جملة أو سؤال آخر

20.5.1   Embedded yes/no questions : السؤال نعم/ لا المضمن بجملة خبرية

We usually use embedded yes/no questions introduced by (*if/ whether+ subject+ verb+ complement*) as a noun clause in a statement, as in:

وهنا يتبع النسق التالي: whether أو if + الفاعل+ الفعل+ التكملة، مثال:

- Was it overcast yesterday?   السؤال: هل كان الجو غائماً بالأمس؟

(This becomes)   يصبح كجزء من سؤال اخر أو جملة أخرى كالاتي:

I don't know **if it was overcast yesterday**.

Embedded question

لا أعلم **اذا ما كان الجو غائماً بالأمس.**

Can you tell me **if it was overcast yesterday**?

Embedded yes/no question

هل لك أن تخبرني **اذا ما كان الجو غائماً بالأمس؟**

20.5.2 Embedded Wh. Questions.   السؤال المضمن: الذي يبدأ بأداة تبدأ بـ Wh

When a Wh- questions is embedded, it becomes a noun clause introduced by the same wh- question word following this pattern (*what/ when...+ subject+ verb+ complement*), as in:

حين يتم تضمين السؤال الذي يبدأ بأداة تبدأ بـ Wh كجزء من سؤال أو جملة أخرى،

يتبع النسق التالي: أداة السؤال التي تبدأ بـ Wh + الفاعل+ الفعل+ التكملة، كما في:

- Where is the best hotel?   أين يقع أفضل فندق؟

I don't know **where the best hotel is**.

Embedded wh- question

لا أعرف **أين يقع أفضل فندق.**

Can you tell me **where the best hotel is**?

Embedded wh- question

هل لك أن تخبرني **أين يقع أفضل فندق** ؟

لاحظ أن صيغة الجملة الخبرية التي يرد بها السؤال المضمن الذي جوابه (نعم/ لا) تتبع الصيغة التالية:

(Subject+ verb (phrase)+ I/ whether+ subject+ verb...)

As in: We don't know **if he is coming**.

لاحظ أن صيغة الجملة الخبرية التي يرد بها السؤال المضمن الذي يبدأ بـWh

تتبع الصيغة التالية:

(Subject+ verb (phrase)+ question word+ subject+ verb...)

As in: We don't know **where the meeting will take place**.

لاحظ أن صيغة السؤال الذي يرد به السؤال المضمن (نعم/ لا) يكون كما يلي:

(Auxiliary+ subject+ verb+ question word+ subject+ verb)

As in: Can you tell me **how far the museum is** from the college?

Fundamental English Grammar Review

20.6   Answers   الاجوبـــــــــة

20.6.1   We use "**Yes+ subject+ auxiliary/ modal**" pattern to answer 'yes/no' questions affirmatively, and we use "**No+ subject+ auxiliary/ modal+ not**" pattern to answer negatively.

للاجابة بالاثبات (بنعم) على سؤال نعم/ لا، نتبع النسق التالي: Yes, +فاعل+ الفعل المساعد.

للاجابة بالنفي (بلا) على سؤال نعم/ لا، نتبع النسق التالي: No, +فاعل+ فعل مساعد+ not .

Yes/ No questions	Answers
Has Hani built a new house?	Yes, he has.
	No, he hasn't.
Can Ali speak English well?	Yes, he can.
	No, he can't.
Is Ali calling his dad on the phone?	Yes, he is.
	No, he isn't.
Does Rami play football?	Yes, he does.
	No, he doesn't.
Do the company employees rarely agree on proposals?	Yes, they do.
	No, they don't.
Did the player compose new songs?	Yes, he did.
	No, he didn't.
Would you go with me?	Yes, I would.
	No, I wouldn't.
Will you turn the tap off?	Yes, I will.
	No, I won't.

20.6.2 Answers to statements: (affirmative agreement)

We الاجابة أو الرد على جمل خبرية بالاثبات (بقصد التأييد/ الاتفاق)

use the following pattern to give an affirmative agreement as a reply for affirmative statement, as in:

'affirmative statement+ and+ <u>so + auxiliary (be/ do/ have/ modal verb)+ subject</u>'

- I'm happy, and *so are you.*
- They will work in the lab tomorrow, and *so will you.*
- A: I'm leaving. B: *So am I.* (وأنا كذلك)
- A: I've a car.   B: *So do I.* (وأنا كذلك)
- A: Arwa can drive a bike. B: *So can Sama.* (وكذلك سما)

يستخدم النسق التالي للرد على جملة خبرية مثبتة: So+ فعل مساعد+ فاعل، بمعنى "وكذلك"
الفعل المساعد يستنبط من الجملة الخبرية التي تريد الرد عليها مراعياً في ذلك نفس الزمن المستخدم في الجملة الرئيسة، وكما في الأمثلة أعلاه.

We use a form of 'do' in the present/ past simple, as in:

- John goes to the school, and *so does my brother.*
- A: I like cinema.   B: *So do I.*
- A: Al- Faisali won.   B: *So did Al- Ahli.*
- A: Rula likes apples. B: *So does Asma.*

نستخدم أحد أفعال (to do) اذا كان الفعل المستخدم في الجملة الخبرية مضارع بسيط
أو ماضي بسيط، وكما في الأمثلة أعلاه.

- You can also follow the following pattern to give affirmative agreement: ويمكن
استخدام النمط التالي أيضا لبيان التأييد والاتفاق

(affirmative statement+ **and+ subject+ auxiliary (be/ do/ have/ modal verb)+ too)**

Examples:
- I'm happy, **and you are too.**
- They will work in the lab tomorrow, **and you will too.**
- John goes to that school, **and my brother does too.**

20.6.3   Negative agreement: الرد على الجملة الخبرية بالنفي (بمعنى عدم التأييد)

We use the following pattern to give a negative agreement as a reply for a negative statement:

'negative statement+ and+ **neither + positive auxiliary (be/ do/ have/ modal verb) + subject'**

- I didn't see Sara this afternoon. *Neither did Ali.*
- She will not go to the meeting. *Neither will Ashraf.*
- The boss isn't at the party. *Neither is the assistant.*ولا حتى المساعد
- John didn't call Sami. *Neither did Ali.*   (ولا حتى علي)
- Rami doesn't speak French. *Neither does Haifa.*   (ولا هيفاء حتى)

يستخدم النسق التالي للرد على جملة خبرية منفية: neither+فعل مساعد+ فاعل
وهي تستخدم بمعنى (ولا حتى). الفعل المساعد يستنبط من الجملة الخبرية التي تريد الرد عليها.
ونستخدم أحد أفعال (to do) اذا كان الفعل المستخدم في الجملة الخبرية مضارعاً بسيطاً
أو ماضٍ بسيط، وكما في الأمثلة أعلاه.

- You can also follow the following pattern to give a negative agreement: ويمكن استخدام
النمط التالي أيضا لبيان عدم التوافق

'negative statement+ **and+ subject + negative auxiliary+ either'**

- I didn't see Sara this afternoon, *and Ali didn't either*.
- She will not go to the meeting, *and Ashraf will not either.*

Exercise (53)

Fill in the blanks with the correct form of either or neither.

1. The boys shouldn't take the medicine, and …..should the girls.
2. We don't plan to join the team, and …..do they.
3. They won't have to work on weekends, and she won't …..
4. I can't stand listening to pop music, and she can't…..

Exercise (54)

Supply the correct form of the missing verb.

1. The boys aren't happy with the programme, and neither…..the girls.
2. We can't study in the library, and they …..either.
3. He didn't know the answer and neither…..I.

Exercise (55)

Correct the underlined errors, so that the questions sound perfect.

1. Rula doesn't drink milk, <u>doesn't</u> she?
2. <u>Where</u> can solve the puzzle? Sami
3. <u>Why</u> is Hani? At home.
4. <u>How far</u> money do you have? 12,000 US.$

Exercise (56)

Make wh-questions for the following statement so that the underlined phrases answer them.

1. <u>We</u> want some food to eat.
Who…………………………..?
2. McCain gave me <u>a bottle of coke</u>.
What …………………………?
3. <u>A picture</u> fell on the floor.
What …………………………?
4. She saw me <u>yesterday</u>.
When …………………………...?
5. I live in <u>Liverpool</u>.
Where …………………………..?
6. Hashim is <u>20 years</u> old.
How old…………………...………?
7. I met <u>the teacher</u> in Manchester.
Whom…………………………...?
8. Mohammad was born in <u>Lisbon</u>.
…………………………………?

9.   I have <u>a sandwich</u> in my luggage.

....?

10.   Ahmad can't leave <u>because his mother is dying</u>.

....?

11.   This is <u>Anne's</u> purse.

....?

12.   I can't figure out <u>the chapter written in French</u>.

....?

Exercise (57):

Add tag questions and give the right responses where necessary.

1.   Mohammad came yesterday, didn't he?

Yes, he did.

2.   I don't live in a palace, ...?

No, ...

3.   Ahmad would like to have some coffee,..........?

....

4.   This is Anne's purse,...............?

....

5.   You have scanned the letter,...........?

Yes, I have.

6.   They couldn't do the exercise, could they?

....

Exercise (58)

Select the correct answer:

1.You love Samia, ...?

    a. don't you   b. do you   c.aren't you

2.Open that window, ...?

    a. will you   b. won't you   c. don't you

3.........does your dad live? In Munich

    a. Where   b. When   c. Who

4.I'm doing my homework this evening.

    a. So am I   b. Neither am I   c. So I am

5.I'm not going out tomorrow.

    a. Neither am I   b. So am I   c. So I am

Exercise (59)

Select the best answer:

1.........Ali and Ahmad studying at the moment?

    a. Is   b. Are   c. Were

2.........you driving fast to reach the top?

    a. Will   b. Were   c. Is

3.........Katrina cut her finger yet?

        a. Has   b. Had   c. Have

4.Must Basil…...his mum?

        a. call   b. calls   c. called

5.........Abdelhadi leave his house yesterday?

        a. Didn't   b. Don't   c. Doesn't

6.Haitham is an officer, ……?

        a. mustn't he   b. is he   c. isn't he

7.She broke the new chair, didn't she?................

        a. Yes, she did   b. Yes, she didn't c. No, she didn't

8.........are you doing? I'm eating pizza.

        a. What   b. Who   c. When

Exercise (60)

Finish these sentences by adding a tag question with the correct form of the verb and the subject pronoun.

1. You're going to Paris next year,………?
2. Harry signed the petition,………?
3. There is a final test,………?
4. She's been studying French for 3 years,………?
5. He should see the dentist,………?
6. You can play tennis today,………?

21. Passive voice

املبني للمجهــــول

In sentences written in active voice, the subject acts and performs the action that is expressed in the verb, as in:

(1) **A stranger** pushed the boy.

'A stranger' is the subject who performed the pushing. But in sentences written in the passive voice, the subject is acted upon and it is the recipient of the action of the verb as well, as in:

(2) **The boy** was pushed by a stranger.

'The boy' is the receiver of the 'push' and so 'push' is in the passive voice. One more example is:

(3) **Mary** was kicked by Ali.

'Mary' is the receiver of the 'kick' and so 'Kick' is in the passive voice.

و   في جمل املبني للمعلوم فان الفاعل في الجملة يكون هو من قام بالفعل كما في املثال (1) حيث أن A stranger فاعل الجملة. أما في جمل املبني للمعلوم فان الفاعل في الجملة هو من وقع عليه الفعل وهو نفسه مستقبل الحدث الذي يعبر عنه الفعل كما في The boy في املثال (2) وكذلك الأمر لـ Mary في املثال (3).

Passive voice is used when the agent is not known or less important than the occurrence. We also use it when we talk about processes. However, the one who does the action may appear in 'by….' Phrase or may be omitted.

يستخدم املبني للمجهول عادة حين يكون الحدث أكثر أهمية ممن قام بالحدث نفسه، ومع هذا يمكن حذف من قام بالحدث من الجملة أو وضعه بنهاية الجملة بعد by.

Note: To change a sentence from active to passive the sentence must have an object.

ملاحظة: لتحويل الجملة من املبني للمعلوم إلى جملة املبني للمجهول فلا بـد للجملة مـن أن تحتوي عـلى مفعول به.

21.1   Steps for changing a sentence from active into passive

خطوات تحويل الجملة من املبني للمعلوم إلى املبني للمجهول

a.   **Place the object of the active sentence at the beginning of the passive sentence**

ضع املفعول به من جملة املبني للمعلوم في بداية جملة املبني للمجهول لتعمل كنائب فاعل.

b.   **Follow the Changes in the table below, which includes:**

اتبع الخطوات الواردة في الجدول التالي والتي تشتمل بشكل رئيس على:

- If the active sentence has any auxiliary, place it after the new subject of the passive sentence, paying attention to the subject- verb agreement.

إذا كان في جملة املبني للمعلوم فعل مساعد ضعه بعد فاعل جملة املبني للمجهول مباشرة، مراعيا في ذلك التوافق ما بين الفعل والفاعل من حيث العدد.

- Place the main verb that is in the active sentence after the auxiliary (in the past participle form).

ضع الفعل الرئيس بصيغة اسم المفعول (التصريف الثالث للفعل) بعد الفعل المساعد.

Active	Passive

* Tense: Present simple
* Form of the change required: (object+ is/ am/ are+ p.p)
'is' for singular objects; 'are' for plural objects; 'am' for 'I')
 	
- Sam <u>drinks</u> <u>tea</u> every morning.
   S   V   O
- Sam <u>eats</u> <u>apples</u> first.
   S   V   O
	
	-**Tea is drunk** every morning.
	
	- **Apples** are eaten first.

* Tense: past simple *** Form of the change required**: (object+ was/ were + p.p) 'was' for sing. objects, 'were' for plural objects	

- Muna <u>bought</u> <u>a bike</u> yesterday.
    S   V   O
- Martin <u>caught</u> <u>two thieves</u>.
    S   V   O
	- **A bike was bought** yesterday.
	
	- **Two thieves were caught.**

* Tense: present progressive *** Form of the change required**: (object+ is/ are/ am+ being + p.p)	

- Nancy <u>is writing</u> <u>a letter.</u>
   S   V   O
- Sylvie <u>is painting</u> <u>three sketches.</u>
   S   V   O
	- **A letter is being written.**
	
	- **Three sketches are being painted.**

* Tense: past progressive *** Form of the change required**: (object+ was/ were+ being+ p.p)	
- Ali <u>was building</u> <u>a house</u> S V O - Ali <u>was helping</u> <u>some people</u>. S V O	- **A house was being built.** - **Some people were being helped.**
* Tense: present perfect *** Form of the change required**: (object+ has/ have+ been+ p.p)	

- Suzan <u>has killed</u> <u>a kidnapper</u>.
  S   V   O
- Suzan <u>has thrown</u> <u>two boxes.</u>
  S   V   O
	- **A kidnapper has been killed.**
	
	- **Two boxes have been thrown.**

* Tense: past perfect *** Form of the change required**: (object+ had+ been+ p.p)	
- Sofia <u>had sold</u> <u>a farm</u>. S V O	- **A farm had been sold.**

- Sofia had stolen some beds. s v o	- **Some beds had been stolen.**
* Modals *** Form of the change required:** (object+ modal verb+ be+ p.p)	
- Jordan will grow rice. s v o	- **Rice will be grown.**
- Salma can freeze two chickens. s v o	- **Two chickens can be frozen.**
(modals perfect) **(modal+ have+ been+ p.p)** - You should have called the boss.	- The boss should have been called.
* be+ to infinitive *** Form of the change required:** (object+ be+ to +be +pp)	
-Phillip is to take a notebook. s to-inf o	- A notebook is to be taken.
- We are to take some notes. s to-inf o	- Some notes are to be taken.
(passive infinitive) -You have to order new books soon. s to inf o	- New books have to be ordered soon.
* With direct/ indirect object	
- Ali gave Sami a gift. s v DO IO	- Sami was given a gift.
- Riyad has offered a job for Sam. s v DO IO	- A job has been offered for Jam.
- Ali gave a gift to Sami. s v DO IO	- A gift was given to Sami.

c.   As we focus on the occurrence in passive sentences, writing the agent/ who does the action is optional. However, you can use the form (by+ the doer) to show the agent-mentioning the name or the object form of pronoun.

The following changes happen to the pronouns preceded by '**by**':

طالما أننا نركز في جمل المبني للمجهول على الحدث فان ذكر من قام بالحدث أمر اختياري، فاذا أردت ذكره فعليك أن تراعي ما يلي:

- اذا كان الذي قام بالحدث هو اسم ظاهر ونود الاشارة اليه في نهاية جملة المبني للمجهول فنضعه كما هو بعدby أما اذا كان من قام بالحدث ضمير فنضعه بصيغة المفعول به.

تاليا التغييرات التي تطرأ على الضمائر عندما تسبقهاby في نهاية جملة المبني للمجهول:

Subject	Object
I	me
you	you
he	him
she	her

it	it
we	us
they	them

For example: the pronoun 'he' in the active sentence '**He** killed the lion' becomes 'him' in passive voice 'The lion was killed **by him**'.

As in:

- Sam drinks tea daily.   (Active)

Tea is drunk every day **by Sam**. (Passive)

- She is writing a story.   (Active)

A story is being written **by her**.   (Passive)

- Phillip is to take notes.   (Active)

Notes are to be taken **by Phillip**.   (Passive)

More examples:

- **Active**: An earthquake destroys a great deal of property every year.

  Passive: A great deal of property is destroyed by an earthquake every year.

- **Active**: A tsunami destroyed fifty buildings.

  Passive: Fifty buildings were destroyed by a tsunami.

- **Active**: The committee is discussing new proposals.

  Passive: New proposals are being discussed by the committee.

- **Active**: The staff was considering new plans.

  Passive: New plans were being considered by the staff.

- **Active**: The government has ordered new weapons.

  Passive: New weapons have been ordered by the government.

- **Active**: The army had ordered new missile systems.

  Passive: New missile systems had been ordered by the army.

- **Active**: The family doctor should attend the clinic today.

  Passive: The clinic should be attended by the family doctor today.

21.2   Have/ get something done

a. Use *'have'* in a passive pattern to mean that *an arrangement made for someone to do something for you* as a professional service.

نستخدم have في صيغة المبني للمجهول لنشير الى أن هناك ترتيبات يتم القيام بها لتمكين شخص ما للقيام بأمر ما بدلا منك باعتباره مختص بهذا الشأن أو يؤده لك كمساعدة.

Examples:

- I *had the furniture delivered.*

(someone else delivered the furniture, not myself)

لقد تم إيصال الأثاث. هذه الجملة تفيد أن شخصا ما قام بإيصال الأثاث نيابة عني. وليس أنا من قام بذلك.

- Sam, you should *have that video fixed.*

(it means by the technician)

تفيد أنه عليك أن ترسل جهاز الفيديو للتصليح. ترسله للتقني المختص.

- Alice *had a new house built.*

(it means by specialists)

تفيد هنا أيضا أن المنزل الذي تم بناءه لها لم تبنه بنفسها، وإنما المختص بأعمال البناء هو من بناه لها.

- I *had my car stolen.*

(it means by someone else)

لقد تم سرقة سيارتي. وتفيد بهذا السياق أيضا أن شخصا ما قام بسرقة سيارتي. (ليس أنا من سرق السيارة).

b. We use *'get'* in a passive pattern to mean exactly what 'have' means.

نستخدمget في صيغة المبني للمجهول لتفيد ما تفيده have تماما، وكما في الأمثلة التالية:

- I must *get the furniture delivered.*

- I *got that video repaired.*

- I'm going to *get my eyes tested.*

- She is *getting her house decorated.*

Exercise (61)

Rewrite the following sentences in passive voice so that the new sentences give the same meaning of the given.

1. My students will have read the book by noon time, tomorrow.

   The book…………………………………..by my students.

2. Two horses were pulling the wagon.

   The wagon ……………………………………………

3. Asma has smashed three windows.

   ………………………………………………by Asma.

4. Aramex sends 2000 boxes of clothes a month.

   …………………………………………..by Aramex

5. Shakespeare wrote Macbeth.

   ………………………………………………

6. She had better return this book before Sunday.

   ……………………………………………….by her.

5. They should have sent this package.

   ……………………………………………… by them.

8. The engineer has performed the project successfully.

   The project………………………………………………..

9. The old man is cutting the trees.

   ……………………………………………….by the old man.

10. Farmers don't grow coffee in Jordan.

    Coffee ………………………………………………..

11. They provided the new house with furniture.

    The new house…………………………………………

12. You ought to sign this document.

    This document…………………………………………

13. They dig wells to get fresh water.

    Wells………………………………………………...

14. She let me in.

    ………………………………………………

15. She spent all the salary on clothes

    All the salary…………………………………………

16. People call Ali 'the smuggler'.

    Ali…………………………………………………...

Exercise (62)

A: **Study the following pair of sentences and answer the question below.**

   a.   I must translate this study into Arabic.

   b.   I must have this study translated into Arabic.

Which sentence indicates that the speaker will ask someone to translate the study?.................

B: **Study the following pair of sentences and answer the question below.**

a.   I've taken my shirt to be shortened.

b.   I've shortened my shirt.

Which sentence indicates that the tailor/ not the speaker has shortened the shirt.
....

C: **Choose the right answer.**

1. The box.......today. (must be/ must be delivered/ must deliver)

2. The report.........two days ago. (wrote/ was written/ were written)

3. This food ....well. (is cooked/ are cooked/ cook)

D: **Complete these sentences using the passive form of the verbs in brackets.**

1. At present, plastic bags ....(see: present simple) as unnecessary evil.

2. Bottles that ....(throw away: present perfect) often end up littering the streets.

22.   Direct and Indirect Speech

الكلام المباشر وغير المباشر

22.1   **Direct speech** is the reporting of speech by repeating exactly the speaker's words, as in:

- 'Peter said, "I'm tired of Arab meetings"
- 'John said, "He is eating an apple"

In direct speech quotation marks are placed at the beginning and end of direct speech piece. We place a comma before the first inverted comma/ quotation marks. (after Peter said/ John asked, etc.).

الكلام المباشر: هو ذكر الكلام الصادر عن الشخص المتكلم كما هو – دون تغيير على كلماته. وفي الكلام المباشر يوضع علامات اقتباس قبل وبعد الجزء الذي قيل. ويوضع كذلك فاصلة بعد الجزء التقديمي وقبل علامة الاقتباس. وكما في الأمثلة أعلاه.

22.2   **Indirect/ reported speech** is reporting what someone has said without using the actual words of the speaker. In reported speech there is usually an introductory verbs and a subordinate 'that' clause, as in:

- He **said** that he was eating apple.

'Said' is an introductory verb, and *that he was eating apple* is a subordinate 'that' clause.

الكلام غير المباشر: نقل ما قاله شخص ما دون الالتزام بالكلمات الصادرة عنه حرفيا. وفي   كما في الكلام غير المباشر/ المنقول نجد هناك فعلاً تمهيدياً/ تقديمياً وجملة تابعة تبدأ بـthat. المثال أعلاه، (حيث الفعل التقديمي في المثال أعلاه هو said).

When you make a change from direct to indirect speech, the pronouns, adverbs of time and place, and tenses are changed and you remove the commas.

عندما تحول الكلام من مباشر إلى كلام غير مباشر فانك تجري تغييراً على الضمائر والظروف الدالة على الزمان والمكان وتغيراً في زمن الفعل وتزيل الفواصل التي كانت مستخدمة في الكلام غير المباشر.

22.3   Changing the direct speech into indirect speech

Those are the changes you should follow when changing direct speech into indirect speech:

تاليا التغييرات التي تجريها عند تحويل جملة الكلام المباشر إلى الكلام غير المباشر:

<u>**Changing statements**</u>. You do the pronouns, verbs and adverbs changes when dealing with statements:

<u>التغيير على الجملة الخبرية</u>. تتبع التغييرات الآتية التي تتم على الضمير والأفعال والضمائر عند التعامل مع الجملة:

Changing pronouns تغيير الضمائر		Changing verbs تغيير الأفعال	
From	**To**	**From**	**To**
I	he/ she/ it	-present simple	-past simple
we	they	-past simple	-past perfect/ past simple
you	I/ we	- past perfect	- past perfect
my	his/ her	-present progressive	-past progressive
our	their	-past progressive	-past perfect progressive
it	it	-present perfect	-past perfect
you (obj)	me/ us	-must	-had to
me	him/ her	-could, might, ought to, would	- (no changes) لا تغيير عليها
us	them	-future, e.g. will, can	-conditional: would, could

Changing adverbs and adjectives تغيير الظروف والصفات	
From	**To**
today	that day
tomorrow	the next day
yesterday	the day before
next (week)	the following (week)
this (month)	that (month)
these	those
here	there
now	then
ago	before

tomorrow morning	the following morning
yesterday evening	the evening before

Changing questions	
التغيير على الأسئلة	
Yes/ no questions	**Wh- questions**
1. Use the introductory verb, e.g. *asked* استخدم فعل تقديمي للسؤال مثل 2. Add: *whether* or *if* أضف 3. Write the **subject**. أكتب الفاعل 4. Do the statement changes. ثم اجر باقي التغييرات التي تتبعها في الجملة الخبرية (التغيير على الضمائر، زمن الفعل و الظروف.	1. Use the introductory verb, *e.g.* *asked* استخدم فعل تقديمي للسؤال مثل 2. Write the **wh-** question **word**, e.g. *What/where*, etc. استخدم أداة السؤال 3. Do the statement changes after the rearrangement of the words order to become as it was in the statement order (S+ V). ثم اجر التغييرات التي تجريها على الجملة الخبرية (التغيير على الضمائر، زمن الفعل و الظروف) ولكن بعد أن تعيد ترتيب الكلمات متبعا الترتيب الذي يتم في الجملة الخبرية وليس الاستفهامية (فاعل+ فعل...) 4. Omit te question mark (?). احذف علامة السؤال (؟)
Changes in commands	**Changes when 'Let's' is used**
التغيير على الجمل الأمرية	التغييرات على الجملة عند استخدامLet's
1. Use the introductory verb, e.g. **ordered** استخدم فعلاً تقديمياً مثل 2. Add (**to**) before the imperative verb. أضف to قبل فعل الأمر المستخدم	Use either of the following forms: - *suggested*+ verb+ ing - **suggested**+ that+ S+ should+ verb (base form) اتبع أيا من الترتيبين الواردين أعلاه

Examples of the changes mentioned above	
Direct Speech	**Indirect Speech**
Statements	
He said, "I study biology"	He said (that) he studied biology.
He said, "I studied biology "	He said (that) he had studied biology.
He said, "I'm studying biology "	He said he was studying biology.
He said, "I was studying physics at 8 o'clock."	He said he had been studying physics at 8 o'clock.
He said, "I have studied biology "	He said he had studied biology.
He said, "I must study biology "	He said he had to study biology.
He said, "I might study biology "	He said he might study biology.
He said, "I will study biology "	He said he would study biology.
Yes/ no questions	
-He asked, "Are you going home?" *But in polite requests as in: -"Could you recommend me a good book on physics?"	=He asked if/ whether I was going home. =She asked me **to recommend** her a good book on physics.
Wh- questions	
He asked, "when does Ali leave?"	He asked when Ali left.
Commands	
He said, "stop there."	He told me to stop there.
He said, "don't stop there."	He told me not to stop there.
With "let's"	
He said "let's go."	- He suggested going. (or) - He suggested that we should go.

More examples:

- Samia to Jamil: My sister is going to Yemen.

  Samia told Jamil that **her sister was going to Yemen**.
- Rashid to Ali: My cousin lives in Jerash.

  Rashid told Ali that **his cousin lived in Jerash**.
- Amal to Samia: Kawthar is pleased about the new mission.

  Amal told Samia that **Kawthar was pleased about the new mission**.

Exercise (63)

Change the following sentences into reported speech.

1.   The lecturer, 'we have a meeting next week.'
The lecturer said that................................

2.   'Lock the door', my mum to me.
My mum ordered me................................

3.   'Have you arrived yet?'
She asked me...

4.   'How many copies do you sell?'
I asked Ali...

5.   'Your story is very good.'
Rabab told Majeda (that)............................

6.   Alia: 'I like your new camera.'
Alia told Ziad (that)....................................

7.   Ibrahim: 'my parents are taking us to India.'
Ibrahim said (that)....................................

8.   'Where is my jacket?'
My friend asked me....................……
(where was my jacket   where is his jacket   where his jacket was)

9.   'We are working here to pay for our new car.'
My parents told me that..

10. 'Yesterday I was in bed with a tempreture.'
He said that...

11. 'If I were you, I wouldn't leave school.'
Ahmad advised Sami...

12. 'Could you recommend me a good book on physics.'
My brother asked me...

23. Relative/ adjective clauses

الجمل الموصولة - العبارات الوصفية

A relative/ adjective clause is a dependent clause that modifies a noun/ or pronoun and it is used to give additional information about that particular noun. A relative clause follows the noun it refers to.

الجملة الموصولة/ أو الوصفية هي جملة تعرف وتحدد الاسم أو الضمير وتستخدم لاعطاء معلومات اضافية حول اسم معين. والجملة الموصولة تأتي مباشرة بعد الإسم الذي تشير اليه، وكما في الأمثلة التالية- حيث أن العبارات التي تحتها خط هي جمل موصولة :

- The book _that is on the table_ is well organized.

"that is on the table" is the relative clause.

- The lady _whom Rakan admires_ is Asma.

"whom Rakan admires" is the relative clause.

- The man _who set up this plan_ is clever.

"who set up this plan" is the relative clause.

23.1 Using 'who', 'which' and 'that' as subject pronouns:

استخدام who, which, that كضمائر فاعل

Pronouns	(1) Examples	(2) The base sentences
Who الذي/ التي تستخدم مع العاقل	I met the lady _who supported me_.	I met the lady. The lady supported me.
أصل الجملة كما في العمود (2) وحل ضمير الوصل who محل The lady في الجملة الثانية وهي فاعل.		
Which الذي/ التي تستخدم مع غير العاقل	The pen _which is there_ is mine.	The pen is mine. It is there
أصل الجملة كما في العمود (2) وحل ضمير الوصل which محل الضمير it في الجملة الثانية		

Note: 'that' is used instead of 'who' and 'which'.

تستخدم that بدلا من كل من who و which -أي أنها تستخدم مع العاقل وغير العاقل.

Note: 'who' is used for people, whereas 'which' is used for things.

تستخدم Who مع الأشخاص و Which مع الأشياء.

23.2 Using 'who(m)', 'which' and 'that' as object pronouns:

استخدام whom, which, that كضمائر مفعول به

Pronouns	(1) Examples	(2) The base sentences
Whom الذي/ التي	The lady _whom I met_ was Rana.	I met the lady. The lady was Rana.
Which الذي/ التي	The pen _which I bought_ was good.	I bought a pen. The pen was good.

<table>
<tr><td colspan="3" align="right">و يمكن استخدامthat بدلا من كل من which و whom.
حل الضمير whom محل المفعول به the lady وكذلك which محل pen .</td></tr>
<tr><td>Whom
الذي/ التي</td><td>She is the lady whom I told you about.</td><td>She is the lady. I told you a bout her.</td></tr>
<tr><td colspan="3" align="center">'Whom' is the object of the preposition 'about'.
 حلت Whom محل المفعول به her المسبوق بحرف الجر about </td></tr>
<tr><td>Which
الذي/ التي</td><td>The music which we listened to yesterday wasn't good.</td><td>We listened to music yesterday. It wasn't good.</td></tr>
<tr><td colspan="3" align="center">'Which' is the object of the preposition 'to'.
 حلت Which محل المفعول به music المسبوق بحرف الجر to </td></tr>
</table>

Note: 'whom' is used for people.   whom تستخدم مع الأشخاص (للعاقل)

Note: 'whom' and 'which' can be omitted when they refer to the object.

يمكن حذف which و whom من الجملة عندما يشيرا الى المفعول به، كما في الأمثلة التالية:

- The lady **whom** I met was Rana.

  The lady I met was Rana.

- The pen **which** I bought was good.

  The pen I bought was good.

- She is the lady **whom** I told you about.

  She is the lady I told you about.

- The music **which** we listened to yesterday wasn't good.

  The music we listened to yesterday wasn't good.

- The lady **whom/ that** I dislike is my ex-wife.

  The lady I dislike is my ex-wife.

- The pen **which/ that** I borrowed was Ali's.

  The pen I borrowed was Ali's.

23.3 Whose, Where and When

Pronouns	(1) Examples	(2) The base sentences
Whose	I met the lady whose van was damaged.	I met the lady. Her van was damaged.
	'Whose' is used to show possession. It is used with 'things' and 'people'. It is followed by a noun. <div align="right">whose تشير الى من تعود ملكية شيء ما، وتستخدم مع الأشخاص والأشياء، ويتبعها اسم.</div>	
Where	- The villa where I live is nice.	I live in that villa. The villa is nice.
	<div align="right">where تستخدم لتعرف أو تضيف معلومات اضافية عن مكان ما (تشير للمكان بمعنى:حيث)</div>	
When	- I will never forget the time when you left me behind.	I will never forget that time. You left me behind at that time.
	<div align="right">when تستخدم لتعرف أو تضيف معلومات اضافية عن زمن ما (تشير للزمن بمعنى:حين)</div>	

23.4 Restrictive and non-restrictive relative/ adjective clause:

العبارة الوصفية المحددة وغير المحددة:

A restrictive clause gives essential information about a noun, and such information cannot be deleted, as in:

1. Shadi who came late to the lesson was rebuked by the teacher.

Restrictive clause

But a non-restrictive clause gives additional information that can be deleted (optional relative clause). It usually comes between commas, as in:

2. Shadi, who is my best friend, was rebuked by the teacher.

Non-restrictive clause

العبارة الوصفية المحددة تعطي معلومات ضرورية عن الاسم ولا يمكن حذفها من الجملة، كما في المثال (1). أما العبارة الوصفية غير المحددة (الإضافية) فتعطي معلومات اضافية عن الاسم والتي يمكن حذفها من الجملة دون احداث تغيير على المقصود من الجملة، وغالبا ما توضع مثل هذه العبارة بين فاصلتين، وكما في المثال (2) أعلاه.

More examples:

- Objects that don't float to the surface should be sold.

Restrictive clause

- My van, which is very large, consumes too much gas.

Non-restrictive clause

Exercise (64)

Identify the relative clause in each sentence.

1. The meeting which I held was great.
   Adjective clause: **Which I held**

2. I know the man whose bike was stolen.
   Adjective clause:

3. The woman who told me the truth is looking at you right now.
   Adjective clause:

4. The villa where I live is by the upper lake.
   Adjective clause:

Exercise (65)

Use (where, which, who, when, whose, or whom) to fill in the blanks.

1.   I'll never forget the day……..I met you.
2.   The town ……..he lives is the old town.
3.   The student……..composition I have already read is excellent.
4.   George W. Bush was the US president……..I told you about.
5.   The programme……..we saw last night was thrilling.
6.   The girl ……..dropped the can was punished severely.

Exercise (66)

Combine the following into one sentence. Make relative clauses by using the relative pronouns in brackets.

1.   Do you know the man? The man lives in the blue building. (**who**)
2.   The coach gave me enough support. I called him.   (**whom**)
3.   The building was hit by missile. We lived in that building. (**where**)

24. Prepositions

حروف الجر

24.1 Prepositions of Place (at, in, and on) حروف جر تدل على المكان

Prepositions of place are used to show the positions of people and things.

<u>In:</u>

	Examples
Enclosed space; **Something around you** تستخدم مع أماكن مغلقة، أو أشياء تحيط بك	in a car, in a taxi, in a helicopter in a boat, in a lift, in a box in a pocket, in a wallet in a building, in an office, in the room in the Kitchen, in the garden in the bathroom
Streets مع الشوارع	in Dallas street, in Oxford street
Countries, cities, towns and **villages** مع الدول والمدن والقرى	in Paris, in Moscow, in New York in Jordan
With ' arrive' بعد الفعل Arrive	arrive in London
Weather مع حالة الطقس	in the rain, in the snow, in the fog
Miscellaneous common *phrases* متفرقة	in the garden, in the sky, in the newspaper, in a row in bed, in a book, in the photo, in the middle, in the back of (a car), in the front of, in back of, in front of

<u>At :</u>

	Examples
Points تشير إلى نقطة محددة	at the corner, at the bus stop, at the door at the top of (the page), at the end of (something), at the cross roads, at the roundabout, at the bottom, at the reception, at the traffic lights,
Street numbers مع الشوارع التي يحدد رقمها	at 17 oxford street
Speed حد السرعة	at a speed of 50 k/ h
Specific place مكان محدد بالضبط	at Heathrow airport, at the cinema, at the pub, at Fred's house
Miscellaneous of *common phrases* متفرقة	at home, at work, at university, at school, at college, at the party, at the meeting, at the football match,

On:

	Examples
Surface/ touching part of something تشير إلى سقف الشيء أو الجزء الملامس لشيء ما بمعنى "على"	on the wall, on the ceiling, on the floor, on the carpet, on the cover of the book, (a sign) on the wall, on the back of an envelope
Directions مع الاتجاهات	on the left, on the right, on the far side
To mean 'by means of something' بمعنى "بواسطة"	on the phone, on the T.V
Levels of a building/ On+ floor مع طوابق المبنى	on the first floor, on the top floor
Parts of the body مع أجزاء الجسم	on my foot, on his leg, on my left arm
Some types of transport مع بعض وسائل النقل	on a bus, on a horse
Miscellaneous of common phrases متفرقة	on this page, on the screen, on the beach

24.2 Prepositions of Time (at, in, and on) حروف جر تدل على الزمن

Prepositions of time are used to show the time of events and activities.

At :

	Examples
Precise time تشير الى وقت محدد	at 5 o'clock, at noon, at midnight at night, at dawn, at lunch time at sunrise, at sunset, at bed time at the moment, at the weekend at the start of June, at present at the same time
With age مع العمر	at the age of 17
Hours مع الساعة	at 6: 30
Calendar seasons المناسبات المحددة بتقويم	at Christmas, at Easter
With meals مع الوجبات	at lunch, at breakfast, at dinner

In:

		Examples
Months	مع أسماء الأشهر	in August, in April
Years	مع السنوات	in 1996, in 2000, in the 1980
Parts of the day	أجزاء النهار الثلاث الرئيسية: الصباح، بعد الظهر، المساء	in the morning, in the afternoon, in the evening
Seasons	مع الفصول	in spring, in summer
Long periods	فترات زمنية طويلة	in 7 months, in the ice age, in the future, in two weeks in two days, in three months
Centuries	مع القرون	in the 20 the century
To refer to the time something takes to be completed لتشير الى الوقت الذي يحتاجه شيء ما ليتم انجازه واتمامه		-1 will finish my paper **in 10 minutes.** -I did the crossword **in half an hour.**

On:

		Examples
Days مع أسماء الأيام		on Monday/ Saturday/ Friday, etc.
A day of the month مع تاريخ يوم محدد ضمن شهر		on 17 February, on 21 march 1968
Days of holiday أيام العطل		on your birthday, on independence day, on Christmas day
Particular time of a day للاشارة الى وقت محدد من اليوم		on Saturday evening, on Thursday morning
Miscellaneous of common phrases متفرقة		on arrival, on your return

24. 3 Other prepositions: after, from…to, to, in time, on time, near between, among, next to, opposite, in front of, in the front of, in back of, in the back of, for and since.

✔ 'After   بمعنى "بعد"

After: is generally used to mean later than, as in:

    Ann was happy **after** she bought a car.

    Ann looked weird **after** crying for two hours.

However 'after' has other meanings, including:

من المعاني الأخرى لها أيضا:

Meaning	behind خلف	chase يطارد/ يلاحق	to have the same name of another's سمي تيمنا
Examples	Ahmad, lock the gate after you, please.	The bear was after Asma.	Alia is named after his grandmother.

✓ 'From.........to/ until/ till' defines the beginning and end of a period, as in: "من...الى" أو "من...ولغاية" وتشير الى بدء ونهاية مدة معينة

The *British Council* will be closed **from 18th July to 15th August**.

✓ 'To' is used to refer to a movement toward something, as in:

"الى/ نحو" وتشير ال اتجاه الحركة

- Ahmad is *cycling* **to** Paris to visit his mother.
- I went **to** Surrey to meet Harith.

It also means 'against مقابل بمعنى as in: 'The score is 7 **to** 4.'

We use 'to' with the following words:

according to	liable to	hard to
give to	prefer to	like to
urge to	beg to	manage to
decide to	eager to	speak to
due to	used to	send to

✓ **In time, On time:**

'In time' means '*before/ not late*', e.g.: تعني "قبل/ ليس بعد"

I arrived **in time** for the 09:00 train.

'On time' means '*exactly at the arranged time*', e.g.:

تعني "بالضبط/ بالوقت المحدد"ليس قبل ولا بعد

My train left **on time**. (Exactly at 9 o'clock/ not after or before)

'Between' is used with two people/ things, and it can be used with more than two when the number is definite, as in:

بمعنى "بين" وتستخدم مع شخصين أو شيئين كما في المثال الأول، ويمكن استخدامها مع أكثر من شخصين حين يكون العدد محدد وقليل كما في المثال الثاني:

1. I divided the portion **between** *Alfred and Helen*.
2. I sat **between** Ali, Ahmad, Yousef and Samia.

✓ 'Among' is used with more than two people/ things and with indefinite number of people/ things, as in:

بمعنى "بين" وتستخدم مع أكثر من شيئين وحين يكون العدد كثير و غير محدد

I slept **among** strange people.

✓ 'Next to'   "بجانب"

It means 'right beside', as in 'look at that picture which is **next to** the blue curtain. It is excellent'.

✓ 'With'   "مع"

It means 'along with', and 'using something- the how'. As in:

- The British fought **with** the Germans.
- Salim hit her **with** a hammer.

We use 'with' with the following words:

satisfied with	familiar with	annoyed with
fill with	consult with	supply with
agree with	endowed with	with confidence
compare with	pleasesd with	covered with

✓ 'Opposite'   "مقابل"

It means 'facing something/ across from', as in:

A: I live in that building.   B: Which one?

A: The building **opposite** to the green grand store.

B: I see. They're facing each other.

✓ 'In front of' "أمام"

It means a head, as in 'Yousef is sitting **in front of** Al.

✓ 'In the front of' "بالجزء الأمامي"

It means 'in the front part of something/ from inside', as in 'The model is **in the front of** the classroom'.

✓ 'In back of' "خلف"

It means 'behind', as in 'The car is **in back of** my house'.

✓ In the back of' "بالجزء الخلفي"

It means 'in the rear part of something', as in 'The teacher is standing **in the back of** the auditorium'.

✓ 'For' is used to indicate to the destination you are going toward. It is also used to express how long an action lasts (length of period),   as in:

تشير الى الوجهة الذاهب اليها بمعنى"الى "، ولطول مدة ما، ومعنى "ل" كما في الأمثلة:

- I'm flying **for** a forum that will be held in Chelsea.
- I have taught English **for seven years**.
- I'll find a job **for** you.

✓ 'Since' is used to refer to the start point of an action, as in:

 I have -وتشير الى نقطة البدء لوقت ما، بمعنى "منذ"، كما في المثال التالي:
been teaching English **since 1987**.

✓ 'Out of' -خارج means the opposite of 'into', as in: '**He walked out of the room.**'

من الأسماء في اللغة الانجليزية ما تأخذ حروف جر ثابتة وكذلك بالنسبة للأفعال و الصفات والتي ينبغي حفظها، وتاليا أمثلة على ذلك:

24.4 Preposition+ noun (e.g. in my opinion) حرف جر+ اسم

on holiday	on a journey	on business	in cash
by cheque	in pen	on television	on the phone
for sale	on the whole	in advance	up to date
on purpose	by chance	by mistake	in my opinion
at a high speed	at first sight	at the invitation of	in charge of
in honor of	on the occasion of		with confidence

by+ transport means: by taxi/ bus/   on foot (means walking)
train/ ship/ sea/ plane/ air

24.5   Verb+ Preposition (prepositional verbs), as in: فعل+ حرف جر
'graduate from', 'spend on' and 'supply with'. Here are some common prepositional verbs:

wait for	belong to	agree with	apply for
apologize for	believe in	care about	deal with
concentrate on	suffer from	talk about	consist of
blame for	provide with	take care of	laugh at
hide from	blame for	cope with	comment on
rely on	depend on	contribute to	stare at
look forward to	congratulate on	take advantage of	dream of/ about
participate in	forget about	vote for	object to
count on	thank for	graduate from	compete with
furnish with	interfere with	mix with	pay for
prevent from	recover from	sit at (the table)	sit in (arm chair)
decide on	detract from	engage in	escape from

24.6   Adjectives+ prepositions (e.g. mad at) صفة+ حرف جر

accustomed to	afraid of	mad at	interested in
expert in	different from	capable of	fond of
rich in	guilty of	detrimental to	partial to
tired of/ from	finished with	absent from	dull of
acquainted with	accused of	innocent of	angry at
jealous of	aware of	bored with	known for
committed to	upset with	dedicated to	discriminated against
content with	proud of	married to	different from
composed of	dressed in	easy for	empty of
full of	superior to	born in	kind to

Exercise (67)

Put in the preposition: in, on or at.

1. Gallagher's room is.........the third floor.
2. I saw Julia Robert holding a parrot.........her hand.
3. I'll meet you ....the airport.
4. There are 23 seats ....the classroom.

Exercise (68)

Add the correct preposition that goes with the verb, adjective, or noun in every sentence:

1. I'm afraid.........parachuting. I hate to jump from high places.
2. Orange is rich.........vitamin (c).
3. People in Congo suffer........ civil war.
4. Don't write...........pen.
5. When you decide to participate in the parliamentary elections, please tell me.......... advance.
6. My firm-report will be declared .... the radio.
7. Water consists........... oxygen and hydrogen.
8. You are well-trained. That is why I can rely......you.
9. I'll be out for few hours. Could you take care......my baby.
10. I've run my website..........2001.(since/ for)
11. He's been there ....over half an hour. (since/ for)
12. He was sitting........the table.   (in/ at)
13. We went to the station.......taxi. (on/ by)
14. I was born .... Holland. (in/on)
15. I'm proud......my king. (of/ at)
16. The child is afraid......the dark room. (of/ by)
17. You're accused ....smuggling. (of/ by)
18. He speaks French ....confidence. (with/ from)
19. He spent a lot of money ...... cassettes. (on/ at)
20. Are you good ....physics? (at/ on)

25.   Emphasis and Distancing the Facts

25.1   Emphasis   التأكيد

There are many ways for emphasizing part of a sentence.

هناك أكثر من طريقة لتأكيد جزء معين من الجملة، وهذه تشمل:

1. **Structures which add emphasis**

    a.   I love Jolie's personality. (base sentence)

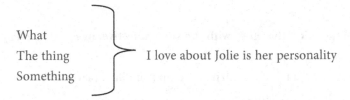

It is Jolie's personality that I love. (cleft sentence)

    b.   He criticizes Bernard constantly. (base sentence)

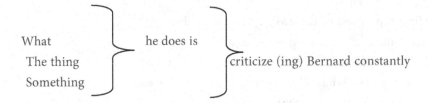

    c.   He criticized Bernard constantly. (base sentence)

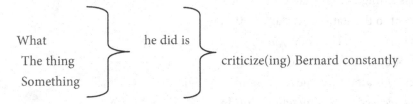

2. **Negative inversion:** Certain negative expressions can be put at the beginning of a sentence for emphasis, as in:

بداية الجملة بكلمة تفيدالنفي **(لتأكيد معنى النفي):** وهنا يستلزم الأمر قلب ترتيب الفعل والفاعل، بحيث يأتي الفعل المساعد بعد الكلمة التي تفيد النفي ثم يأتي الفاعل بعد الفعل المساعد، ثم الفعل الرئيسي. ومن هذه الكلمات:

(never, rarely, not only, scarcely, seldom, etc.).

Examples:

- I'll never forget the day when I first met her.

Never will I forget the day when I first met her.

- People rarely fall in love at first sight.

Rarely do people fall in love at first sight.

3. **Emphatic do/ does/ did:** استخدام مجموعة الفعل "يعمل" للتأكيد

- Finally I did find the keys.   تضع did قبل الفعل المصدر في جملة الماضي
(Finally I found the keys.)   أصل الجملة كما يلي:
- I do like Mrs. Bonnet.   تضع do قبل الفعل المصدر في جملة المضارع اذا كان الفاعل جمع
(I like Mrs. Bonnet.)   أصل الجملة كما يلي:
- She does love her dad.   تضع does قبل المصدر اذا كان الفعل مضارع والفاعل مفرد
(She loves her dad.)   أصل الجملة كما يلي:

25.2   Distancing the Facts (hedging)

These are the ways of how you can give information putting distance between yourself, as a speaker, and the facts:

تاليا الطرق التي يمكنك اتباعها ليبدو الكلام صادراً عن مصدر ما غيرك أنت متجنبا اعطاء كلام قاطع- كلام غير ملزم (بالعربية يستخدم هذا الأسلوب مع كلمات مثل: يقال، يذكر أن، يبدو، كثير من الناس يؤمنون أن...)

1.   Passive constructions.   استخدام أسلوب المبني للمجهول

Look at these sentences:

-   They say Hanna works in the hotel.
-   People assume Kate is wasting her time with Angelina.
-   Everyone thought Mogabi had made his fortune in tobacco.

These sentences can be expressed in the passive in two ways, beginning with 'it' or the 'name/pronoun':

الجمل الواردة أعلاه تصبح كما يلي في صيغة المبني للمجهول بحيث تبدأ بـ It أو اسم/ ضمير. وتستخدم أفعالا مثل say, think, assume بمعنى (يقال أن/ يعتقد أن/ يفترض أن).

-   **It is said that** Hanna works in the hotel.
-   **It is assumed that** Kate is wasting her time with Angelina.
-   **It was thought that** Mogabi had made his fortune in tobacco.

(You can use phrases like: it is believed that/ it is expected/ it is alleged/ it is reported/ etc.)

(or)

-   **Hanna/ He is said to** work in the bar.
-   **Kate/She is assumed to** be wasting her time with Angelina.
-   **Mogabi/He was thought to** have made his fortune in tobacco.

2.   Seem and appear.   "يبدو"

حيث يمكن أن تضع بعد الفعل seem/ appear فعل مصدر مسبوق بـ to ، والطريقة الأخرى أن تأتي بجملة that بعد seem/ appear.

-   He **appears to have** scanned my family photos.
-   The Sunday **seems to have** found the required details from reliable sources.
-   Benjamin's declaration **seems to be** more factual.
-   **It appears that** the president dealt with the circumstances confidently.

Exercise (69)

Rewrite these sentences to make them more emphatic.

1. Love changes the course of your life. ....
2. She always disagrees with me. ....
3. I admire Arthur's courage. ....
4. I've never been humiliated in my life. ....

26. Punctuation Marks

علامات الترقيم

Punctuation marks are symbols used in punctuating a written text including: full stop, comma, question mark, colon, exclamation mark, apostrophe, etc.

أدوات الترقيم هي رموز تستخدم لترقيم نص مكتوب، وهي تضم قائمة من الرموز أبرزها: النقطة، الفاصلة، علامة الاستفهام، نقطتين رأسيتين، علامة التعجب، و الفاصلة العلوية. وهذه الرموز هي التي سنقتصر على ذكرها في هذا المقام.

26.1   Full stop. It is a small dot (.) whose main use is as follows:

النقطة واستخداماتها الرئيسة :

1. To indicate the end of a sentence which is not a question or an exclamation, as in:

في نهاية الجملة الخبرية (ليس للسؤال ولا عبارات التعجب)

- Miller is really embarrassed.
- Rebecca is studying applied linguistics.

2. At the end of an abbreviation that involves the first few letters of a word, as in:

في نهاية الاختصارات التي تشتمل الحروف الأولى للكلمة

Feb. / Jan. / Aug. / Tue. /etc. / Mr.

3. In decimal fractions, as in "3.5 feet".   في الكسور العشرية

4. At the end of a reported/ indirect sentence, as in:

في نهاية جملة الكلام المباشر وغير المباشر.

- He said he would help her.

26.2   Comma (,). It is mainly used: الفاصلة: واستخداماتها الرئيسية

1. Between individual items in a list of three or more items, e.g.: بين أجزاء القائمة الواحدة التي تتكون من أكثر من عنصرين

- I like football, tennis, basketball and table tennis.
- I can speak English, Arabic and French.

2. To separate clauses or phrases that can be removed from a sentence without changing the basic meaning of the sentence, as in:

لفصل العبارة الوصفية التي تضيف معلوما ت اضافية يمكن حذفها من الجملة، كما في:

- My father, *who is Irish*, is smart.

3. When the subordinate clause precedes the main clause, as in:

حين تأتي الجملة التابعة قبل الجملة الرئيسية اذ توضع حينها الفاصلة بعد الجملة التابعة.

- *Although she was sick,* she went to school.

4. To separate a question tag, as in "It is hot, isn't it?"

قبل الأسئلة المذيلة، لتفصلها عن الجملة التي قبل السؤال.

5. Before a quotation, as in: قبل الاقتباس

- I boldly cried out, 'what a bad day!'

6. In numbers of four or more figures, to separate each group of three consecutive figures, starting from the right, as in:

في الأرقام المؤلفة من أربع خانات وأكثر، لتفصل كل مجموعة أرقام مكونة من ثلاث خانات على

حدا ابتداء من الجهة اليمنى، كما في:

(11,234,657)

26.3 Question mark (?). It is placed at the end of a question or interrogative sentence, as in:

- Who is she?

- What did you say?

أداة الاستفهام: وتوضع في نهاية السؤال، كما في الأمثلة أعلاه.

26.4 Colon (:). It is used:
النقطتان الرأسيتان: وتستخدم

1. To introduce a list of items, as in:

تسبق قائمة من الأسماء التي تشكل عناصرا في مجموعة ما، كما في المثال التالي:

- I have a list of what we need for lunch: potatoes, tomatoes,   garlic and bread.

2. In numerals as in "it is 7:30 pm".   في الأرقام كما في الوقت

3. To explain and clarify what has gone before it, as in:

لتوضيح ما سبق ذكره في الجملة، كما في:

- I have some good news: Alzamalik won the championship.

4. Before a quotation, as in: قبل الاقتباس

- The godfather wrote these words: I owe you a grand.

26.5 Exclamation mark (!). It is used after an exclamatory word, phrase, or a sentence expressing absurdity, contempt, emotion, enthusiasm, sorrow, a wish, or a wonder, as in:

- What a sunny day!

- What a beautiful lady!

- Alas!

علامة التعجب: وتستخدم بعد كلمة أو شبه جملة أو جملة تعبر عن تعجب، ازدراء، تقليل من شأن أمر ما،
عاطفة ما، حماس، حزن، أمنية.

26.6 Apostrophe ('). It is used: الفاصلة العلوية: وتستخدم

1. To show the possession case, as in 'This is **John's** book.

لتبين على من تعود ملكية الشيء

2. To show omission, as in '**John's** angry.' which is the short form of '**John is** angry.' لتبين أن حرفا ما تم حذفه

Do not= **don't**, is not= **isn't**, etc.

26.7 Semicolon (;).

1. It is mainly used between clauses that are not joined by any form of conjunction, as in:

الفاصلة العلوية وتوضع بين عبارتين/ جملتين لم يتم ربطهما بأداة ربط، وكما في الجملة التالية:

- We had a wonderful holiday; sadly they didn't.

2. It is also used to form subsets in a long list of names so that the said list seems less complex, as in:

وتستخدم أيضا لتفصل بين مجموعات صغيرة في قائمة من الأسماء لتبدو القائمة المذكورة
أقل تعقيدا، كما في:

- He has applied to The Guardian in London; The Mail in Toronto; AlRai in Jordan.

3. It is sometimes used before 'however, nevertheless, hence, etc.', as in:

كما وتستخدم أحيانا قبل أدوات ربط مثل: however, nevertheless, hence كما في:

- It is freezing; *nevertheless*, he'll go out.

Note: It is key to learn that you should use capital letters in the following situations whilst writing a text:

ملاحظة: من المهم أن تعرف أنه عليك استخدام الحرف الكبير في المواقف التالية من كتابتك لأي نص.

1. Initial letter of proper nouns, days of the week, and months of the year. (Ahmad, Jordan,Cairo, Saturday, Sunday, May)

بداية الأسماء العلم، وأيام الأسبوع وأشهر السنة.

2. Initial letter of the first word of each sentence, as in:

أول حرف من أول كلمة لكل جملة

Ruling a state isn't easy.

3. Initial letter of titles, as in (**Mr, Dr, Miss**) بداية الألقاب

27.   Redundancy

الحشو

A redundant part of a sentence is where some information is unnecessarily repeated. It is necessary to learn which word/ or part of the sentence should be crossed out to make a sentence sound correct. The following is a list of words that students usually tend to use making a sentence redundant.

الجملة المطولة هي جملة تحتوي على كلمات مكررة بلا داعي (وهو ما يعرف أيضا بالحشو). ومن الضروري تعلم أي كلمة أو جزء من الجملة ينبغي حذفه لتصبح الجملة صحيحة. تالياً قائمة من الكلمات عادة ما يميل الطلاب الى استخدامها متسببين بإدخال حشو في الجملة لا ضرورة له.

Reason...because السبب...لأنه

The <u>reason</u> I want to borrow some money is that <u>because</u> I want to by a new house. (incorrect)

The <u>reason</u> I want to borrow some money is that I want to by a new house. (correct)

Repeat again أعد ثانية

Mary <u>repeated</u> the question <u>again</u>. (incorrect)

Mary <u>repeated</u> the question. (correct)

New innovations ابتكارات جديدة

- We should come up with <u>new</u> <u>innovations</u> to improve our way of living. (incorrect)

- We should come up with <u>innovations</u> to improve our way of living. (correct)

Join together يشترك معا:

My father asked me to <u>join</u> the team <u>together</u>. (incorrect)

My father asked me to <u>join</u> the team. (correct)

Sufficient enough كافٍ بشكل كافٍ

We have <u>sufficient enough</u> money. (incorrect)

We have <u>sufficient</u> money. (correct)

We have <u>enough</u> money. (correct)

Return back يرجع للوراء أو يعود للوراء

I <u>returned</u> <u>back</u> last night. (incorrect)

I <u>returned</u> last night. (correct)

Progress forward يتقدم للأمام

  The Israeli-Palestinian peace talks <u>progressed forward</u>. (incorrect)

  The Israeli-Palestinian peace talks <u>progressed</u>. (correct)

Advance forward يتقدم للأمام

  The army <u>advanced forward</u> after the main battle. (incorrect)

  The army <u>advanced </u>after the main battle. (correct)

Proceed forward يتقدم للأمام

  The teacher <u>proceeded forward</u> to discuss the puzzle. (incorrect)

  The teacher <u>proceeded </u>to discuss the puzzle. (correct)

Same identicalمطابق نفس الشيء

  The twins have the <u>same</u> <u>identical</u> birthmarks. (incorrect)

  The twins have <u>identical</u> birthmarks. (correct)

Two twins توأم اثنان

  My brother wants to play with the <u>two</u> <u>twins</u>. (incorrect)

  My brother wants to play with the <u>twins</u>. (correct)

Two halves نصفين اثنين

  I split the group into <u>two</u> <u>halves</u>. (incorrect)

  I split the group into <u>halves</u>. (correct)

The time when الوقت حين

  It is <u>the time when</u> I'll meet her. (incorrect)

  It is <u>the time </u>I'll meet her. (correct)

The place where المكان حيث/ أين

  This is <u>the place</u> <u>where</u> I dropped her. (incorrect)

  This is <u>where</u> I dropped her. (correct)

28. **Guide for Finding Writing Errors**

دليل ايجاد الأخطاء الكتابية

While you are reading any sentence, you had better memorize the following basic hints to determine whether the sentence is correct or not.

بينما وأنت تقرأ أية جملة ينصح بتذكر النقاط التالية لتحدد ما اذا كانت الجملة صحيحة أم خطأ.

i. **Subject- verb agreement (singular/ plural agreement)**

التوافق بين الفعل والفاعل:

- *I has* written three short stories. (**x**)

I have written 3 letters. (√)

ii. **Word form**   شكل الكلمة واشتقاقها

- I met a *beauty girl.* (**x**)

I met a *beautiful girl.* (√)

- He is *gooder* than Ali. (**x**)

He is *better* than Ali. (√)

iii. **Verb tense**   زمن الفعل

- Yasar *is play* tennis now. (**x**)

Yasar *is playing* tennis now. (√)

iv. **Add or omit a word/ article, etc.**   اضافة أو حذف كلمة أو أداة

- I *want see* you soon. (**x**)

I *want to* see you soon. (√)

v. **Word order**   ترتيب الكلمات

- I bought a *car black.* (**x**)

I bought a *black car.* (√)

vi. **Incomplete sentence**   جملة غير تامة المعنى

- I went home. *Because I felt tried.* (**x**)

I went home because I felt tired. (√)

vii. **Spelling**   التهجئة

- The red car *stoped.* (**x**)

The red car *stopped.* (√)

viii. **Punctuation**   الترقيم

- Who is that. (**x**)

Who is that? (√)

ix. **Capitalization**   البدء بحرف كبير

she is going to *japan.* (**x**)

She is going to *Japan.* (√)

Exercise (70)

Find the errors and then correct them in the following sentences:

1.   I have be living in London since 2001.
2.   Don't repeat the song again.
3.   He have been to Paris twice.
4.   Ive three children.
5.   I have two son.
6.   Sami buyed this house 20 years ago.
7.   John didn't attend the class. Because he was sick.
8.   ali bought a good van.
9.   What is your name.
10.   An Earth rotates round the sun.
11.   Didn't you saw that sign?
12.   If I were a bird , I will fly to Canada.
13.   I quit to smoke.
14.   Suzan and Julia is coming to dinner

Exercise (71)

Imagine you are an editor in Aljazeera international channel, you are asked to edit the following lines taken from an advertisement. There are six underlined mistakes; correct them.

- Stop **look** for a new computer.
- **your** best personal computer is now available.
- Our aim is to provide you with the **lateste** technology.
- Your computer was made in **england**.
- Now it **have** the best options.
- **Dont** think twice. You won't regret it.
- Do you still have any doubts**,**

29.   Problem Words

29.1   lie/ lay, sit/ set, and rise/ raise.

These verbs sometimes cause problems. And to solve the problem you should remember which verbs are transitive and which are intransitive.

يصعب أحيانا التمييز بين هذه الأفعال، ولحل هذا النوع من الخلط بينها عليك أن تتذكر أيا من هذه الأفعال لازمة وأيها متعدية.

29.1.1   lie, sit, and **rise** are intransitive verbs.

هذه الأفعال هي لازمة (لا تأخذ مفعولا به مباشر).

Infinitive	Past simple	Past participle	Meaning
lie	lay	lain	rest, be situated in a place
sit	sat	sat	take a seat
rise	rose	risen	get up, increase

Examples:

- Ahmad lay on the grass just few minutes ago.
- I'll lie down for a nap.
- I'll sit in the shade.
- Ali sat on the beach.
- The sun rises early in the summer.

29.1.2.   lay, set and **raise**

هذه الأفعال متعدية (تأخذ مفعولا به مباشر).

Infinitive	Past simple	Past participle	Meaning
lay	laid	laid	to put something/ or somebody on a surface
set	set	set	put
raise	raised	raised	lift, elevate, to increase something

Examples:

- Ahmad laid his clothes on the bed.
- I'll set my favourite flowers in the sun.
- Raise your hands.
- The government is going to raise the price of oil.

29.1.3   'Lie' which means 'to say something that is not true' has the following verb forms.

(lie) إن هذا الفعل يستخدم أيضا بمعنى (يكذب) ويصرف كما يلي:

Infinitive	Past simple	Past participle	Meaning
lie	lied	lied	to say something that is not true

29.2 Some people fail to distinguish between some words due to their similarity in spelling or pronunciation. The following are some of them with their meanings:

Word	Meaning in English	Meaning in Arabic
acetic	acid used in vinegar, sour	حامض، الخل
ascetic	self-denying	زاهد
angel	heavenly being	ملاك
angle	a figure formed by to lines meeting at a certain point	زاوية
adverse	hostile, unfavorable	معادي، مناوئ
averse (to)	having dislike, unwilling	كاره، مبغض
cite	quote as an example	يقتبس، يدلل، يشير للمرجع
site	location	موقع
sight	view, aiming device	منظر، مُوَجِه (أداة تسديد)
costume	clothing	لباس
custom	a traditional practice of a particular group of people	تقليد
descent	lineage, downward motion	انحدار، هبوط، ينحدر من سلالة ما
decent	suitable	ملائم، جيد
dessert	pudding, the final course of a meal	حلوى، مايؤكل بعد الوجبة الرئيسية، العقبى
desert	abandon, dry place	صحراء، يترك
later	a time in the future	فيما بعد، مستقبلا
latter	last of two things mentioned	اللاحق
loose	opposite of tight	فضفاض
lose	opposite of win, mislay	يخسر
peace	opposite of war	سلام
piece	part of a whole	قطعة، جزء من كل
principal	main, director of a school	رئيسي، مدير مدرسة
principle	fundamental rule	جوهر الشيء
quiet	serene	هادئ
quite	completely	تماما
quit	stop	يترك
their	possessive adjective	صفة ملكية (بمعنى:لهم)
there	opposite of here	هناك(عكس هنا)

they're	contraction of 'they+are'	اختصار لـ they+are
two	number (2)	رقم 2
too	excessively, also	بإفراط، أيضا
weather	atmospheric conditions	الطقس
whether	if	إذا
whose	relative pronoun	ضمير وصل
who's	contraction of 'who+is/ who+has'	اختصار لـ who+is/has
accept	take the given	يقبل
except	excluding	باستثناء
advice (n)	counseling	نصيحة، مشورة
advise (v)	counsel	ينصح
affect (v)	to make a change	يؤثر
effect (n)	consequence	تأثير
device	plan	خطة، اختراع
devise	invent	يخلق، يضع خطة
elicit	draw out	يوضح
illicit	unlawful	غير قانوني
explicit	direct, clear	مباشر، واضح
implicit	implied, unquestioning	متضمن، مطلق/ غير قابل للجدل
formerly	previously	سابقا
formally	officially	رسمي
immortal	Incapable of dying	أبدي، سرمدي
immoral	bad	غير أخلاقي، سيء
persecute	torture	يعذب
prosecute	to bring suit against	يدعي على، يوجه تهمة ضد
precede	to come before	يسبق
proceed	continue after interruption	يستأنف
beside	next to	بجانب
besides	in addition to	بالإضافة الى
aside	to one side	الى جانب واحد
considerable	rather large amount	ضخم
considerate	polite, thoughtful	لبق، متعقل
credible	believable	يمكن تصديقة
creditable	worthy of praise	يستحق الثناء
hard	difficult	صعب، قاس
hardly	barely	لا يكاد
liquefy	change to a liquid state	يذيب، يحول الى سائل

liquidate	eliminate, change to cash	يصفي، يحول الى كاش
amiable	friendly, agreeable (people/moods)	ودود، لطيف، أليف (تستخدم لوصف الأشخاص والحالة الذهنية)
amicable	characterized by goodwill (relationships/documents)	سلمي، ودي، حسن النية (تستخدم لوصف العلاقات والمعاهدات والوثائق)
biannual	twice a year	مرتين بالعام الواحد
biennial	every two years	كل عامين
cannon	a large gun	مدفع
canon	a ruling	قانون، القانون الكنسي
censor	to examine publications	يتفحص، يدقق
censure	to blame, criticize severely	ينتقد بشدة
defective	having a fault	معطل
deficient	having a lack	معوز، ينقصه (الكفاءة)
discomfit	to embarrass	يحرج
discomfort	lack of comfort	غير مريح
exercise	physical exertion, a piece of school work	تمرين
exorcise	to rid of evil spirits	يتعوذ، يتخلص من الأرواح الشريرة
extant	still in existence	باق
extinct	no longer in existence	منقرض
fatal	causing death	قاتل، مميت
fateful	important and decisive	هام، وحاسم
hail	frozen rain	برد
hale	healthy and strong	قوي وبصحة جيدة
hyper-	above (hypertension)	فوق، متجاوز الحد بالارتفاع
hypo-	under (hypothermia)	دون الحد
illegible	impossible to read	غير مقروء
eligible	qualified, suitable	مؤهل، ملائم
literal	word for word	حرفيا
literate	able to read and write	قادر على القراءة والكتابة (عكس أمي)
luxuriant	profuse, growing thickly and strongly	ينمو بكثرة وبقوة، غزير
luxurious	referring to luxury	مترف

momentary	lasting for a very short time	لحظي، يستمر لفترة قصيرة
momentous	very important	مهم، الأبرز
moral	concerning the principles of right and wrong	أخلاقي
morale	state of confidence	معنويات
noticeable	obvious	واضح
notable	remarkable	مدهش
perpetrate	to commit	يرتكب
perpetuate	to cause to continue	يبقي على، يساهم بإبقاء صورة ما في أذهان الآخرين، يؤثر
personal	of a person	شخصي
personnel	the people employed in a work place	قوى بشرية، العمال في مشروع ما...
plain	easy to see, frank, simple, not beautiful	واضح، صريح، بسيط من دون تكلف، ليس جميلاً
plane	aeroplane	طائرة
pray	to speak to god	يصلي، يدعو
prey	to hunt and kill	يفترس
reign	the time during which the king reigns	فترة الحكم
rein	one of the leather straps that control a horse	لجام (حزام من الجلد يستخدم للسيطرة على الخيل)
stationary	standing still	ثابت، غير متحرك
stationery	writing materials	قرطاسية
wet	to cover with moisture	يبلل
whet	to sharpen, to stimulate	يبري(السيف)، يحفز(الشهية)

Exercise (72)

Select the correct word in parentheses to complete the meaning of the sentence.

1. A beautiful (angel/ angle) visited me.
2. I have (your/ you're) notes in my notebook.
3. It is a (costume/ custom) in Jordan to eat lamb on wedding parties.
4. (Weather/ Whether) we run or walk depends on the roads conditions.
5. Although my brother doesn't like (dessert/desert), I prefer something sweet.
6. James and Fredrick teach kindergarten; the (latter/later) works in Nepal.
7. King Abdullah II is of the Hashemite (decent/descent).
8. You need to (site/sight/cite) your references when you write an essay.
9. My shirt came (lose/loose) and it needed to be tightened.
10. Asma had to (quit/quiet/quite) eating sweets to be healthier.
11. Your remarks greatly (effected/affected) Kaite.
12. After declaring bankruptcy, General Motors was forced to (liquefy/liquidate) its assets.

Comprehension Tests

Test (1)

Q1. <u>Error analysis:</u> Every sentence of the following has one error out of the underlined words/ phrases/ clauses. Find the error and then correct it.

1. He <u>have</u> <u>been</u> to Paris <u>twice</u>.

2. I <u>have</u> <u>study</u> English linguistics <u>for</u> three years.

3. Sam <u>usually</u> <u>wake up</u> at six o'clock.

4. <u>Ive</u> three <u>children</u>.

5. I <u>have</u> two <u>son</u>.

6. <u>I</u> saw a <u>beauty</u> girl.

7. He <u>is</u> <u>been</u> three <u>since</u> 2007.

8. Sami <u>buyed</u> this house 20 <u>years</u> ago.

9. John didn't <u>attend</u> the class. <u>Because he was sick</u>.

10. <u>ali</u> <u>bought</u> a good van.

11. What is <u>your</u> name<u>.</u>

12. <u>An</u> Earth <u>rotates</u> round <u>the</u> sun.

13. <u>Last</u> night I <u>saw</u> a dog. <u>A</u> dog was chasing a cat.

14. You must <u>to write</u> your <u>article</u>.

15. I <u>don't</u> <u>has</u> <u>any</u> money.

16. <u>Too much</u> people use the <u>subway</u> to get <u>their</u> work in time.

Q2. <u>Error analysis:</u> **Find and correct the errors in the following sentences:**

1. She don't have any money.

2. That is your pen, aren't they?

3. Everyone took the test , didn't he?

4. Ann doesn't drink coffee, does she.

5. I am supposed to leave now, aren't we?

6. Does your plane left at seven?

7. Didn't you saw that sign?

8. When did you do last night? I studied.

9. Why can answer the question? Ali

10. Why is she? At home.

11. How much is she? 12

12. Where book should I buy? This one.

13. I is a student.

14. George is carelessly .

15. Ali speaks English good.

16. She asked him an easily question.

17. That house looks perfectly.

18. Birds flies.

19. he has never met her.

20. It is rain now.

21. I have to study hard because of my course is difficult.

Fundamental English Grammar Review

Q3. Choose the best answer.

1. Have you …….. to Paris?
   a. be ever   b. been   c. were

2. Dave has already …….. the meeting.
   a. inaugurated   b. inaugurate   c. inaugurating

3. Niss …….. my glasses.
   a. broken   b. broke   c. break

4. Sali …….. this portrait by herself.
   a. do   b. did   c. done

5. Ali …….. enter this theatre. It's forbidden.
   a. mustn't   b. don't have   c. might

6. I have a toothache. You …….. see the dentist.
   a. should   b. can   c. ought

7. I'm not familiar …….. this teacher's way of testing.
   a. with   b. to   c. from

8. I graduated…….. Mutah university.
   a. from   b. of   c. on

9. …….. my opinion, she is ugly.
   a. In   b. At   c. On

10. My father is named …….. his grandfather
    a. before   b. after   c. about

11. I was born …….. Tokyo.
    a. in   b. on   c. at

12. Miss Ruby always comes late. She's never …….. time.
    a. on   b. at   c. by

13. I came …….. foot. I didn't catch the train.
    a. on   b. in   c. by

14. I …….. for you for 3 hours.
    a. have been waiting   b. has being waited   c. wait

15. Seldom …….. Dr. Khattab.
    a. have I met   b. I have met   c. met

16. Killing animals is unlawful. You …….. hunt dogs.
    a. mustn't   b. don't have to   c. can't

17. Could I have a …….. of Jam?
    a. Jar   b. slice   c. loaf

18. Can I have a …….. of tea?
    a. cup   b. bottle   c. dozen

19. Can I have a ………of chocolate?
    a. bar   b. head   c. dozen

20. When I came in, I saw her…….. football.
    a. play   b. playing   c. is playing

21. He …….. in 2001.
    a. died   b. has died   c. was dying

22. I .... to leave now.

    a. have   b. can   c. must

23. None of my friends .... a good friend.

    a. are   b. is   c. am

24. One of the students .... in trouble.

    a. was   b. were   c. are

25. The number of males........ more than the females.

    a. is   b. are   c. were

26. A number of my friends .... flying tonight.

    a. is   b. are   c. was

27. I have .... pure water, so I should buy some more.

    a. little   b. a little   c. few

28. I got up .... 7: 30 .

    a. in   b. on   c. at

29. She looks .... than I do.

    a. happier   b. more happy   c. happyer

30. Did you .... tennis yesterday ?

    a. played   b. play   c. playing

31 . I .... a dream.

    a. has   b. am   c. have

32. If you take advantage of Rami's experience, you.................. .

a. are going to succeed   b. would succeed   c could have succeeded.

Q4.   **Study the following pair of sentences and answer the questions below.**

        a.   I'm going to have the walls painted.

        b.   I'm going to paint the walls.

        Which sentence means that the speaker will not do the painting himself.

        ....

Q5. Correct the underlined mistakes in the following sentences:

      1.   I'm <u>interesting</u> in Salim's idea.

      2.   How many <u>peoples</u> have you invited?

      3.   When I came back, everything <u>is</u> fine.

Q6. The following is incomplete sentence. Beneath the sentence you will see three words or phrases. Choose the one word or phrase that best completes the sentence.

- During the early period of ocean navigation,.......any need for sophisticated instruments of techniques.

    a.   so that hardly

    b.   hardly was

    c.   there was hardly

Test (2)

Q1. Complete the sentences with the correct form of verbs in brackets.

1. The teacher made the student………the class. (leave)
2. Mr. Robert had his wife………the food. (prepare)
3. My father had his house……….. His elder son painted the house. (paint)
4. I made my students…………the classroom's windows. (wash)
5. George got some children…………his garage (clean)
6. I ……… the car boot after I hit a truck. (damage)
7. It ………heavily in Mumbai in June and July. (rain)

Q2. Give the correct 'ing' form/ gerund and the past form of the following words:

stop: *stopping* / *stopped.*

open: …….. /…….. .

control:…….. /…….. .

try: …….. /…….. .

lie: …….. /…….. .

Q3. Give the correct past form of the following words:

argue: *argued*

destroy:……….

prefer: ………

study: ………

play: ………

Q4. Use either the present simple or the present progressive of the verbs in brackets to fill in the blanks.

1. Diana can't help you right now. She …………… (take) a shower.
2. Dove……………. (wash) his hair every weekend .
3. The sun…………. (rise) from the east.
4. Please be quiet. I …………… (try) to write a letter.
5. I'm glad that you…………… (visit) Petra this month.
6. She can't afford that car. It ………… (cost) a lot of money.
7. Right now I ……….. (check) the student's exercise books.
8. That pen…………. (not/ belong) to me.
9. This evening Laura……….. (help) Jim with his homework.
10. I ……….. (not / love) Jerry. I really ……… (hate) him.
11. She………… (need) you to help her husband now.
12. I ………… (want) to check in right now or I'll miss the flight.

Q5. Choose the correct word in brackets.

1. The boy …………… (raised / rose) his hands.
2. Water ………… (boils/ boiles) at 100 degrees.

3. Brown .... (set/ sat) in a chair because he was exhausted.

4. I .... (set / sat) you pen over there an hour ago.

5. Johnson .... (laid / lay) on his bed.

6. If I were you, I would .... (lie / lay) down and sleep.

7. Yesterday I .... (sleeped / slept) at 10. p.m.

8. I usually .... (deal/ deals) with honest people.

9. The plane .... (flew / flied) a few hours ago.

10. The police .... (catched / caught) the thief last week.

Q6. Select the appropriate preposition to complete the sentences.

1. Are you interested .... teaching English?

   a. to   b. in   c. of

2. Can you visit me .... noon time?

   a. at   b. in   c. on

3. Would you mind calling me .... 7 o'clock?

   a. at   b. on   c. in

4. Iran was .... war with Iraq for 10 years.

   a. in   b. at   c. on

5. He learnt French .... 5 weeks.

   a. in   b. at   c. on

6. It is usually hot .... summer.

   a. in   b. at   c. on

7. He was walking .... the snow.

   a. in   b. at   c. on

8. She hasn't seen me .... last year.

   a. for   b. since   c. at

9. She stayed at home .... 7 o'clock to 10 o'clock.

   a. from   b. on   c. about

Q7: Using the dictionary entry below, choose the correct form to fill in the blanks.

Magic (n): mysterious charm

Magical (adj): charming

Magician (n): a person skilled in magic

---

1. The tricks of the............ astonished the viewers.

2. I'm touched by the .... of Shakespeare's novels.

Q8: **Rewrite the following sentences avoiding the errors where necessary.**

1. dr ali is the english teacher at amman private university.

2. A: Are you a teacher?

   B: no, I'm not

3. the womens' mosque is to your left.

4. Are you happy to join the team.

5. Because I'm optimistic I won the championship.

6. I bought Tims car.

7. I bought a pen a book and a table.

Q9. **Put the words in the correct order to make sentences.**

1. shining/ The/ yesterday/ was/ sun

2. You/ last night/ were/ jeans/ wearing

3. bought/ scarf/ She/ cotton/ a/pretty

Q10. **According to the subject-verb agreement, decide whether the sentences are correct or incorrect?**

1. People from the south of Cork is so friendly. (   )

2. You and I am supposed to live together in Geneva. (   )

Q11. **Choose the correct preposition.**

1. Chuck lives ………21 Piccadilly Street, doesn't he?

   a. in   b. at   c. on

2. Adiga will be able to leave Albania ……..10 minutes.

   a. in   b. on   c. at

3. Angela doesn't get mad ………you unless you interrupt her.

   a. in   b. on   c. at

Q12. **The following is incomplete sentence. Beneath the sentence you will see three words or phrases. Choose the one word or phrase that best completes the sentence.**

- Simple photographic lenses cannot…..sharp, undistorted images over a wide field.

   a. to form

   b. are formed

   c. form

   d. forming

Test (3)

Q1. Use the past simple or the past progressive to correct the verbs in brackets.

1. I………. (have) an accident last week.
2. While I ………. (drive) down King's Street, a red car ……. (hit)mine.
3. Three years ago, the Sudanese government………. (decide) to build ten dams. At that time, many farmers in the country side………. (starve) because of the drought.
4. I ……… (fall) down as I ………. (run)in the corridor barefoot.
5. What ……… (wear/ Asmahan) at last night's party?

Q2. Fill in the gaps with the correct form of verbs by using the past simple or the present perfect.

1. Suha………. (not / attend) any meetings since January.
2. Bill………. (go) to Spain last night.
3. He………just ………. (return) from Honolulu.
4. In her whole lifetime, Helena………. (never/ see) snow.
5. Up to now, William ……….. (finish) four exams.
6. I ……… (have) this car for ten years.
7. I ………never ……… (win) a lottery.
8. How long ……... you………. (stay) in Grand Tulip Hotel?
9. ……….Sam …….. (feed) his dog before he came in? Yes, he did.
10. The weather……… (be) nice lately.
11. I ………. (release) three thieves so far this week.

Q3. Use the past perfect or past simple for sentences (1-3).

1. Bush ……… (make) an apple pie after we got home.
2. My little son ………. (fall) asleep before we got home.
3. He ……….. (become) a businessman after he……. (become) a T.V reporter.

Q4. Find and correct the errors in the following sentences.

1. I visit my son in law three times when I was in Paris.
2. She is living at 37 Pennsylvanian Avenue since last June.
3. Amman have changed its name four times.
4. While I am writing my poem last night, Ali knocked the door.

Q5. Use (in, on, or at) to supply an appropriate preposition for each of the following sentences.

1. I'll meet Sam ……….the evening.

2. Sue always stays home ....night .

3. I'll call you............10:30.

4. I was born............August 6th , 1980.

5. .... the moment I'm reading a short story.

6. I don't like to go swimming............the winter.

Q6. Use (a, b, or c) to fill in the gaps with the appropriate answer.

1. Neither Sami .... Ahmad attended the class.

    a. nor   b. but also   c. never

2. .... Ahmad or the teacher is at risk.

    a. Either   b. Not only   c. Although

3. Not only did she drop the basket .... lost her keys.

    a. but also   b. neither   c. but

4. Layth works as a physician .... funds many poor people.

    a. but   b. and   c. when

5. He is rich .... he has no car.

    a. but   b. if   c. because

6. Both Sami and Rashid .... broke.

    a. is   b. are   c. was

7. Neither Ali nor his friends .... here.

    a. is   b. are   c. be

8. .... she is sick, she works hard.

    a. Although   b. Unless   c. Because of

9. He had lung cancer .... he was a heavy smoker.

    a. since   b. despite   c. but

10. .... the cold weather, he is sitting outside.

    a. In spite of   b. Although   c. Because

Q7. Write the following sentences in reported speech.

1. Rasha says, 'My relatives are coming to visit Petra this week.' Rasha said (that)..

2. Ahmad says, 'I think Jerash is the most beautiful city in Jordan.' Ahmad said (that)..

3. Josef says, 'My parents have moved their house.
    Josef said (that)..

Q8.   **Select the best answer.**

1. A: I am sick.

  B: You....... see the doctor

    a. can't   b. must   c. don't have to

2. Sámi....... at 7:00 every morning .

    a. wake up   b. wakes up   c. woke up

3. You can't drive quickly in this street. It is not wide enough.

    a. It is too narrow   b. it is narrow too   c. too it is narrow

4. There are……. people outside.

    a. too many   b. too much   c. too far

5. He ate……. the biscuits. The box is empty.

    a. all   b. some   c. any

6. It is peaceful there. There aren't ……. cars.

    a. any   b. many   c. all

7. Do you want ……. water?

    a. some   b. many   c. a few

8. I ……. live in the countryside.

    a. used to   b. would   c. am

9. Do you know how people live in……. city?

    a. a   b. the   c. x

10. ……. people in Switzerland can speak French, but not many.

    a. some   b. many   c. all

11. Mr. Hayek, ……. is a teacher at my school, is leaving soon.

    a. who   b. which   c. where

12. Thank you for taking me to the exhibition, ……. I enjoyed a lot.

    a. who   b. which   c. when

13. Fredrick wishes he ………younger so he could play basketball.

    a. were   b. had been   c. is

14. Could I have a……..of ice cream?

    a. jar   b. container   c. scoop

Q9. The following is incomplete sentence. Beneath the sentence you will see three words or phrases. Choose the one word or phrase that best completes the sentence.

- ……..of tissues is known as histology.

    a.   Studying scientific

    b.   The scientific study

    c.   To study scientifically

Q10. The following sentence has four underlined words or phrases. Identify the one word or phrase that must be changed in order for the sentence to be correct.

- Of the <u>much</u> factors that <u>contributed</u> to the <u>growth</u> of international

           a   b   c

tourism in 1990s, <u>one</u> of the most important was the advent of Internet

                  d

in 1990.

Test (4)

Q1. Find and correct the errors in the form of modals or the verbs they precede in the following sentences:

1. Rose can to play well.
2. Rose wills play well.
3. Rose should had played better.
4. Can Rose to behave well?
5. Do you can run faster than Jim?
6. They don't can go to Amman by bus.
7. I must going now.
8. I don't have depart now.
9. I have to playing basketball.
10. You ought study tonight.
11. The driver shoulds slow down.
12. You had better got a visa.
13. I was able reach the mountain top.

Q2. Change the following sentences from active into passive:

1. Sam opens the red window every other morning.

……………………………….. by Sam .

2. Sam is painting the brown barrels.

The brown barrels ……………………………

3. The policemen have smashed the gate.

 The gate……………………………….by the policemen.

4. The taxi driver shook the red wine bottle.

The red wine bottle……………………….

5. Lee was washing the cars.

…………. …………………………by Lee.

6. Tom and Jeff had served the old women.

…………………………………. by Tom and Jeff.

7. Jeffery will set up a new plan.

………………...………………. by Jeffery.

The government is going to establish a new hospital.

………………………………….. by the government

Q3. Rewrite the following sentences so that they give the same meaning:

1. The English company made 20,000 pairs of trousers last week.

    …………………………………………………………

2. My father built our house in 1990.

    …………………………………………………………

3. My mother will complete my rug tomorrow.

    …………………………………………………………

4. I have dropped a large vase.

....

5. You should teach your son how to behave.

....

Q4. Complete the following sentences using either a gerund or to- infinitive.

1. Jim avoided looking / to look at her.
2. Do you enjoy playing / to play soccer?
3. Keep taking/ to talk . I'm listening to you.
4. I suggest visiting/ to visit Jordan next week.
5. I'd like talking/ to take a shower.
6. Mary planned build/ to build a new house.
7. Do you mind closing/ to close the door? Thank you.

Q5. Choose the correct answer.

1. She is----------- chemist.

   a. a   b. the   c. an   d. x

2. I visited --------------USA twice.

   a. a   b. the   c. an   d. x

3. It is usually warm in -------------- south of Jordan.

   a. the   b. a   c. an   d. x

4. ----------- hotel seems nasty place.

   a. These   b. Those   c. This   d. that is

5. ---------are Alison's pamphlets.

   a. This   b. That   c. These   d. which

6. The underlined letter in the word *looks* is pronounced:

   a. /s /   b. /z/   c. /ez/   d. /iz/

7. The underlined letter in the word *'cite'* is pronounced:

   a. /s/   b. /k/   c. /ng/   d. /si/

8. The underlined letter in the word *'helped'* is pronounced:

   a. /t/   b. /d/   c. /ed/   d. /id/

Q6. Select the meaning of the underlined modals/ phrases in the following sentences:

1. **It is possible** that David comes tonight.

     a. May   b. Must   c. Will

2. She **should** call her husband.

     a. Ought to   b. Have to   c. Could

3. I **can** lift this luggage.

     a. I am able to   b. Should   c. Had better

4. **Would you mind** calling you after midnight?

     a. Ability   b. Request   c. Obligation

     5. You **must** pull over your car right now.

              a. necessity   b. Strong obligation   c. Prohibition

Q7. Correct the words in brackets to fit the meaning of each sentence.

1. I was thinking about my English homework when the phone…..(ring).

2. When I……. in the town, I used to spend my free time with my friends.(live)

3. What……. you usually……. when you get home from school? (do)

4. A: What……. your father usually……. (do)

   B: He ……. a newspaper reporter. (be)

5. Sue used to……. when she was a child. (smoke)

6. She……. her tea yet. (not drink)

7. Fatima……. Just……her lunch. (eat)

8. ……. you ever ……. to London?(be)

9. I ……. my ankle once, in a basketball match.(sprain)

10. A tourist stopped to ask me for directions. He…. (lose) his map.

11. I had already cooked the dinner by the time my mother……. (come) home.

Q8. In the following questions each sentence has four underlined words or phrases. Identify the one word or phrase that must be changed in order for the sentence to be correct.

   1. Mohammad <u>studied</u> many <u>different</u> cultures, and he was one

                     a   b

   <u>of the first</u> anthropologists to photograph <u>him</u> subjects.

      c   d

   2. A food <u>additive</u> is <u>any chemical</u> that food manufactures <u>intentional</u> add

             a   b   c

   to their <u>products</u>.

         d

Test (5)

Q1. The underlined letters in the following words are pronounced:

1. lift   a. /I/   b. /e/

2. cold   a. /g/   b. /k/

3. good   a. /g/   b. /k/

Q2. Select the correct answer.

1. There are two .... in our town.

     a. travel agents   b. travels agent   c. travels agents

2. I have five............

     a. sister- in- laws   b. sisters- in- law   c. sisters- in- laws

3. I have ten............

     a. childs   b. childrens   c. children

4. I met seven ....

     a. police mans   b. polices man   c. policemen

5. I divided the class into ....

     a. haves   b. halves   c. halfes

6. We had few............ we need to square them away.

     a. crisises   b. crises   c. crisis

7. I have 300 ....

     a. aircrafts   b. aircraftes   c. airscraft

8. The committee .... changing their plans.

     a. is   b. was   c. are

9. Physics............ the most interesting subject.

     a. is   b. are   c. be

10. .... students passed the test.

     a. Few   b. Little   c. Too much

11. This amount of coffee is not enough for five people.

     There is............ left.

     a. little   b. a little   c. few

Q3. Select the appropriate answer.

1. The food smells............

     a. deliciously   b. delicious   c. deliciousness

2. Ann is............ than Sal.

     a. taller   b. tallest   c. more tall

3. This exam is the .... ever.

     a. bad   b. worse   c. worst

4. She is the............ girl in the village.

     a. pretty   b. prettyest   c. prettiest

5. This house has............ tables than ours.

     a. less   b. least   c. the least

6. The movie was............ I almost slept.

    a. bored   b. boring   c. boringly

7. Luna is as .... as Sylvia.

    a. pretty   b. prettier   c. more pretty

8. Ma'an is .... than Amman.

    a. far   b. further   c. furthest

9. Ali walks ....

    a. slow   b. slowly   c. slower

10. He drive ....

    a. fast   b. fastingly   c. fastly

11. He drives ....

    a. careful   b. carefully   c. carfulness

12. .... did you wake up? At 7o'clock.

    a. Where   b. When   c. Which

13. .... did you meet him? In Asab.

    a. Where   b. When   c. Who

14. .... car do you prefer? The Mercedes .

    a. Whom   b. Why   c. Which

15. .... didn't you attend the class? I was sick.

    a. Why   b. Who   c. Where

16. .... is it to Amman ? 80 km .

    a. How much   b. How far   c. How many

Q4. Select the best preposition.

1. I am fond .... adventure films.

    a. of   b. in   c. on

2. My students are accustomed .... my way of tackling issues.

    a. to   b. in   c. about

3. David is good .... physics.

    a. to   b. from   c. at

4. You are my best friend. I can really rely .... you.

    a. on   b. of   c. from

5. He went .... Washington by train.

    a. to   b. in   c. by

6. I live .... 10 Jones Street.

    a. in   b. at   c. on

7. I will wait you .... the second circle.

    a. at   b. in   c. on

Test (6)

Q1. Adding 'ed' or 'ing' to the words in brackets, make adjectives so that they fit the meaning of the sentences.

1. Last night I had a very .... (excite) day. That is why I'm still a little bit .... (please).
2. You made fun of Conrad. He is really .... (embarrass).
3. The test was .... (disappoint). No one passed it.
4. You look .... (tire). Was your job .... (exhaust).
5. Can you turn the T.V down? It is .... (annoy).

Q2. Correct the verbs in brackets. Use present simple, present progressive, past simple or past progressive:

1. Farah never............. as sad as today. (sound)
2. Dan .... his grandfather regularly. (visit)
3. Rick .... to London, this winter, to meet wife. (fly)
4. Look, Sal .... to solve the problem (try)
5. My roommate .... me...... every day. (wake up)
6. It .... last night when the power went off. (snow)
7. Al .... TV as his mother was cooking. (watch)
8. Ricky .... his radio set this time yesterday. (fix)
9. Jessie .... to the school after she had breakfast. (go)
10. I .... my wallet while I was looking for my keys. (lose).

Q3. Use the present perfect or the past perfect of the verbs in brackets:

1. Kirby ...... his calculator. He is looking for it right now. (lose)
2. Jones was sad. He .... the test (fail).

Q4. Circle the correct answer:

1. The rate of crime .... in the USA this year.
    a. decrease   b. is decreasing   c. decreased

2. Lucy often .... letters to her ex-husband.
    a. was sending   b. sends   c. is sending

3. Suzy and I .... when my father came in.
    a. was fighting   b. were fighting   c. fight

4. The food we ate yesterday ....well.
    a. tastes   b. tasted   c. was tasting

5. What a good day! The sun .... and the sea is calm.
    a. shines   b. is shining   c. is shinning

6. Rula is a good teacher. She .... for 5 years
    a. teaches   b. has been teaching   c. is teaching

7. My neighbor ………….. in Washington for 10 years. Then he moved to New York.

    a. lives   b. is living   c. lived

8. The sun………….. in the west.

    a. set   b. sets   c. is setting

9. The driver was talking on phone while he …………..

    a. was driving   b. drove   c. is driving

10. Sumaya quit dancing two years ago. She ………….for 10 years.

    a.had been dancing   b. has danced   c. will dance

11. I cashed my cheque. I ………….. my sister tonight.

    a. will visit   b. am going to visit   c. had visited

12. My family ………….. Tokyo before the volcano erupted.

    a. have left   b. has left   c. had left

13. If you want to meet Samia tomorrow morning, she ………….. you at Guildford pub main gate.

    a. will be waiting   b. will have waited   c. was waiting

Q5. Select the correct answer.

1. He said he …………. a good villa.

    a. had   b. has   c. is having

2. He asked ………….

    a. where did she go   b. where she went   c. where is gone

3. The waitress…………. won the lottery is Mrs. Bartlett.

    a. who   b. whom   c. which

4. The coach …………. I cheated was clumsy.

    a. whom   b. which   c. where

5. The apartment …………. I live is attractive.

    a. when   b. where   c. whom

6. January month is …………. I met Mrs. Tyre.

    a. where   b. which   c. when

7. The cat …………. fur is disgusting is his.

    a. whose   b. which   c. who

8. …………. having the authority, he can fire you.

    a. because of   b. so   c. despite

9. Seldom…………such a dreg.

    a. I have talked to   b. have I talked to

10. Look how slippery the road is! It ……….last night.

    a. must have rained   b. could have rained

Test (7)

Q1: Choose the appropriate answer for the following situations:

Situation (1): Hemingway is a good person, but he didn't call for help because he didn't see the accident.

❖ If Hemingway ……………the accident, he would have phoned for help.

a. saw   b. had seen   c. sees

Situation (2): Alma has good computer skills, so that she can do her searches.

❖ It …………possible for Alma to do her searches if she didn't have good computer skills.

a. wouldn't be   b. hadn't been   c. won't be

Q2: Read the following pairs of sentences and answer the questions.

Pair (1):

a. John has been reading a book about the history of English language

b. John has read a book a bout the history of English language.

● Which sentence indicates that *reading is in progress*?

Pair (2):

a. Who's that man? He must be my boss.

b. I must go now.

● In which sentence does *'must'* express necessity?

Pair (3):

a. I have been studying English literature since 1999.

b. I am interested in this article since I like literature.

● In which sentence can *'since'* be replaced by 'because'?

Pair (4):

a. My lady had already eaten the meal before I got the house

b. My lady was eating when I got the house.

● Write the sentence which expresses that the eating was completed when I arrived.

Pair (5):

a. I will be writing a letter at 7:30 tomorrow morning.

b. I will have written a letter by 7:30 tomorrow morning.

▪ Which sentence means that writing a letter will be finished at 7:30?

Q3 : Select the correct answer.

1. This is a ………… Christmas holiday plan.

a. complete   b. completely   c. completion

2. Mr. Brown is ………… That is why he can't go to school.

a. sick   b. sickness   c. sickly

3. Your skin feels ....

      a. hot   b. hotly   c. hotness

4. Don't press the 'ok' button before.........the possible consequences.

      a. know   b. knowledge   c. knowing

5. You can leave if you ....finished the writing section of the test.

      a. complete   b. completely   c. completion

6. Have you ....your project?

      a. final   b. finalized   c. finally

7. Mr. Dove didn't talk to ....in his group. I think he is upset.

      a. anybody   b. nobody   c. somebody

8. Give me ....opportunity, please.

      a. another   b. the other   c. any body

9. Can you turn the light off? It is ....It hurts my eyes.

      a. too bright   b. bright enough   c. very bright

10. She decided to buy ....apartment.

      a. a five- room   b. five- a room   c. a five rooms

11. She gave me a ....project.

      a. well planed   b. well- planned   c. planned well

12. Qatar is a............. country.

      a. gas- producing   b. gas- produced   c. producing gas

13. Sam hasn't finished the mission and my brother hasn't..............

      a. either   b. neither   c. too

14. ....them regularly takes a lot of time.

      a. Monitor   b. Monitoring   c. To monitor

15. No news ....good news

      a. is   b. are   c. were

Q4: Circle the appropriate answer.

1. I used to ....a lot when I was 20 years old.

      a. smoke   b. smoking   c. smoked

2. He told her ....him again.

      a. not to visit   b. to not visit   c. not visit

3. I can't tell ....my dad was upset or not.

      a. weather   b. whether   c. we there

4. ....going with me?

      a. Whose   b. Who's   c. How

5. Reading Shakespeare's novels had a great ....on Jiff.

      a. effect   b. affect   c. affects

6. It is not easy to.............your terms.

      a. accept   b. except   c. exccept

7. My elephant is eating ....food

      a. it's   b. its   c. it was

8. You have to control your employees and I have to supervise........ .

    a. my   b. mine   c. meen

9. They may find a good ....for a new national college in Bella.

    a. site   b. sight   c. cite

10. The lake seems ....

    a. quite   b. quiet   c. quietly

11. Jim received his letter and Rania got ......letter too.

    a. hers   b. her   c. mine

12. ....rooms are in the Sultan of Brunei's palace?

    a. How many   b. How much   c. How far

13. Sali doesn't have .... about opium.

    a. much knowledge   b. many knowledge c. a few knowledge

14. ....are too many options to select.

    a. They're   b. There   c. Their

Q5. Select the appropriate answer.

1. Have you.......... Fairouz's new CD?.

    a. bought   b. buying   c. buy

2. The word for someone who produces TV programmes is a......

    a. producer   b. producer   c. product

3. He has been a teacher.......... 2002.

    a. for   b. since   c. ago

4. My brother has a shirt with long sleeves. He's got a.......... .

    a.long-sleeved shirt   b. longed- sleeve shirt

5. I am .... of spiders.

    a. terrified   b. terrifying   c. terrify

6. Fairouz is a.......... person.

    a. popular   b. popularity   c. popularize

7. .... players are there in a football team?

Eleven.

    a.   How many   b.   When   c. Who

8. .... did the Derby race start?   In 1989

    a. Where   b. When   c. How

Test (8)

Choose the correct answer a, b, c, or d.

1. They have lived in Dubai .... six years.

    a. since   b. between   c. for   d. among

2. Hosam would have called the security if he ...... the accident.

    a. sees   b. had seen   c. saw   d. have seen

3. Did Mr. Mobaidin ....a lot of homework yesterday.

    a. has   b. have   c. had   d. having

4. Mustafa ......when I called her.

    a. is eating   b. has eaten   c. was eating   d. ate

5. Bill and John ....since 7 o'clock.

    a. are waiting here   b. wait here

    c. had waited here   d. have waited here

6. The cabinet is straight ahead. It is ......

    a. close to you   b. in back of you

    c. opposite to you   d. in front of you

7. Al-Khattab enjoyed ....my biographical essay.

    a. to read   b. read   c. be read   d. reading

8. I'm interested ....meeting your sister.

    a. for   b. in   c. to   d. with

9. Please, ...all the gates.

    a. open   b. opens   c. opened   d. opening

10. The rain prevented us from........for the port.

    a. leave   b. to leave   c. leaving   d. left

11. Why don't you wait until Sali ....?

    a. come   b. comes   c. came   d. had come

12. ....is a very important skill.

    a. Speak   b. To speak   c. Spoke   d. Speaking

13. I would help you with your test if I ....time.

    a. has   b. had   c. have had   d. having

14. The professor said, "can you tell me ......"

    a. where he is from   b. where is he from

    c. if he is from   d. whether is he from

15. Is the preparatory test ......by the P.T. Instructor?

    a. given   b. to give   c. gives   d. be given

16. You can't run that fast, ...?

    a. can you   b. could you   c. can't you   d. do you

17. Heat can be .... through iron.

    a. transmitted   b. is transmitted   c. transmits   d. transmitting

18. That is the train ....to Sharm Al-Sheikh.

    a. which goes   b. that go   c. go   d. has gone

19. Fred's park is not as attractive as Jane's. Jane's garden is.....than Fred's.

a. much attractive   b. more attractive

c. the most attractive   d. less attractive

20. She had come across a woman ......name was so strange.

     a. whose   b. who   c. whom   d. where

21. Math ....in all Jordanian schools.

     a. is taught   b. teaching   c. taught   d. were taught

22. There are many villages similar ......mine.

     a. to   b. for   c. at   d. of

23. Rasmi weighs 200 pounds. His son weighs 210 pounds.

     a. Rasmi is lighter than his son   b. Rasmi's son is heavier than his dad

     c. They are alike   d. They weigh the same

24. They aren't going to Salvador next week, ...?

     a. are they   b. aren't they   c. They aren't   d. they are

25. Choose the correct sentence:

     a.Her necklace is as valuable as yours.

     b. Her necklace valuable as is yours.

     c. Her necklace is more valuable as yours.

     d. Her necklace is your as valuable as.

26. I haven't got used to......this amount of dessert.

     a. eat   b. eating   c. eaten   d. ate

27. A few men came to the ceremony. ....came.

     a. Not many   b. Not much   c. None   d. plenty

28. All philosophers must...... before his majesty the king arrives.

     a. sign in   b. signed in   c. signing   d. signature

29. Banks don't work ......Christmas.

     a. in   b. on   c. at   d. in front of

30. Before he became broke, he ....buy anything.

     a. has to   b. could   c. should   d. ought to

31. We replaced the ......tables.

     a. break   b. breaking   c. broke   d. broken

32. The headmaster didn't meet me, and ....I.

     a. didn't too   b. either did   c. neither did   d. so did I

33. Do you know how much ....?

     a. a car costs   b. costing a car   c. a car does cost   d. is a car costing

Comprehension Tests' Answer Keys
Test (1)

Q1	1. have= has	2. study= studied	3. wake up= wakes up
	4. Ive= I've	5. son= sons	6. beauty= beautiful
	7. is= has	8. buyed= bought	9. .Because he was sick= because he was sick (omit the full stop)
	10. ali= Ali	11. (.)= ?	12. an= the
	13. A=The	14. to write= write	15. has= have
	16. Too much = Too many		
Q2	1. don't= doesn't	2. aren't they= isn't it	3. didn't he= didn't they
	4. does she.= does she?	5. aren't we= aren't I	6. left= leave
	7. saw= see	8. when= what	9. why= who
	10. why= where	11. How much= How old	12. where= which
	13. is= am	14. carelessly= careless	15. good= well
	16. easily= easy	17. perfectly= perfect	18. flies= fly
	19. he= He	20. rain= raining	21. because of= because
Q3	1. b	2. a	3. b
	4. b	5. a	6. a
	7. a	8. a	9. a
	10. b	11. a	12. a
	13. a	14. a	15. a
	16. a	17. a	18. a
	19. a	20. b	21. a
	22. a	23. b	24. a
	25. a	26. b	27. a
	28. c	29. a	30. b
	31. c	32.	
Q4	a		
Q5	1. interested	2. people	3. was
Q6	c		

Test (2)

Q1	1. leave	2. prepare	3. painted
	4. wash	5. to clean	6. damaged
	7. rains		
Q2	stopping/ stopped	opening/ opened	controlling/ controlled
	trying/ tried	lying/lay	
Q3	argued	destroyed	preferred
	studied	played	
Q4	1. is taking	2. washes	3. rises
	4. am trying	5. are visiting	6. costs
	7. am checking	8. doesn't belong	9. is helping
	10. don't love...hate	11. needs	12. want
Q5	1. raised	2. boils	3. sat
	4. set	5. lay	6. lie
	7. slept	8. deal	9. flew
Q6	1. b	2. a	3. a
	4. b	5. a	6. a
	7. a	8. b	9. a
Q7	1. magician	2. magic	
Q8	1. Dr. Ali is the English teacher at Amman private school.		
	2. B: No, I'm not.		
	3. The women's mosque is to your left.		
	4. Are you happy to join the team?		
	5. Because I'm optimistic, I won the championship		
	6. I bought Tim's car.		
	7. I bought a pen, a book and a table.		
Q9	1. The sun was shining yesterday.	2. You were wearing jeans last night.	3. She bought a pretty cotton scarf.
Q10	1. incorrect	2. incorrect	
Q11	1. a	2. a	3. c
Q12	c		

Test (3)

Q1	1. had	2. was driving...hit	3. decided...were starving
	4. fell...was running	5. was Asmahan wearing	

Q2	1. hasn't attended	2. went	3. has...returned
	4. has...seen	5. has finished	6. has had
	7. has never won	8. have you stayed	9. Has Sam fed
	10. has been	11. have released	

Q3	1. made	2. had fallen	3. became...had become

Q4	1. visit= visited	2. is living= has been living	3. have= has
	4. am= was		

Q5	1. in	2. at	3. at
	4. on	5. at	6. in

Q6	1. a	2. a	3. a
	4. b	5. a	4. b
	7. b	8. a	9. a
	10. a		

Q7	1. her relatives were coming to visit Petra that week.
	2. he thought Jerash was the most beautiful city in Jordan.
	3. his parents had changed their house.

Q8	1. a	2. b	3. a
	4. a	5. a	6. a
	7. a	8. a	9. b
	10. a	11. a	12. b
	13. a	14. c	

Q9	a

Test (4)

Q1	1. to play= play	2. wills= will	3. had= have
	4. to behave= behave	5. Do you can run…= Can you run…	6. don't can= can't
	7. going= go	8. don't have= don't have to	9. playing= play
	10. ought= ought to	11. shoulds= should	12. got= get
	13. was able= was able to		

Q2	1. The red window is opened by Sam every other morning.
	2. The brown barrels are being painted by Sam.
	3. The gate has been smashed by the policemen.
	4. The red wine bottle was shaken by the taxi driver.
	5. The cars were being washed by Lee.
	6. The old women had been served by Tom and Jeff.
	7. Anew plan will be set up be Jeffery
	8. A new hospital is going to be established by the government.

Q3	1. 20,000 pairs of trousers were made by the English company last week.
	2. Our house was built by my father in 1999.
	3. My rug will be completed by my mother tomorrow.
	4. A large vase has been dropped by me.
	5. Your son should be taught how to behave.

Q4	1. looking	2. playing	3. talking
	4. to visit/ visiting	5. to take	6. to build
	7. closing		

Q5	1. a	2. b	3. a
	4. c	5. c	6. a
	7. a	8. a	

Q6	1. a	2. a	3. a
	4. b	5. b	

Q7	1. rang	2. was living	3. do…do
	4. A: does…do B: is	5. smoke	6. hasn't drunk
	7. has…eaten	8. Have…been	9. sprained
	10. had lost	11. came	

Q8	1. d	2. c	

Test (5)

Q1	1. a	2. b	3. a
Q2	1. a	2. b	3. c
	4. c	5. b	6. b
	7. a	8. c	9. a
	10. a	11. a	
Q3	1. b	2. a	3. c
	4. c	5. a	6. b
	7. a	8. b	9. b
	10. a	11. b	12. b
	13. a	14. c	15. a
	16. b		
Q4	1. a	2. a	3. c
	4. a	5. a	6. a
	7. a		

Test (6)

Q1	1. exciting…pleased	2. embarrassed	3. disappointing
	4. tired	5. annoying	
Q2	1. sounded	2. visits	3. is flying
	4. is trying	5. wakes…up	6. had snowed
	7. was watching	8. was fixing	9. went
	10. lost		
Q3	1. has dropped	2. has failed	
Q4	1. b	2. b	3. b
	4. b	5. b	6. b
	7. c	8. b	9. a
	10. a	11. b	12. c
	13. a		
Q5	1. a	2. b	3. a
	4. a	5. b	6. c
	7. a	8. a	9. b
	10. a		

Test (7)

Q1	Situation (1): b	Situation (2): b	
Q2	Pair 1: a	Pair 2: b	Pair 3: b
	Pair 4: a	Pair 5: b	
Q3	1. a	2. a	3. a
	4. c	5. b	6. b
	7. a	8. a	9. a
	10. a	11. b	12. a
	13. a	14. b	15. a
Q4	1. a	2. b	3. b
	4. a	5. a	6. a
	7. b	8. b	9. a
	10. b	11. b	12. a
	13. a	14. b	
Q5	1. a	2. a	3. b
	4. a	5. a	6. a
	7. a	8. b	

Test (8)

Q1	Q2	Q3	Q4	Q5	Q6	Q7	Q8	Q9	Q10	Q11	Q12	Q13
C	B	B	C	D	D	D	B	A	C	B	D	B
Q14	Q15	Q16	Q17	Q18	Q19	Q20	Q21	Q22	Q23	Q24	Q25	Q26
A	A	A	A	A	B	A	A	A	B	A	A	A
Q27	Q28	Q29	Q30	Q31	Q32	Q33						
A	A	C	B	D	C	A						

APPENDICES

Appendix (1) Irregular verbs

Infinitive	Past	Past participle
arise	arose	arisen
awake	awoke	awoke
be	was; were	been
beat	beat	beaten
become	became	become
befall	befell	befallen
behold	beheld	beheld
bend	bent	bent
bereave	bereft	bereft
beseech	besought	besought
beset	beset	beset
bet	bet	bet
bid	bid	bid; bidden
bind	bound	bound
bite	bit	bit; bitten
bleed	bled	bled
blow	blew	blown
break	broke	broken
breed	bred	bred
bring	brought	brought
broadcast	broadcast	broadcast
build	built	built
burn	burnt	burnt
burst	burst	burst
buy	bought	bought
cast	cast	cast
catch	caught	caught
choose	chose	chosen
come	came	come
cost	cost	cost
creep	crept	crept
cut	cut	cut
deal	dealt	dealt
dig	dug	dug
do	did	done
draw	drew	drawn
dream	dreamt	dreamt
drink	drank	drunk
drive	drove	driven

eat	ate	eaten
fall	fell	fallen
feed	fed	fed
fight	fought	fought
find	found	found
flee	fled	fled
fling	flung	flung
fly	flew	flown
forbid	forbade	forbidden
forecast	forecast	forecast
forget	forgot	forgotten
forgive	forgave	forgiven
freeze	froze	frozen
get	got	got; gotten
go	went	gone
grind	ground	ground
grow	grew	grown
have	had	had
hear	heard	heard
hide	hid	hidden; hid
hit	hit	hit
hold	held	held
hurt	hurt	hurt
keep	kept	kept
kneel	knelt	knelt
know	knew	known
lay	laid	laid
lead	led	led
lean	leant	leant
leap	leapt	leapt
learn	learnt	learnt
leave	left	left
lend	lent	lent
let	let	let
lie	lay	lain
light	lit	lit
lose	lost	lost
make	made	made
mean	meant	meant
meet	met	met
mistake	mistook	mistaken
misunderstand	misunderstood	misunderstood
mow	mowed	mown

overcast	overcast	overcast
pay	paid	paid
put	put	put
read	read	read
rend	rent	rent
rid	rid	rid
ride	rode	ridden
ring	rang	rung
rise	rose	risen
run	ran	run
saw	sawed	sawn
say	said	said
see	saw	seen
seek	sought	sought
sell	sold	sold
send	sent	sent
set	set	set
shake	shook	shaken
shed	shed	shed
shine	shone	shone
shoot	shot	shot
show	showed	shown
shrink	shrank	shrunk
shut	shut	shut
sing	sang	sung
sink	sank	sunk
sit	sat	sat
sleep	slept	slept
slide	slid	slid
sling	slung	slung
smell	smelt	smelt
speak	spoke	spoken
spent	spent	spent
spin	span	spun
split	split	split
spread	spread	spread
spring	sprang	sprung
stand	stood	stood
steal	stole	stolen
stick	stuck	stuck
sting	stung	stung
stink	stank	stunk
stride	strode	stridden

strike	struck	struck
string	strung	strung
swear	swore	sworn
sweep	swept	swept
swim	swam	swum
swing	swung	swung
take	took	taken
teach	taught	taught
tear	tore	torn
tell	told	told
think	thought	thought
throw	threw	thrown
thrust	thrust	thrust
understand	understood	understood
upset	upset	upset
wake	woke	waken
wear	wore	worn
weave	wove	woven
weep	wept	wept
win	won	won
withdraw	withdrew	withdrawn
write	wrote	written

Appendix (2)

British English and American English equivalent

British English	American English
mobile phone	cell phone
biscuit	cookie
chemist's/ chemistry	drugstore
pavement	sidewalk
autumn	fall
cupboard	closet
lorry	truck
holiday	vacation
underground	subway
lift	elevator
windscreen	windshield
trousers	pants
cooker	stove
aborigine	eggplant
sweets	candy
bonnet (on car)	hood
boot (on car)	trunk
rubbish	garbage
dressing gown	bathrobe
cinema	movie theatre
angry	mean (of mood)
mean	cheap
clever/ intelligent	smart
smart	well dressed

Cardinals

1 one	2 two	3 three	4 four
5 five	6 six	7 seven	8 eight
9 nine	10 ten	11 eleven	12 twelve
13 thirteen	14 fourteen	15 fifteen	16 sixteen
17 seventeen	18 eighteen	19 nineteen	20 twenty
21 twenty one...	30 thirty	31 thirty one...	40 forty
50 fifty	60 sixty	70 seventy	80 eighty
90 ninety	100 one hundred	101 one hundred and one	1000 one thousand

1000000 million   1000000000 billion

Ordinals

1st first	2nd second	3rd third	4th fourth
5th fifth	6th sixth	7th seventh	8th eighth
9th ninth	10th tenth	11th eleventh	12th twelfth
13th thirteenth	14th fourteenth	15th fifteenth	16th sixteenth
17th seventeenth	18th eighteenth	19th nineteenth	20th twentieth
21st twenty first...	30th thirtieth	40th fortieth	50th fiftieth
60th sixtieth	70th seventieth	80th eightieth	90th ninetieth

100th hundredth

Dates

Examples (written)	Read
3/4/1989 (or) 3 April 1989	The third of April, nineteen eighty-nine (or) April the third, nineteen eighty-nine
2000	Two thousand
2009	Two thousand and nine
1500	Fifteen hundred
1510	Fifteen hundred and ten

Fractions

Examples (written)	Read	Examples (written)	Read
1/4	A quarter (or) fourth	4/10	Four tenths
1/2	A half	2/3	Two thirds
3/4	Three quarters	2 .2/3	Two and two thirds
3/6	Three sixths	2/5	Two fifths

Decimals and Percentages

Decimals		Percentage	
Examples (written)	Read	Examples (written)	Read
0.2	Point two	30%	Thirty percent
2.4	Two point four	30.5%	Thirty point five percent
3.5	Three point five	26%	Twenty six percent

Timing

Examples (written)	Read	Examples (written)	Read
10:00	Ten o'clock	10:10	Ten past ten
10:15	Quarter past ten (or) ten, fifteen	10:35	Thirty five past ten (or)Ten, thirty five
10:30	Half past ten (or) ten, thirty	10:25	Twenty five past ten (or) Ten, twenty five
10:45	Quarter to eleven	10:55	Five to eleven

Appendix (4):

Nationalities

Country	Nationality
Egypt	Egyptian
Portugal	Portuguese
Iran	Iranian
Poland	Polish
Germany	German
Greece	Greek
Holland	Dutch
Japan	Japanese
Switzerland	Swiss
China	Chinese
France	French
Spain	Spanish
Syria	Syrian
Lebanon	Lebanese
Jordan	Jordanian
America	American
England	English
Turkey	Turkish
Iraq	Iraqi
Palestine	Palestinian
Russia	Russian
Canada	Canadian
Italy	Italian
Sweden	Swedish
Denmark	Danish
Pakistan	Pakistani
Thailand	Thai
Scotland	Scottish
Djibouti	Djiboutian
Timor	Timorese
Europe	European
Korea	Korean
Kuwait	Kuwaiti
Morocco	Moroccan
Yemen	Yemeni
Zimbabwe	Zimbabwean

Appendix (5):

Examples of phrasal verbs

Phrasal verb	Meaning in English	Meaning in Arabic	Example
back out	withdraw, cancel	ينسحب من، يلغي	Our company backed out of the deal with Fastlink.
back down	yield, admit defeat	يتنازل عن(مطلب)، يتراجع	Addison was going to see the monster, but then he backed down when he saw that the monster was giant.
back up	to drive in reverse, to move backwards	يرجع للخلف	Sal backed the car up to the garage gate.
back up	protect, preserve, to make a protection copy	يحتفظ بنسخة احتياط، يحمي	The computer users ought to back up their important files.
back up	defend, to confirm facts, support	يدعم، يسند	Fahed backed Razan's story up. He told the students the same facts that she said.
break down	to crash, dismantle, destroy	يدمر، يفكك	The robbers broke the bank's door down before they came in two days ago.
break down	analyze, revise	يحلل، يراجع	When we broke the costs down, we found that we had been stolen.
break down	to stop working	يتعطل	Asma's car broke down last night.
break in	get in, make the team, to make sb. included	يروض، يدرب، يجعل فلان جزءا من الفريق	One of the commander's duties is to break the new soldiers in.
break into	to enter forcefully, burglarize	يقتحم عنوة، سطو	Shukri broke into a house and stole a satellite receiver. Now, he's behind bars.

bring up	introduce, discuss, launch	يطرح موضوعا للمناقشة	I brought up the issue at the meeting but nobody wanted to talk about it.
bring up	to raise, rear	يربي	I was brought up with very strict religious rules.
come back	return to one's memory, flood back	يعود للذاكرة	The events of the past are slowly coming back to me.
come by	get, obtain, acquire	يكسب، يحصل على	She came by a lot of money recently and is now enjoying her life.
come-down	a lowering in status/ income/ influence or energy	هبوط، أن ينحسر مكانه	His new job was a real come-down.
come down with	catch, become ill with	يصاب بـ	Hilton came down with Swine flu when she arrived at Heathrow airport.
count in	include	يشمل، يضم ، يحسب حساب فلان	Please, count Sura in if she likes to visit Spain.
count on	depend on	يعتمد على، يثق بـ	You can never count on him to do anything right.
count out	exclude, dismiss	يستثني، يشطب، يطرد	Count Sam out if he doesn't like to go to Spain.
cut out	eliminate, stop	ينقطع عن ، يتوقف عن	She decided to cut out chocolate in order to lose weight.
do without	manage without something	يستغني عن	If there is no sugar, we'll have to do without it.
draw in	make/become shorter	يقصر	Days in winter time draw in.
draw out	make or become longer	يطول، يمتد	Days in summer time draw out.

get along	to have a friendly relationship	ينسجم مع	Do you get along with family?
get a move on	hurry up	أسرع	Please get a move on. We are already over three hours late.
get around	to avoid having to do something	يتجنب	The men tried to get around doing the dishes.
get at	to try to prove or make clear, mean	يبلغ، يقصد، يحاول أن يثبت أو يوضح	I couldn't understand what Sami was getting at. He didn't make any sense.
get away	succeed in leaving, escape	يفلت من ، يفر	I was able to get away early from work today so I went shopping for a while.
get on	to enter a large, closed vehicle	يركب، يعتلي	Quick! Get on the train, it's about to leave.
get on in years	to advance in age	يتقدم بالسن	He is getting on in years and is not very healthy
get over something	recover from an illness or shock, overcome a difficulty	يتعافى،يتغلب	She has been having a lot of trouble getting over her father's death.
get (something) over with	finish, end	ينهي	He wants to get his exams over with so that he can begin to relax again
hand in	to submit work you have done	يسلم	Harold handed his report in. His boss really liked it.
hand-me-down	something given away after another doesn't need it (especially clothing)	جاهز ورخيص، مستعمل	She was very poor when she was a child and always wore hand-me-down clothing.
hand out (v)	give things of the same kind to several people	يوزع	The teacher decided not to hand out the tests sheets.

hand-out (n)	sheets of paper given to students or people who attend a meeting, etc.	نشره	Everyone at the meeting was given a hand-out on how to save and invest money.
hand over	give control or possession to someone, give something to another person	يعيد، يسلم (شيئا) لآخر ، تسليم	The criminals were forced to hand over the stolen money to the police.
hang around	pass time or stay someplace without any real purpose or aim, staying around	يمضي وقتا أو يبقى في مكان ما دون هدف ، يتسكع	We decided to stay home and hang around on Sunday rather then go out to the game.
hang back	stay some distance behind or away, hesitate or be unwilling to do something	يتردد، يتخلف عن الآخرين، لا يرغب بالتطوع بفعل أمر ما	He lacks self-confidence and always hangs back when his boss asks for volunteers.
go along with	agree	يتفق، يتماشى مع	Hamad always goes along with what his employer wants to do.
look at	glance	ينظر بسرعة/ خلسة	He looked at his watch quickly.
look through	search	يفتش	The robbers looked through the whole villa for money.
throw away	toss	يرمي	When she got her test back, she was so disappointed that she threw the calculator away.
put into	pour	يصب، يسكب	The waiter put Pepsi into my glass.
move out of	disappear	يختفي، يغادر	It was foggy and I watched my friend move out of the house.
watch out for	be alert	يحذر، يبقى يقظا	You have to watch out for the little children while driving.

Appendix (6):

Common expressions with prepositions

1. **Out of:**

   Out of town: away

   Out of date: old

   Out of work: unemployed

   Out of the question: impossible

   Out of order: not functioning

2. **By:**

   By then: before a time

   By way of: via

   By the way: incidentally

   By far: considerably

   By accident: not intentionally

3. **At:**

   At least

   At once

   At present

   At the moment

   At times (occasionally)

   At first

4. **On:**

   On the sidewalk

   On the way

   On the right

   On the left

   On sale

   On the whole

   On the other hand

Appendix (7):

Problem Words (Vocabulary)

1. Old cars are not as they ___.
   a. seam (closure)
   b. seem (appear)

2. On the ___, she is a kind person.
   a. whole (entire)
   b. hole (gap)

3. I ___ a lot better but I did it anyway.
   a. knew (past of know)
   b. new (fresh)

4. Good traders buy low and ___ high.
   a. sell (trade)
   b. cell (unit)

5. Didn't Sami ___ you when you called him?
   a. hear (perceive sound)
   b. here (opposite of there)

6. Do not ___ in others' affairs.
   a. medal (award)
   b. meddle (interfere)

7. Do you really ___ a new van?
   a. knead (message)
   b. need (require)

8. During weekends I work as a tour ___.
   a. guide (lead)
   b. guyed

9. I told ___ not to call her but he would not listen.
   a. him (pronoun)
   b. hymn (chant)

10. My car broke down last night, so I called for a ___ truck.
    a. toe (of the foot)
    b. tow (pull)

11. Every time I sleep with ___ hair I catch a cold.
    a. wet (damp)
    b. whet (sharpen)

12. I want to ___ you for your achievements.
    a. complement (balance)
    b. compliment (praise)

13. You are not ___ to stay up later than 12 p.m.
    a. allowed (permitted)
    b. aloud (audibly)

14. My nephew has ___ 15 centimeters since last winter.
    a. groan (moan)
    b. grown (past participle of grow)

15. Mary___ flowers to her father on Fathers' Day.
    a. scent (smell)
    b. sent (send)

16. Are those cakes ___ or artificial?
    a. real (actual)
    b. reel (roll)

17. You need to read the text carefully to detect a hidden ___.
    a. clause (part)
    b. claws (claw)

18. The rope you gave me was ___.
    a. taught (teach)
    b. taut (tight)

19. The animal has mud all over its ___.
    a. pause (gap)
    b. paws (paw)

20. Is it possible to ___ minerals from Jordan valley?
    a. leach (filter)
    b. leech (tick; vampire)

21. I served in a ___ base for two years.
  a. naval (marine)
  b. navel (part of the body)

22. She traveled for ___ with a lot of money.
  a. days (day)
  b. daze (astonish)

23. The manager is planning to ___ out the project in three main stages.
  a. faze (put off)
  b. phase (stage)

24. You must ___ in that wild horse.
  a. reign (time in power)
  b. rein (control)

25. I've got a new rod and ___.
  a. real (actual)
  b. reel (roll)

26. Jolie served in the armoured ___ .
  a. corpse (dead body)
  b. corps (unit)

27. The dessert was a sliced ___ on a bar of chocolate.
  a. pair (couple)
  b. pare (peel)

28. We planned ___ vacation carefully
  a. hour (60 minutes)
  b. our (pronoun)

29. The ___ waited for ten hours.
  a. patience (endurance)
  b. patients (sick)

30. I learned to ___ when I was six.
  a. sew (stitch)
  b. so

31. An egg has the white part and the ___.

    a. yoke (repression)

    b. yolk (inner yellow part of an egg)

32. Many people believe that passengers should have the exact ___ ready. a. fair (pale)

    b. fare (charge)

33. Do you ___ the way to the British Council?

    a. know

    b. no

34. A wedding party is a beautiful ___.

    a. right (correct)

    b. rite (ritual)

35. Do you ___ the money for dinner?

    a. halve (devide)

    b. have (possess)

36. There is a worldwide ___ on ivory trade.

    a. ban (forbid)

    b. van (front)

37. A ___ is the short way of referring to an animal doctor.

    a. bet (gamble)

    b. vet (animal doctor)

38. The judge decided that Samir could be released on a 200 J.D ___.

    a. bail (surety; payment)

    b. veil (covering)

39. The ship had a leak, so we had to ___ out the water.

    a. bail (remove out)

    b. veil (covering)

40. This computer is the ___ of my work! It keeps logging off.

    a. vain (ineffective)

    b. bane (nuisance)

41. He likes to ___ his wife with gifts and flowers.

    a. lavish (to make something bountiful)

    b. ravish (of rape)

42. The president was ___ from his country and forced to live in Spain.
    a. vanished (missing)
    b. banished (expel)

43. Najeeb Mahfouz received the ___ prize for literature.
    a. Novel (work of fiction)
    b. Nobel (name of an award)

44. Sending printed-false information could result in a charge of ___.
    a. rival (competitor)
    b. libel (defamation)

45. The winner has time to ___ in his success party.
    a. rebel (revolt)
    b. revel (drink)

46. One symptom of measles is having a red ___.
    a. rash (reaction)
    b. lash (tie)

47. Cats are preferred as pets because they have a strong sense of ___.
    a. loyalty (faithfulness)
    b. royalty (monarchs)

48. The painful ___ in my neck was caused by hunching over the TV for long time.
    a. click (tick)
    b. crick (spasm)

49. I think it's hard to concentrate while hearing the sharp, loud ___ of the typewriters.
    a. clack (click)
    b. crack (break)

Appendix (8):
Acronyms

College and graduate school entrance exam

ACT	American College Testing Assessment
CLEP	College Level Examination Program
DAT	Dental Admission Test
GMAT	Graduate Management Admission Test
GRE	Graduate Record Examinations
LSAT	Law School Admission Test
MCAT	Medical College Admission Test
SAT	Scholastic Assessment Test
TOEFL	Test of English as a Foreign Language
TSE	Test of Spoken English
TWE	Test of Written English
IELTS	International English Language Testing Services
CAE	Certificate of Advanced English
FCE	First Certificate in English

United Nations programmes, funds, and agencies

UNDCP	UN Drug Control Programme
UNDP	UN Development Programme
UNEP	UN Environment Programme
UNHCR	UN High Commissioner for Refugees
UNICEF	UN Children's Fund
UNIFEM	UN Development Fund for Women
UNRWA	UN Relief and Work Agency (for Palestine Refugees in Near East)
WFP	World Food Programme
FAO	Food and Agriculture Organization
IBRD (The World Bank')	International Bank for Reconstruction and Development
ILO	International Labour Organization
UNESCO	UN Educational, Scientific, and Cultural Organization

Exercises (1-72)

Answer Keys

Exercise (1)

Select the appropriate answer:

1.   a. /s /

2.   b. /z/

3.   a. /n /

4.   a. /s/

5.   b. /k/

6.   b. /g/

7.   c. /et/

Exercise (2)

/t/	/d/	/ð/	/i/	/⊠/	/v/	/⊠/	/ʃ/	/ed/
sack**ed** laugh**ed**	play**ed** entangl**ed**	**th**ese	ch**ea**p rep**ea**t rec**ei**ve	cons**u**mption ded**u**ction	**v**an	**th**in	**sh**arp	paint**ed** affect**ed**

Exercise (3)

A:

noun	Robert
verb	helped
adjective	rich
adverb	very
preposition	at
determiner	a few
pronoun	She
conjunction	If

B:

1. <u>Fadi</u> <u>is buying</u> <u>a new house</u> <u>in Amman.</u>

    subject   verb   complement   modifier

2. <u>Eddi</u> <u>has been shopping</u> <u>downtown.</u>

    subject   verb   modifier

Exercise (4)

1. <u>was playing</u>   (verb phrase)
2. <u>Macbeth</u>   (noun phrase)
3. <u>absolutely idle</u>   (adjective phrase)
4. <u>in the pool</u>   (prepositional phrase)
5. <u>before you arrive</u>. (adverbial phrase)

Exercise (5)

1. (simple)
2. (complex)
3. (compound)
4. (complex)
5. (simple)
6. (simple)
7. (compound)
8. (complex)

Exercise (6)

1. was eating
2. was sleeping
3. was studying
4. went
5. was looking

Exercise (7)

1. has seen
2. swam
3. has read
4. I have not begun
5. has traveled

Exercise (8)

1. had read, met
2. had washed
3. joined

Exercise (9)

1. leaves
2. go
3. gets
4. rises
5. am working
6. is buying

Exercise (10)

    A:

    1. leave

    2. repair

    3. to type

    4. write

    5. sign

    6. to play

    7. to swim

    B: a.   I've taken my shirt to be shortened.

Exercise (11)

    1. to hear

    2. to see

    3. smoking

    4. boring

    5. leave

    6. to fetch

    7. repair

    8. to walk

    9. looking

    10. playing

    11. talking

    12. to visit

    13. to come

    14. our

    15. Fadi's

Exercise (12)

Verbs	Gerund	Past form
stop	stopping	stopped
die	dying	died
argue	arguing	argued
agree	agreeing	agreed
enjoy	enjoying	enjoyed
fix	fixing	fixed

Exercise (13)

    1. have not visited

    2. are presenting

3. had called

4. have been driving

5. A: have you been teaching

6. was figuring out

7. drinks

8. were studying

9. watch

10. were having

11. is

12. am running

13. walk

14. swimming

15. are....wearing

16. Have....seen

17. have been observing

Exercise (14)

1	a. to keep
2	a. Eating
3	a. been
4	b. thinking
5	a. He's
6	a. looks
7	a. is
8	b. are
9	b. are
10	a. is
11	a. is
12	c. am

Exercise (15)

Next year, our college tennis team **will use** new fields and courts for training. They **weren't** that professional last year; but now they've **become** more and more well trained and organized.

Exercise (16)

      1.   Mrs. Bartlett has read a poem of Blake.

Exercise (17)

1.	Jim had <u>a great time</u>.	object
2.	<u>Everybody</u> was brilliant.	subject
3.	I <u>liked</u> your suggestion.	verb
4.	I'm <u>happy</u> today.	complement (adjective)
5.	She visits her grandmother <u>weekly</u>.	adverb
6.	I love <u>Silvia</u>.	object

Exercise (18)

Make sentences by putting the following words in the correct order. You can refer to the simple sentence forms.

    1.   Ali is going to meet some people.

    2.   I have 15 buildings.

    3.   Aaron was sick yesterday.

    4.   He is looking at Gabriel.

    5.   They gave him a Swiss watch.

Exercise (19)

A:

1	c. was born
2	c. drinks
3	b. will study
4	c. take
5	b. went
6	c. am
7	a. has
8	a. do

Exercise (20)

    1. I'm not going to see my friend.

    2. My father will not/ won't come back soon.

    3. I don't/ do not want to sell my apartment.

    4. These shirts don't/ do not cost too much.

5. My T-shirt didn't/ did not cost a lot of money.

6. She didn't/ did not shake hands with me.

7. Don't/ Do not put this letter in the envelope.

8. He couldn't/ could not leave early.

9. She doesn't have two daughters.

10. You didn't have to come by ship.

11. Rice isn't/ is not grown in Egypt.

Exercise (21)

1. bought

2. will leave

3. is

4. are

5. has already bought

6. had

7. left

8. eat

Exercise (22)

1. Ali lives in Amman.

Exercise (23):

1.   Jack doesn't/ does not live in Barcelona.

2.   Hitler didn't/ did not live in Germany.

3.   Steve and Ross don't/ do not prefer pop music.

4.   Mrs. Obama doesn't/ does not have two daughters.

6.   We aren't/ are not close friends.

Exercise (24)

(1)   The project we have is very **successful**.

(2)   The boss told me that it was so important to **succeed** in the test.

(3)   What a great **success**!

Exercise (25)

(1)   Henry decided to visit Petra after reading an **advertisement** about it.

(2)   It isn't cheap to **advertise** on TV.

Exercise (26)

1. quiet
2. care
3. easily
4. certainty
5. immediate
6. fast
7. wonderful
8. perfectly

Exercise (27)

A:

1. <u>are</u> (incorrect). It must be <u>is</u>.
2. <u>are</u> (incorrect). It must be <u>is</u>.
3. <u>too many</u> (incorrect). It must be <u>too much</u>..
4. <u>I</u> (incorrect). It must be <u>me</u>..
5. <u>to take</u> (incorrect). It must be <u>taking</u>.

B: Change the following sentences so that they are parallel.

1.   Melissa is a scholar, an athlete, and ***artist***.
2.   Children love playing in the mud, running in streets, *and **getting** very dirty*.

Exercise (28)

1. is
2. brings
3. aren't
4. are
5. are
6. is
7. are

Exercise (29)

A:

1. I will visit Abdelrahman tomorrow.
2. They called **us** on the phone.
3. Johnson told **her** a story.
4. Alfred will make his presentation after **he** finishes his exercise.
5. Mugabi is eating **his** dinner.
6. **My** sitting room is freezing.

7. I go to the school with **him** every day.

8. She speaks to **us** every day.

9. I hurt **my** leg.

10. John **himself** went to the meeting.

11. Hussein and **I** would go to Essex.

12. **Her** car didn't go as fast as **ours**.

B:

Countable nouns	Mass nouns
television	news
car	furniture
person	water
tooth	money
minute	information
cup	economics

Exercise (30)

1	c. few	2	a. a lot of
3	B. boys'	4	a. mens'
5	b. children	6	a. stories
7	b. loaves	8	a. too much
9	a. enough	10	a. is
11	b. some	12	a. traffic
13	b. myself		

Exercise (31)

1	a. an	2	a. the
3	a. a	4	d. x
5	c. the	6	c. the
7	b. the	8	c. This
9	c. These	10	a. somebody
11	b. him	12	a. we
13	c. x/the	14	c. the/the
15	d. x		

Exercise (32)

1. Ali crossed **the** Mississippi.

2. Mount Rum is one of **the** highest mountains in Jordan.

3. **The** Alps lies in (**nothing**) Europe.

4. The shepard gave me **an** animal.

5. You need **a** pen and **an** exercise book to practice well.

6. **A** million people received my text message at Christmas Eve.

7. **A** few people were fortunate to escape the fire.

8. French is **an** easy language to learn.

9. My father is **an** honorable man.

10. (**nothing**) Gold is very precious metal.

Exercise (33)

1. The old man was sick.

2. I finished my task three years ago.

3. My parents moved into a new apartment.

4. Alia speaks English well.

5. Did I tell you about the new job?

6. I met a few people in the school.

7. Prevention is better than cure.

Exercise (34)

1. Mary hurt **herself**.

2. We helped the old woman **ourselves**.

3. Did you see Alison **yourself**?

4. Alia's coat is red; **mine** is brown.

5. Lucy is preparing **her** clothes.

6. Is that **your** motor cycle?

Exercise (35)

1. <u>can dance</u>

2. <u>will</u>

3. <u>should have</u>

4. <u>play</u>

5. <u>I'm able to</u>

Exercise (36)

1. **Beethoven may be English.**

   - It is possible that Beethoven is English.

Or - Beethoven is possibly English.

2. **Mills will probably leave this summer.**

   - It is probable that Mills will leave this summer

3. **It is likely that Rashid flies tomorrow morning.**

   - Rashid may fly tomorrow morning.

Exercise (37)

1	a. Ability
2	a. Ought to
3	a. Be able to
4	b. Request
5	c. Prohibition
6	b. Lack of necessity
7	a. Internal obligation

Exercise (38)

1	**b. holds back** 30 cubic meters of water.
2	**give** it **up**
3	I think I'll **take** my coat **off**. It is too hot here.
4	a. **put up** the picture you bought to me
5	c. **mix** me **up**
6	d. **look after** your child
7	e. **get over** them

Exercise (39)

1	**b. delicious**
2	**a. fitter**
3	**b. best**
4	**b. most gorgeous**
5	**b. more**
6	**b. interesting**
7	**a. healthy**
8	**b. slowly**
9	**a. fast**
10	**b. brown-eyed**

Exercise (40)

1. most interesting
2. easier
3. the longest
4. worse than

5. more painful

6. larger

7. more comfortable

8. highest

9. not as good as

10. as strong as

Exercise (41)

1	a. a seven-star hotel
2	b. a five-bedroom house
3	b. a ten-letter word
4	a. a dark-haired mother
5	a. a 110-year-old man

Exercise (42)

Adjective	Comparative	Superlative
fine	finer	the finest
short	shorter	the shortest
few	fewer	the fewest
exciting	more exciting	the most exciting
nice	nicer	the nicest
fat	fatter	the fattest
difficult	more difficult	the most difficult
dim	dimmer	the dimmest
ugly	uglier	the ugliest
early	earlier	the earliest
dry	drier	the driest
young	younger	the youngest
narrow	narrower	the narrowest
much/ many	more	the most
little	less	the least
far	further/ farther	the furthest/ the farthest

Exercise (43)

1. I feel **a bit better** today.

2. The shop is **much more expensive** than the mall.

3. The missile went **higher and higher** into the sky.

Exercise (44)

1. Dove is **more talented** than Maccaine.

2. This month is **as hot as** last month.

3. A new apartment is **much more expensive** than an old one.

4. A new apartment is **much better** than an old one.

5. My dog runs **faster** than yours.

Exercise (45)

1. Salma is **the happiest** person we know.

2. Ben's car is **faster** than Dan's.

3. This picture is **more colourful** than the old one.

4. Hamad is **the least** athletic of all men.

5. Ahmad has **few** opportunities to join the team.

Exercise (46)

1. would travel

2. will break

3. would have finished

4. keep

5. expands

6. would tell

7. will be

8. had listened

9. will not get

10. didn't marry

11. will give

12. would have lived

13. would buy

14. can eat

15. are

16. studied

17. had seen

18. would have gone

19. would ride

20. had

Exercise (47)

1. Unless I was sick, I would attend the session.

2. Unless you call her, she will not be grateful.

3. I wish Shadi was telling me the truth.

4. I wish I could pay attention.

5. I wish I had woken up early this morning.

Exercise (48)

1	a. Provided	2	c. although
3	a. Because	4	a. While
5	a. are	6	a. are
7	a. nor	8	b. although

9	a. for	10	a. so am I
11	a. as soon as	12	a. so
13	b. However	14	a. nevertheless
15	c. carefully	16	a. clever

Exercise (49)

1. In spite of sleeping early, I couldn't wake up on time.
2. Because of the war in Iraq, Ahmad postponed his flight.

Exercise (50)

1	because	2	because
3	because of	4	because of
5	because of		

Exercise (51)

1. The sun is shining **so** brightly that I have to put on my sunglasses.
2. Deema is **such** a powerful runner that she always wins the races.

Exercise (52)

A:

1. Mr. Eyad speaks **not only** Spanish **but also** English.
2. I have villas **both** in the country **and** in the city.

B:

1. We had **such** a bad night that we couldn't sleep.
2. She gave me **so** good a stereo that I was very grateful to her.
3. The day was **so** hot that everyone went to the sea.
4. The motel has **such** a comfortable room that I don't want to leave.
5. It was **so** dark that I couldn't see my finger.
6. That restaurant has **such** delicious food that I can't stop eating.

Exercise (53)

1. The boys shouldn't take the medicine, and **neither** should the girls.
2. We don't plan to join the team, and **neither** do they.
3. They won't have to work on weekends, and she won't **either**.
4. I can't stand listening to pop music, and she can't **either**.

Exercise (54)

1. The boys aren't happy with the programme, and neither **do** the girls.
2. We can't study in the library, and they **can't** either.
3. He didn't know the answer and neither **did** I.

Exercise (55)

1. <u>does</u>
2. <u>Who</u>
3. <u>Where</u>
4. <u>How much</u>

Exercise (56)

1. Who wants some food to eat?
2. What did McCain give me?
3. What fell on the floor?
4. When did she see me?
5. Where do you live in?
6. How old is Hashim?
7. Whom did you meet in Manchester?
8. Where was Mohammad born ?
9. What do you have in your luggage?
10. Why can't Ahmad leave?
11. Whose purse is this?
12. Which chapter can't you figure out?

Exercise (57):

1. Mohammad came yesterday, didn't he?
Yes, he did.
2. I don't live in a palace, do I?
No, you don't.
3. Ahmad would like to have some coffee, wouldn't he?
Yes, he would.
4. This is Anne's purse, isn't it?
Yes, it is.
5. You have scanned the letter, haven't you?
Yes, I have.
6. They couldn't do the exercise, could they?
No, they couldn't

Exercise (58)

1	a. don't you	2	b. won't you
3	a. Where	4	a. So am I
5	a. Neither am I		

Exercise (59)

1	b. Are	2	b. Were
3	a. Has	4	a. call
5	a. Didn't	6	c. isn't he
7	a. Yes, she did	8	a. What

Exercise (60)

1. You're going to Paris next year, aren't you?

2. Harry signed the petition, didn't he?

3. There is a final test, isn't it?

4. She's been studying French for 3 years, hasn't she?

5. He should see the dentist, shouldn't he?

6. You can play tennis today, can't you?

Exercise (61)

1. The book will have been read by noon time tomorrow by my students.

2. The wagon was being pulled by two horses.

3. Three windows have been smashed by Asma.

4. 2000 boxes of clothes are sent a month by Aramex.

5. Macbeth was written by Shakespeare.

6. This book had better be returned before Sunday by her.

7. This package should have been sent by them.

8. The project has been performed successfully by the engineer.

9. The trees are being cut by the old man.

10. Coffee isn't grown in Jordan by farmers.

11. The new house was provided with furniture by them.

12. This document ought to be signed by you.

13. Wells are dug by them to get fresh water.

14. I was let in by her.

15. All the salary was spent by her on clothes.

16. Ali is called 'the smuggler'.

Exercise (62)

A:

    b.   I must have this study translated into Arabic.

B:

    a.   I've taken my shirt to be shortened.

C:

1. must be delivered

2. was written

3. is cooked

D:

1. are seen

2. have been thrown away

Exercise (63)

1. The lecturer said that they had a meeting the following week.

2. My mum ordered me to lock the door.

3. She asked me if I had married.

4. I asked Ali how many copies he sold.

5. Rabab told Majeda (that) her story was very good.

6. Alia told Ziad (that) she liked his camera.

7. Ibrahim said (that) his parents were taking them to India.

8. My friend asked me where his jacket was.

9. My parents told me that they were working there to pay for their new car.

10. He said that yesterday he had been in bed with temperature.

11. Ahmad advised Sami not to leave school.

12. My brother asked me to recommend him a good book on physics.

Exercise (64)

1. Adjective clause: **which I held**

2. Adjective clause: **whose bike is stolen**

3. Adjective clause: **who told me the truth**

4. Adjective clause: **where I live**

Exercise (65)

1.	when.	2.	where	3.	whose
4.	whom	5.	which	6.	who

Exercise (66)

1. Do you know the man who lives in the blue building?

2. The coach whom I called gave me enough support.

3. The building where we lived was hit by missile.

Exercise (67)

1. Gallagher's room is on the third floor.

2. I saw Julia Robert holding a parrot in her hand.

3. I'll meet you at the airport.

    4. There are 23 seats in the classroom.

Exercise (68)

1. I'm **afraid of** parachuting. I hate to jump from high places.
2. Orange is **rich in** vitamin (c).
3. People in Congo **suffer from** civil war.
4. Don't write **in pen**.
5. When you decide to participate in the parliamentary elections, please tell me **in advance**.
6. My firm-report will be declared **on the radio**.
7. Water **consists of** oxygen and hydrogen.
8. You are well-trained. That is why I can **rely on** you.
9. I'll be out for few hours. Could you **take care of** my baby?
10. I've run my website **since** 2001.(since/ for)
11. He's been there **for** over half an hour. (since/ for)
12. He was sitting **at the table**. (in/ at)
13. We went to the station **by taxi.** (on/ by)
14. I was **born in** Holland. (in/on)
15. I'm **proud of** my king. (of/ at)
16. The child is **afraid of** the dark room. (of/ by)
17. You're **accused of** smuggling. (of/ by)
18. He speaks French **with confidence.** (with/ from)
19. He spent a lot of money **on** cassettes. (on/ at)
20. Are you **good at** physics? (at/ on)

Exercise (69)

1. Love **does change** the course of your life.
2. She **does** always **disagree** with me.
3. I **do admire** Arthur's courage./ **It is Arthur's courage** what I admire./ **What I admire is** Arthur's courage.
4. **Never have** I been humiliated in my life.

Exercise (70)

1. I have **been** living in London since 2001.
2. Don't **repeat** the song.
3. He **has** been to Paris twice.
4. **I've** three children.
5. I have two **sons**.
6. Sami **bought** this house 20 years ago.
7. John didn't attend the **class because** he was sick.

8. **Ali** bought a good van.

9. What is your name**?**

10. **The** Earth rotates round the sun.

11. Didn't you **see** that sign?

12. If I were a bird, I **would** fly to Canada.

13. I quit **smoking**.

14. Suzan and Julia **are** coming to dinner.

Exercise (71)

- Stop <u>looking</u> for a new computer.

- <u>Your</u> best personal computer is now available.

- Our aim is to provide you with the <u>latest</u> technology.

- Your computer was made in <u>England</u>.

- Now it <u>has</u> the best options.

- <u>Don't</u> think twice. You won't regret it.

- Do you still have any doubts<u>?</u>

Exercise (72)

1. A beautiful **angel** visited me.

2. I have **your** notes in my notebook.

3. It is a **custom** in Jordan to eat lamb on wedding parties.

4. **Whether** we run or walk depends on the roads conditions.

5. Although my brother doesn't like **dessert**, I prefer something sweet.

6. James and Fredrick teach kindergarten; the **latter** works in Nepal.

7. King Abdullah II is of the Hashemite **descent.**

8. You need to **cite** your references when you write an essay.

9. My shirt came **loose** and it needed to be tightened.

10. Asma had to **quit** eating sweets to be healthier.

11. Your remarks greatly **affected** Kaite.

12. After declaring bankruptcy, General Motors was forced to **liquidate** its assets.

This book has been prepared by referring to: Objective IELTS, Michael Black and Annetta Capel, Cambridge University Press, England 2008; The Oxford Dictionary of Current English, R E Allen, England, 1984; TOEFL Test Preparation Kit Workbook, ETS, USA, 1998; Oxford practice grammar, John Eastwood, Oxford University, 1994; Translation with Reference to English and Arabic: A Practical Guide, Fargal M. & Shunnaq A., Dar Alhilal for Translation, 1998; A Course in Phonetics, Peter Ladefoged, Harcourt Brace, Florida, 1993; Understanding and Using English Grammar, Betty Azar, Washington, 1989; Action Pack 10, Simon Haines, Pearson Educational Ltd- York press, England, 2008; Webster's concise edition of spelling, grammar and using, English thesaurus, Scotland 2002; Focus on Language, Aida Alemami, Amman, 1998.

KNOWLEDGE HAS BITTER ROOTS
BUT SWEET FRUITS

Notes

Printed in the United States
By Bookmasters